MICROSOFT® OFFICE
EXCEL 2007

Editions ENI

http://www.eni-publishing.com

Collection directed by Corinne HERVO

Foreword

This is a book for anyone who uses Excel 2007 (the version of Excel included in the Office 2007 application suite). It is designed so that you can look up the task you want to perform and find a clear description of how go about it. The screens illustrated throughout these pages add to the efficacy of the explanations, by showing the dialog box corresponding to a particular command, or by giving a precise example. This book is made up of thirteen parts :

Excel tables and pivot tables   p. 283 to 298

Excel allows you to manage Excel tables (tables presented as list of datas) and to create pivot tables.

Group work   p. 299 to 315

Techniques for using shared worksheets, including protecting data and macros digitally and setting access and data entry conditions.

Various advanced features   p. 316 to 362

Deals with other Excel features, such as using smart tags and hyperlinks, importing and exporting data, creating macros and managing Web pages.

You can find techniques and commands more quickly by using the comprehensive index at the back of the book.

Typographic conventions

To help you find the information you require quickly and easily, the following conventions have been adopted.

These typefaces are used for:

bold   showing which menu option or dialog box to use.

italic   giving an explanation of the command you are following, or of any changes on the screen.

Ctrl   showing which keys you should press. When two keys are displayed together they must be pressed simultaneously.

The following symbols indicate:

⏏   An action you should perform (activating an option, clicking with the mouse).

      A general comment on the command being used.

      A useful tip.

      A technique which involves the mouse.

      A keyboard technique.

      A technique which uses options from the menus.

Table of contents

Microsoft Excel 2007

Table of contents

Managing documents

Workbooks

Templates

Entering/editing data

Moving/selecting

Entering data

Table of contents

Worksheets

Table of contents

Table of contents

Table of contents

Table of contents

⊟ **Outlines**

Printing data

⊟ **Page setup**

⊟ **Printing**

Charts and objects

⊟ **Creating charts**

Table of contents

Excel tables and pivot tables

⊡ Excel tables

⊡ Pivot tables

⊡ PivotChart

Group work

⊡ Protection

Table of contents

Table of contents

Table of contents

Part 1
Microsoft Excel 2007

Starting Microsoft Excel 2007

⊡ Click the **Start** button.

⊡ Move the mouse to **All Programs** then **Microsoft Office**.

⊡ Click **Microsoft Office Excel 2007**.

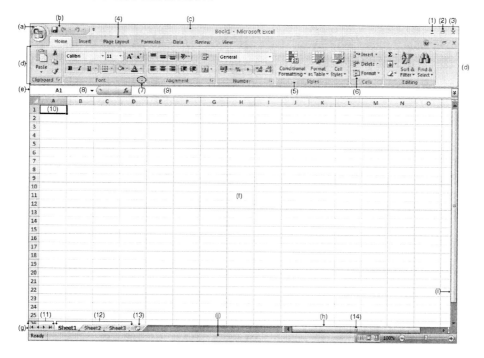

A workbook named Book1 appears.

⊟ The **Microsoft Office** button (a) replaces the **File** menu from previous versions of Excel. It opens a menu with the basic features of the application (such as create new spreadsheet, open, save or close a spreadsheet, print, etc) and more advanced features such as sharing a file and changing Excel settings.

⊟ The **Quick Access Toolbar** (b) contains the most frequently used tools. You can customise it by displaying it under the ribbon or adding new tools to it (see Customisation Chapter).

⊟ The **Title bar** (c) displays the name of the spreadsheet (called **Book*n*** if it has not been saved) followed by the name of the application (**Microsoft Excel**). On the right are the **Minimize** (1), **Maximize** or **Restore** (2) and **Close** (3) buttons.

⊟ The **Minimize Window** and **Restore Window** buttons for the workbook are below.

⊟ The **Ribbon** (d) contains most of the application's commands, and replaces the menus and toolbars from previous versions of Excel. These commands are grouped by tasks, with each task represented by a **tab** (4). When certain objects are selected (such as an image), more tabs, called contextual tabs, appear. These tabs are displayed to the right of the normal tabs and contain the commands relevant to each selected object. Each tab has several **groups** (5) of commands (or sub tasks) containing **command buttons** (6) which perform most tasks. Some groups have a **dialog box launcher** (7), displaying a dialog box or an Office pane with more options.

⊟ The **Formula bar** (e) contains the **name box** (e) and the **formula area** (9): the name box displays information about the active cell while the formula area is where you enter and edit data. Both areas can be resized (see Display chapter).

⊟ The **workspace** (f) is made up of cells arranged in rows and columns. Rows are represented by numbers while columns are represented by letters. With Excel 2007, you have 1 048 576 rows and 16 384 columns (identified as XFD). Each cell is a combination of the column letter and the row number in which it is situated. For example, a cell at the intersection of the third column and second row is called **C10**. When you click a particular cell it becomes **active** (10) and its reference appears at the left of the formula bar. The black square at the bottom right corner of the active cell is called the **fill handle**.

⊟ A workbook consists of several sheets (3 by default). Excel identifies them in the **workbook tab** bar at the bottom of the book window. This bar contains the worksheet scroll buttons (11), the worksheet tabs (12) and the **Insert a worksheet** tab (13).

The **scroll bars** are for moving across (h) or up and down (i) the active worksheet. The rectangles on the scroll bars (14) are called **scroll cursors** or **scroll boxes**.

The **status bar** (j) displays information about the work environment, the view mode, the Zoom button and the Zoom cursor. You can change the information displayed in the bar (see Customisation chapter).

Leaving Microsoft Excel 2007

Click the **Microsoft Office** button 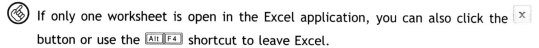 then **Leave Excel** in the lower right of the menu.

If necessary, save the modified workbooks.

If only one worksheet is open in the Excel application, you can also click the [×] button or use the [Alt][F4] shortcut to leave Excel.

Using/managing the ribbon

The ribbon contains most of the application's commands, and replaces the menus and toolbars from previous versions of Microsoft Excel.

Click the name of a tab to display its contents.

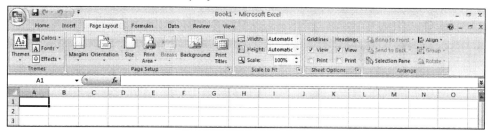

*Each tab is divided into several groups. For example, in the **Page Layout** tab, which is for managing the presentation of worksheets, there are five groups of commands: **Themes**, **Page Setup**, **Scale to fit**, **Sheet options** and **Arrange**.*

If you want more screen space you can temporarily minimise the ribbon by double clicking a tab or with the [Ctrl][F1] shortcut.

Only the tabs remain displayed, providing a larger work area.

To display the whole ribbon again, click a tab or use the [Ctrl][F1] shortcut keys.

⊟ To permanently minimise the ribbon, click the **Customize Quick Access Toolbar** button ⬛, and check **Minimize the ribbon.** To use the ribbon when it is minimized, click the tab you want to use, then the option or command you want.

⊟ To display the dialog box or Office pane for a particular group, click the ⬛ button in the bottom right corner of the relevant group of commands.

⊟ To access the ribbon with the keyboard, press the Alt key.

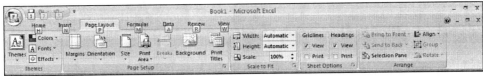

The shortcuts from the quick access toolbar and tabs are displayed.

Press the letter in the ribbon corresponding to the tab you want to activate.

Every command in the active tab has a shorcut key.

Press the letter corresponding to the option you want to use. If two letters are associated with an option, type the letters one after the other.

You can also use a shortcut to activate a tab. For example, Alt *R activates the* **Review** *tab.*

Shortcuts are automatically hidden after the command has been carried out. However, if you don't need to perform a command, press the Alt *key to hide the shortcuts.*

Although the ribbon replaces the menus and toolbars from previous versions, the shortcut menus remain. A shortcut menu is displayed when you right click an item. It only displays the commands related to that item.

Undoing the last actions

- To cancel the last action, click the **Undo** tool button ⤺ in the **Quick access toolbar** or use the Ctrl Z shortcut.

- To cancel the last actions, click the arrow on the **Undo** tool ⤺ to open the list of last actions then click the last action to cancel (that action and all the following actions will be cancelled).

Some actions, such as opening or saving a worksheet, cannot be undone. In these cases, the **Undo** tool button is replaced by **Can't undo**.

Redoing the last cancelled actions

- To redo the last cancelled action, click the **Redo** tool button ⤼ (in the **Quick access** toolbar) once or use the Ctrl Y shortcut.

- To redo the last actions cancelled, click the **Redo** tool button ⤼ as many times as you need.

Repeating the last action

You can repeat your last action instead of redoing it several times over and again.

- If required, select the relevant cells.

- Click the **Repeat** tool button ↻ in the **Quick access** toolbar or use the Ctrl Y shortcut or F4.

The **Redo** ⤼ and **Repeat** ↻ tool buttons are never displayed at the same time in the **Quick access** toolbar. They occupy the same position in the toolbar, with either one or the other visible depending on your action. For example, if you have just cancelled an action, you see the **Redo** ⤼ tool button, while if you have just formatted a cell you see the **Repeat** ↻ tool button.

———————————— ▪▪ ————————————

Starting/leaving the Microsoft Office Excel 2007 help function

You are strongly advised to be online when you use the Microsoft Office Excel help function. You will have access to a more comprehensive and up-to-date help menu.

Click the **Microsoft Office Excel Help** tool button ⓦ on the right of the ribbon or in a dialog box, or press ⌐F1⌐.

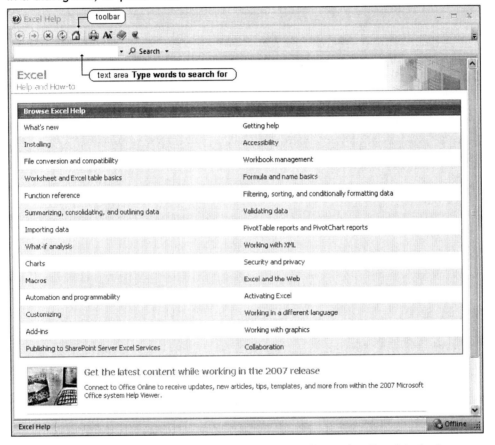

The Excel - Help window appears. If you are online, the Excel help home page, called Excel help and how to, appears after information is downloaded from the Microsoft Office Online site. The message Connected to Office Online is displayed in the bottom right of the window. Alternatively, the Offline message is displayed.

⊟ To leave the help application, click the **Close** tool button ⊠ or use the Alt F4 shortcut.

To switch from online to offline help, click the connection status button (**Connected to Office Online** or **Offline**) in the bottom right of the window then activate one of the two options: **Show content from Office Online** or **Show content only from this computer**. Your choice will be active the next time you open the help window.

Searching from the home page

⊟ Start the Excel help function.

⊟ In the help window toolbar, click the **Home** tool button 🏠 to display the help home page.

⊟ Point to the help link you want to consult.

When you point to a link, it appears underlined, and the pointer takes the shape of a hand with a pointing finger.

⊟ Click the link to display the help topics.

The 🔘 *icon appears to the left of the help topics.*

⊟ To consult a topic, point to it and click it.

You can display the previous pages using the ← and → tool buttons.

Searching from the table of contents

⊟ Start the Excel help function.

⊟ In the help window toolbar, click the **Show the table of contents** 🔖 tool button.

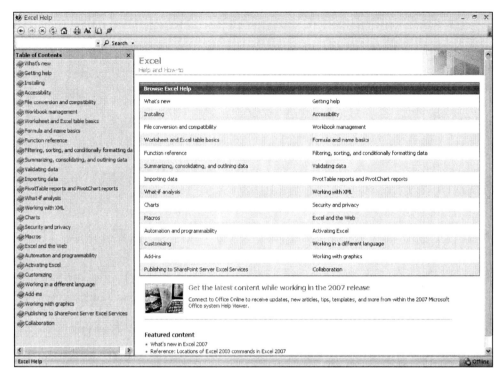

The table of contents is displayed in the left of the help window. It consists of help categories represented by a closed book or an open book depending on whether they are expanded or not. When a category is expanded, the different topics are preceded by the icon.

- To expand a topic category, click the corresponding "closed book" symbol.
- To minimize a topic category, click the relevant topic category name.
- To display the detail of a topic, click its name.

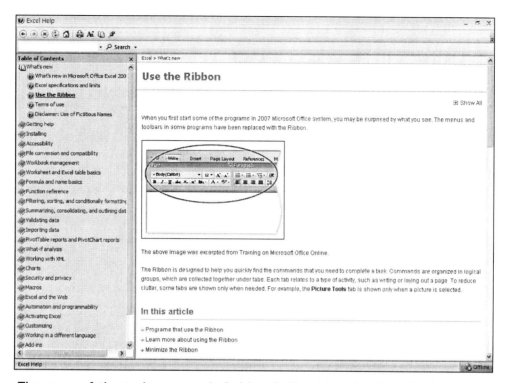

The name of the topic appears in bold underlined type in the left of the window, while the topic content is displayed in the right of the window.

The connection may be disabled if you do not use it. If this happens, just click the **Refresh** tool button to update the topics.

Searching with keywords

- Start the Excel help function.
- Enter the words in the **Type words to search for** box.
- Click the **Search** button or press Enter .

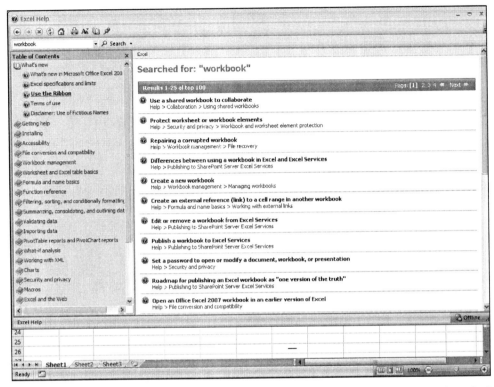

The titles of the topics matching the search criteria appear in the help window. The number of topics found is displayed in the top of the results window, above the first topic. If many topics are found, they are displayed on several pages.

Go to the page containing the help topic you want to read by clicking the relevant page number on the top right of the results window.

You can also use the   and   tool buttons to access the previous and following pages.

Click the name of the topic to display its contents.

If the table of contents is displayed, the topic content is displayed in the right of the window. The table of contents is expanded and the title of the topic is in bold underline type.

To search using recently used keywords, open the list on the **Type words to search for** box then click the text you want to search from. The topics matching the search criteria are displayed automatically, without having to click the **Search** button. This list is cleared automatically each time you close the window.

To restrict the search to a specific subject area, open the list on the help window **Search** button, then click the relevant subject (**All Excel** is selected by default).

Managing the help window

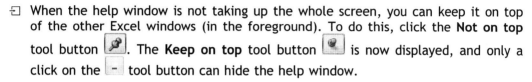

⊟ When the help window is not taking up the whole screen, you can keep it on top of the other Excel windows (in the foreground). To do this, click the **Not on top** tool button 🖉. The **Keep on top** tool button 🖉 is now displayed, and only a click on the 🖳 tool button can hide the help window.

⊟ If you want the help window to be hidden by the Excel application windows, click the **Keep on top** 🖉 tool button. The **Not on top** 🖉 tool button is displayed. By activating an Excel window the help window is hidden. To display it again, you need to click the relevant button in the task bar.

⊟ To change the size of the text in the help window, click the 🄰 tool button, then click the option matching the size of the text you need. The **Medium** option is selected by default.

⊟ To update the contents of the help window if you are online, click the 🄯 tool button in the toolbar. The 🞮 tool button stops a page from opening.

⊟ To add/delete tools from the toolbar, click the tool button in the top right of the help window then point to the **Add or remove buttons**. Next, check the options corresponding to the tools you want to add and uncheck the tools you want to remove. The **Reset toolbar** option restores the toolbar to its default setting.

Moving the Quick Access toolbar

⊟ Click the **Customize Quick Access Toolbar** tool button ▪ and click **Show below the ribbon**.

To put the Quick Access toolbar back over the ribbon, click the **Customize Quick Access Toolbar** tool button ▪, then check **Show above the ribbon**.

Customising the Quick Access toolbar

⊟ Click the **Customize Quick Access toolbar** tool button ▪, then click **More commands**.

*The **Excel Options** dialog box opens with the **Customize** group activated.*

⊟ Specify whether the customization applies to all worksheet or just the active one. To do this, open the **Customize Quick Access toolbar** list and select either **For all documents (default)** or **For active document**.

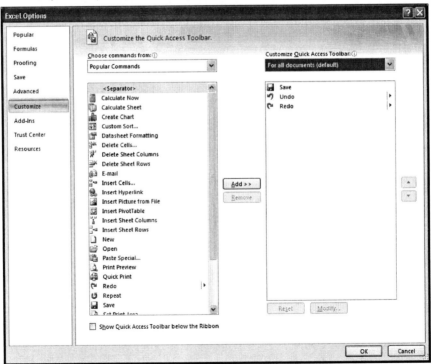

Customising

- ⊟ Make your changes (see following sub-headings) then, when you are ready, click **OK** in the **Excel options** dialog box.

Adding a command to the Quick Access toolbar

- ⊟ Open the list under **Choose commands from** then click the category containing the command to add.

- ⊟ In the list of commands from the selected category, click the command to add.

- ⊟ Click **Add**.

Removing a command from the Quick Access toolbar

- ⊟ Open the list under **Choose commands from**, then click the category containing the command to remove.

- ⊟ In the list of commands on the **Quick Access** toolbar, on the right of the dialog box, click the command to remove.

- ⊟ Click **Remove**.

Changing the order of commands in the Quick Access toolbar

- ⊟ In the list of commands on the **Quick Access** toolbar, on the right of the dialog box, click the command you want to move.

- ⊟ Click the [▲] tool button or the [▼] tool button, according to where you want to move the command.

- To restore the **Quick Access** toolbar, click **Reset** in the **Excel options** dialog box and confirm by clicking **Yes**.

Displaying/hiding the screentips

By default, when you point to a ribbon command, a descriptive text is displayed in a window called ScreenTip. You can hide the ScreenTips or display only the command name without its description. Below, you can see the description of the **Wrap text** *command in an advanced ScreenTip:*

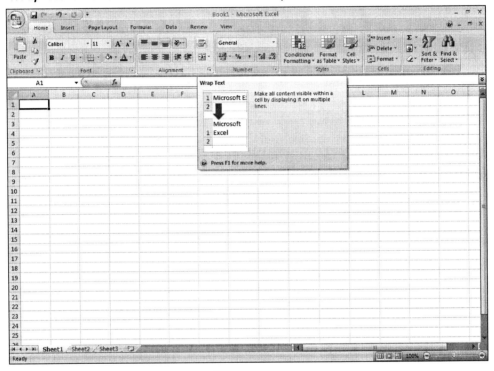

⊟ Click the **Microsoft Office** button 🔵 then click **Excel Options**.

⊟ In the left part of the dialog box, select **Popular**.

⊟ Go to the **Top options for working with** Excel area, open the **ScreenTip style** list and click one of the following options:

Show feature descriptions in ScreenTips: this option activates advanced ScreenTips. The name of the command you are pointing to followed by its description appears in the ScreenTip window. If there is a shortcut for the command you are pointing to, it appears in brackets to the right of the command name.

26

Don't show feature descriptions in ScreenTips: this option deactivates advanced ScreenTips. Only the name of the command you are pointing to and the shortcut (if there is one) are displayed in the ScreenTip window.

Don't show ScreenTips: this option deactivates the ScreenTips. No ScreenTip appears when you point to a command.

🔲 Click **OK**.

 If you have activated advanced ScreenTips, when you point to certain commands, you will see **Press** F1 **for help**. In this case, you just need to press F1 to open the help topic relating to the command you are pointing to.

Customising the status bar

You can hide or display the indicators displayed on the status bar.

🔲 Right click the status bar.

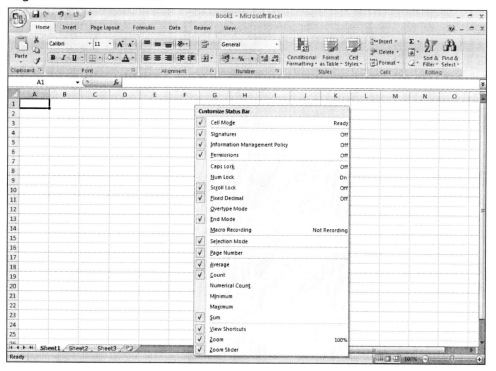

The checked options are indicators that can be displayed, depending on the function you perform.

⊟ Click the required options to activate or deactivate them.

⊟ When you have finished, click outside the status bar to confirm.

Display

Changing the display mode

Microsoft Office Excel 2007 offers three main displays.

Normal view

Normal view is the default view.

In the **View** tab, go to the **Workbook Views** group and click **Normal**, or click the tool button on the right of the status bar.

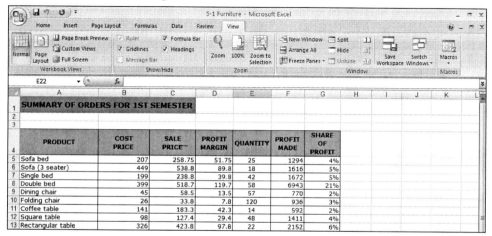

Page Layout view

In the **View** tab, go to the **Workbook Views** group and click the **Page Layout** tab, or click the tool button on the right of the status bar.

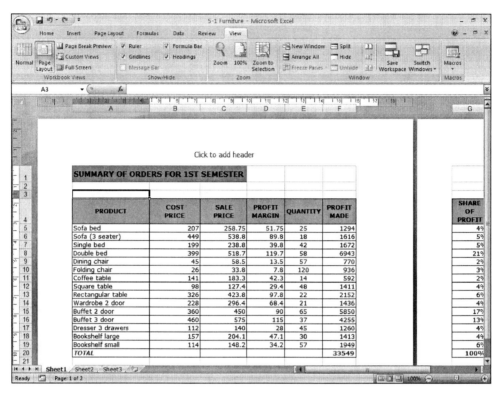

In Page Layout view, Excel displays the general layout of the worksheet as it would appear on the printed page. You see the top of two pages. You can correctly position objects and views, and directly modify page margins in the worksheet with the horizontal and vertical rulers. You can also create and modify the page headers and footers.

Page break preview

In this view you can view and move existing page breaks.

⊡ In the **View** tab, go to the **Workbook Views** group and click the **Page Break Preview** button, or click the ▥ tool button on the right of the status bar.

A dialog box appears, indicating that you can drag the page breaks to move them.

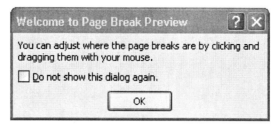

⊟ If you want, check **Do not show this dialog again**, then click **OK**.

Page breaks are indicated by blue lines, continuous for manual page breaks and dotted for automatic page breaks. You can work normally in the worksheet (enter, edit data, etc).

⊟ To move a page break, point to the blue line then drag it to its new position.

Activate full screen view

*Whichever view you are using, fullscreen view displays only the workbook, without the **Quick Access** toolbar, the ribbon and the status bar.*

⊟ Activate the view you want (**Normal**, **Page Layout** or **Page Break Preview**).

⊟ In the **View** tab, go to the **Workbook views** group and click the **Full screen** button.

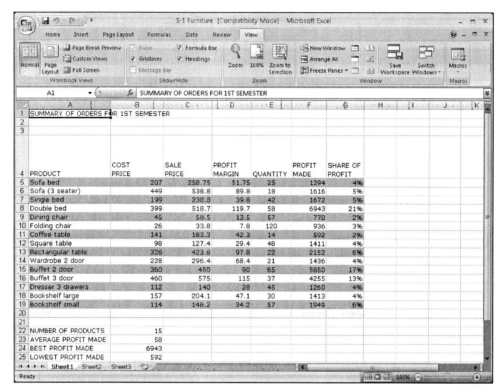

*Here, the worksheet is in Normal and full screen view. You no longer see the **Quick Access** toolbar, the ribbon or the status bar.*

⊡ Click Esc to go back to the previous view.

Modifying the formula bar display

Remember that the formula bar has two boxes that you can re-size.

⊡ To increase or reduce the size of the name box in relation to the formula box, point to the intersection (the mouse pointer takes the shape of a horizontal two-headed arrow) and drag it either to the left or the right.

⊡ To increase or reduce the size of the formula box, point to the bottom of the box (the pointer takes the shape of a vertical two-headed arrow) and drag towards the top or bottom.

Display

When the formula box includes a scroll bar, this means that not all its content is displayed.

⊟ To automatically adjust the formula box according to its contents (i.e. according to the number of lines of text in the active cell) point to the bottom of the box (the pointer takes the shape of a vertical two-headed arrow) and double click.

⊟ To expand the formula box by at least three lines or to reduce it to a single line, click the ⮛ tool button at the end of the formula bar, or use the Ctrl Shift U shortcut.

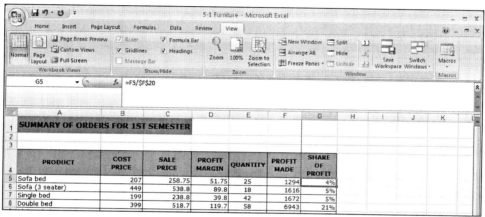

⊛ To hide the formula bar, activate the **View** tab, go to the **Show/Hide** group and uncheck the **Formula bar** box.

Displaying/hiding gridlines, line and column headers

⊟ Activate the **View** tab.

⊟ To hide the gridlines, go to the **Show/Hide** group and uncheck the gridlines box. To redisplay the gridlines, check the box.

⊟ To hide the letters indicating the columns and the numbers indicating the rows, go to the **Show/Hide** group and uncheck the **Headings** box. To display them, check the box.

Changing the zoom setting

⊟ To quickly change the zoom level, drag the **Zoom cursor** 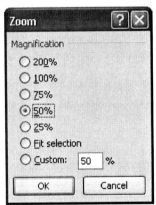 situated on the status bar, or click the **Zoom in** ⊖ or **Zoom out** ⊕ buttons as many times as required.

You can also press the Ctrl *key and turn the mouse scroll button forward or backward. The zoom percentage for the workbook is displayed in the status bar.*

⊟ To zoom in to one part of the workbook, select the cells you want to zoom in to, go to the **View** tab, **Zoom** group and click the **Zoom to Selection** button.

⊟ To specify a particular zoom setting, activate the **View** tab, go to the **Zoom** group and click the **Zoom** button, or click the button in the status bar that displays the **Zoom** percentage.

*The **Zoom** dialog box appears.*

Click the zoom setting you require, or enter a zoom value in the **Customized** box.

*The **Fit selection** option zooms in to selected cells.*

⊟ Click **OK**.

Activating a window

When several workbooks are open, or when you have opened several windows within a single workbook (cf. next heading), you need to know how to activate one window or the other.

⊟ Activate the **View** tab, go to the **Window** group and click the **Switch Windows** button.

Display

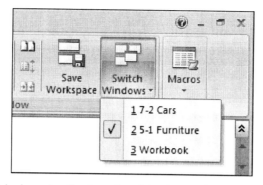

The list of open windows is displayed, with the active window checked.

⊟ Click the window you want to activate.

🖑 If all the windows are displayed on the screen (see Rearranging the window layout), click the window you want to activate. You can also click the button corresponding to the window to activate in the Windows task bar.

Creating a window from an active window

You can create several different views of the active workbook. This allows you, for example, to view non-adjacent cells from the same workbook or two worksheets from the same workbook.

⊟ In the **View** tab, go to the **Window** group and click **New Window**.

A new window called workbook name.xlsx:2 opens over the original window.

🖑 Working in any of the windows modifies the workbook, not just the sheet that is active in the window.

Arranging the window view

You can display different windows from one or more workbooks at the same time.

⊟ Activate the windows for the workbook.

⊟ In the **View** tab, go to the **Window** group and click **Arrange all**.

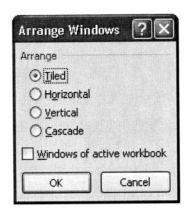

Use the dialog box to choose the window layout.

⊟ Choose the layout you want for your windows. **Tiled** displays all windows side-by-side; **Cascade** displays the windows in a cascade style, one on top of the other, with the title bar visible.

⊟ To display all windows of the active workbook, check **Windows of active workbook**.

⊟ Click **OK**.

Displaying/hiding a window

You can hide a window without in Excel closing it.

⊟ Activate the window you want to hide.
In the **View** tab, go to the **Window** group and click the **Hide** button.

⊟ To display a hidden window, go to the **Window** group and click **Unhide**.
In the **Display** dialog box that opens, click the name of the window to display then click **OK**, or double-click the name.

Display

Freezing/unfreezing rows or columns

This function freezes lines and/or columns on screen so you can view data at opposite ends of the worksheet.

⊡ Activate the **View** tab.

⊡ To lock a line, scroll down the window to display the relevant line as the first row of the window. Go to the **Window** group and click **Freeze Panes** and check **Freeze top row**.

⊡ To lock a column, display it as the first column in the window. Go to the **Window** group, click **Freeze Panes** and select **Freeze first column**.

⊡ To lock the first rows and columns of the window, click in the cell to the right of the column and below the rows you want to lock. Next, go to the **Window** group, click the **Freeze Panes** button and select **Freeze Panes**.

⊡ To unlock rows or columns, go to the **Window** group, click the **Freeze Panes** button and select **Unfreeze Panes**.

Splitting/unsplitting the window

Much like freezing a row or column, you can split a window into two or four panes. You can independently scroll through the content of each pane at the same time.

⊡ To split the window, click the cell below and to the right of the place where you want to split the worksheet.

⊡ Activate the **View** tab, go to the **Window** group and click the **Split** button .

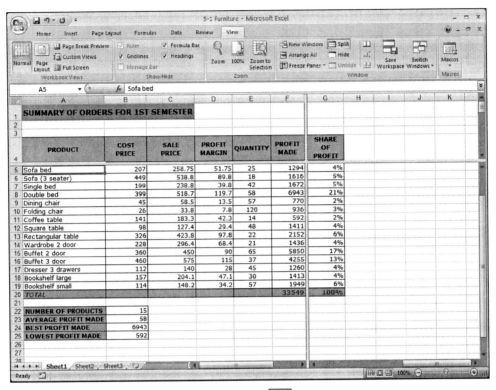

↴ To remove the split, click the **Split** button ▦ again.

You can also split the window by pointing to the split bars located at the top of the vertical scroll bar ▭ and at the far right of the horizontal scroll bar ▯ depending on whether you want to split vertically or horizontally. Once the pointer looks like a two-headed arrow, drag the split bar down and/or to the left until your window looks the way you want it.

Part 2
Managing documents

Documents created in Microsoft Office Excel 2007 are called workbooks.

Creating a new workbook

⊟ Click the **Microsoft Office** button 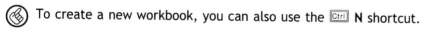, then **New**.

⊟ In the **New Workbook** dialog box, make sure that the **Blank Workbook** button is selected in the **Blank and recent** pane.

⊟ Click **Create**.

A new blank window appears, called Book, followed by a number.

To create a new workbook, you can also use the Ctrl N shortcut.

Creating a workbook from a template

You can create a workbook from a different template to the one used to create the blank workbook by using either a predefined template that is installed with Excel, a template you have created yourself (cf. Chapter: Templates – Creating a customised workbook template), or a template downloaded from the Microsoft site.

⊟ Clic the **Microsoft Office** button , then **New**.

Creating a workbook from a predefined template

⊟ In the **New Workbook** dialog box, click **Installed Templates**, under **Templates**.

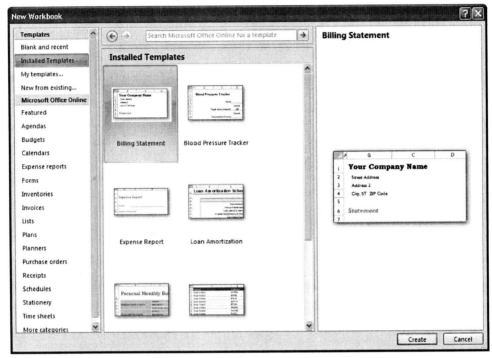

The predefined Excel 2007 templates appear in the centre of the dialog box, in the Installed Templates pane.

⊟ Click the template you want to use.

⊟ Click **Create**.

A new window opens, containing the data from the installed template.

⊟ Make the changes you require and save the workbook as a new workbook.

Creating a workbook from a customized template

⊟ In the **New workbook** dialog box, go to the **Templates** category and click **My templates.**

*The **New** dialog box opens, displaying the list of templates you have saved. The customized templates are normally saved in a dedicated templates folder (C:\Documents and Settings\username\Application Data\Microsoft\Templates).*

⊟ Double click the template you want to use.

A new window opens, containing the data from the template. This window has the same name as the template, followed by a number.

⊟ Enter your data and save the workbook as a new workbook.

Creating a workbook from a downloaded template

⊟ In the **New workbook** dialog box, under the **Templates** pane, in the **Microsoft Office Online** category, click the category of template you want to download.

⊟ Depending on the category you choose, several sub-categories may be displayed in the centre of the dialog box. If so, click the link relating to the category of template you want.

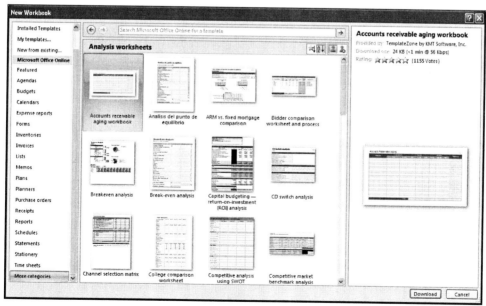

*The list of templates available on the **Microsoft Online** site is downloaded and is displayed in the centre of the dialog box.*

*The name of the category or the sub-category is displayed at the top of the pane. If the templates are part of a sub-category, there is a link to the corresponding category above the **Sort by** box. Click the link if you want to activate that category.*

🖸 To sort the list of templates by name, click the **Sort by name** tool button ▦.

🖸 To sort the list of templates by rating, click the **Sort by customer rating** tool button ▦.

Internet users can rate each template on the Microsoft Online site. You can use this option, which is active by default, to sort templates from best to worst according to their rating.

By default, templates appear as thumbnails.

🖸 Select the template you want to use: its preview as well as its properties (name, size, rating, etc) are displayed in the right pane.

🖸 Click the **Download** button or double click the relevant template.

After downloading, a new window opens, containing the data from the new template. This window also has the same name as the template, followed by a number.

🖸 Make your changes and save the workbook as a new workbook.

Ⓜ The list of **Recently used templates** is displayed in the **New workbook** dialog box, in the **Blank and recent** category. To create a workbook from one of these templates, simply double click the name of the workbook you want to use. If no templates have been previously used, you will not see a list. To remove a template from this list, right click the name of the template you want to remove, then click **Remove template**. To remove all templates from this list, right click the name of one of the templates, then click **Remove all recent templates**.

To look for a template on the Microsoft Office Online site, enter one or more keywords in the **Search Microsoft Office Online for a template** box then start searching by clicking the →| button. If there are any, the templates matching your search will be displayed in the centre pane of the dialog box. If the search goes on for too long, click the **Stop** button: there are no templates matching your search.

Creating a workbook from an existing workbook

⊡ Click the **Microsoft Office** button , then click **New**.

⊡ In the **New workbook** dialog box, go to the **Templates** pane and click **New from existing**.

*The **New from existing workbook** dialog box opens.*

⊡ Access the folder containing the template you want to use and double click its name.

The window that opens contains the data from the selected workbook, but does not exist as a workbook; it has the same name as the workbook it is based on, followed by a number.

⊡ Make your changes and save the workbook as a new workbook.

Opening a workbook

⊡ Click the **Microsoft Office** button , then click **Open**, or use the Ctrl O shortcut.

⊡ Indicate the workbook location using the **Look in** drop-down list, or using the buttons from the **My places** bar (situated in the left of the dialog box).

*The **My recent documents** button displays the last 50 files/folders used.*

The **Desktop** button accesses the shortcuts installed on your Windows desktop.

The **My documents** button opens the **My documents** folder.

The **My computer** button displays the contents of your computer.

The **My network places** button accesses your networks.

The **Look in** list contains all the drives on your computer, including the hard drive (c), the CD or DVD drive, your network places or the Internet (FTP sites).

⊟ Select the drive where your document is located (A:, C:, D: etc) if it is on your computer, or click **My network places** to access a network drive.

⊟ Double click the icon name to access the folder where the workbook is located, and if required, access the sub-folders using double-clicks.

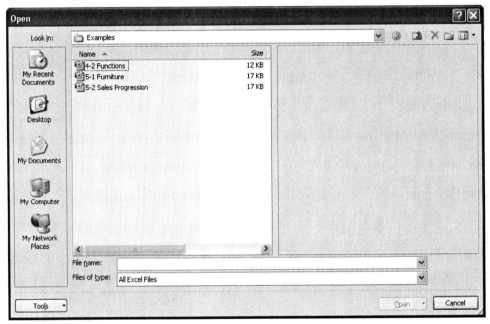

The ⌷ button displays the contents of the parent folder (parent folder), while the ⊕ ▾ button displays the contents of the last folder you have accessed.

⊟ To change the view of the list of documents in the active folder, click the ⊞ ▾ tool button and select:

Thumbnails	displays a large icon (showing the file type) and the name of each document.
Tiles	displays a medium-sized icon, the name, the type and the size of each document.
Icons	displays a small icon and the name of each document.
List	displays a small icon of each document followed by its name, in list form.
Details	displays a small icon, the name, size, type and date last modified for each document, in list form.
Properties	displays the properties of the selected document. Click the name of the document to see its properties displayed in the pane on the right.
Preview	displays a preview of the selected document. Click the name of the document in the centre pane to preview it in the right hand side of the dialog box.

To open a workbook, double-click its name. To open several workbooks at the same time, click the first workbook to open, then:

- if the workbooks follow each other , press the `⇧ Shift` key and click the last workbook to open.

- if the workbooks do not follow each other, press the `Ctrl` key and click each workbook to open.

Click **Open**.

 To add a shortcut for a document or folder to the **My places** bar, go to the

Look in list (if you are in the **Open** dialog box) or the,

Save in list (if you are in the **Save as** dialog box).

Next, select the relevant document or folder, right click in the empty space in the **My places** bar, then click **Add "document/drive name"**.

Opening a recently used workbook

⊟ To open a recently used file quickly, click the **Microsoft Office** button 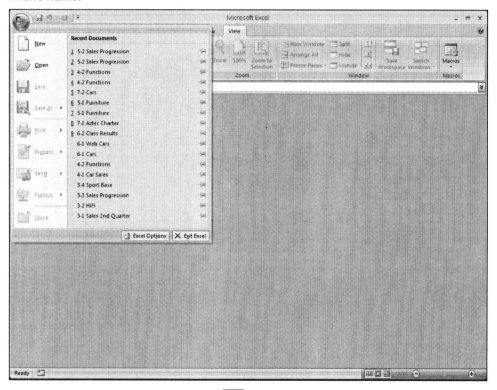, then click the name of the workbook to open in the **Recent documents** list.

By default, the last nine documents used are displayed in this list; Each time you open a document, the last document in the list disappears and its place is taken by the document you have just opened, which goes to the top of the list.

⊟ To keep a document in the list of **Recent documents**, click the **Pin this document to the recent documents list** tool button ⊸⧄, displayed to the right of the document name.

The symbol is displayed in green ⧆. *To cancel, simply click the symbol. The document will disappear automatically when it has reached the last position on the list.*

⊟ To change the number of documents displayed in the **Recent documents** list, open the **Excel Options** dialog box (🔲 – **Excel Options**), then click **Advanced**. Go to the **Display** category and specify a value in the **Show this number of recent documents** list.

A maximum of fifty documents can be displayed in this list.

⊟ Click **OK**.

Saving a workbook

Saving a new workbook

A workbook that has never been saved does not have a name. It only exists in the computer's memory. As the memory is unstable, all its data is permanently erased from the computer when you turn it off.

⊟ Click the **Microsoft Office** button 🔲 then **Save**, or click the **Save** tool button 🔲 from the **Quick Access** toolbar, or use the Ctrl S shortcut.

⊟ Select the drive where you want to save the workbook using the **Save in** drop-down list, or the icons from the **My Places** bar.

⊟ Double-click the icon of the folder where you want to save the workbook and, if required, one of the sub-folders. If you want to create a folder, access the folder in which the new folder should be created, and click the 🔲 tool button. Enter the name you want to give to the folder and click **OK**.

⊟ Double-click in the **File name** box then enter the workbook name.

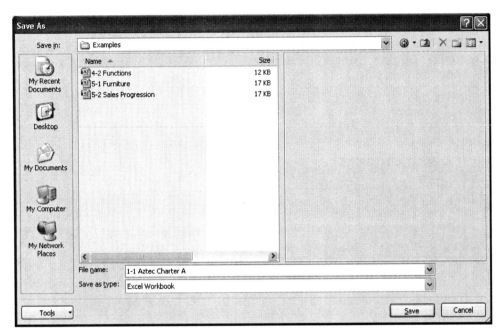

⊟ Click **Save**.

Excel documents now have the **.xlsx** extension (even if it is not displayed). This file format, based on XML language, reduces the size of files, make them more secure, and easier to use in other professional applications. Note, however, that you can still save a workbook in a pre-2007 version of Excel (cf. Using workbooks from pre-Office 2007 versions of Excel).

Saving an existing workbook

When you are working on an existing workbook, you are making changes to it. To keep these changes, you must save them.

⊟ Click the **Microsoft Office** button , then **Save**, or click the **Save** tool button from the **Quick Access** toolbar, or use the Ctrl **S** shortcut.

When you are making many changes, a progress bar is displayed in the status bar.

Excel memorizes the active cell when the workbook is saved.

Using Office Excel 2007 workbooks in previous versions

A new file format, based on XML language, is associated with workbooks created in Microsoft Office Excel 2007. They now have the extension .xlsx whereas workbooks created in previous versions have the extension .xls (binary format).

You can still save a workbook in a previous version of Excel (97 – 2003), but it is worthwhile checking its compatibility first.

Checking the compatibility of a workbook

This task detects and resolves any possible compatibility problems that might cause a loss of information with previous versions of Excel.

⊟ In Microsoft Office Excel 2007, open the relevant workbook.

⊟ Click the **Microsoft Office** button 🔘 , then **Prepare**, then **Run compatibility checker**.

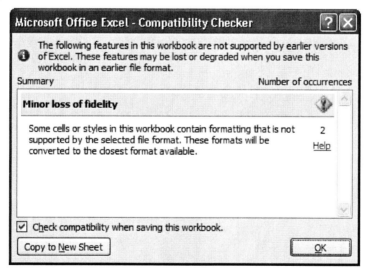

⊟ To check the compatibility of a workbook each time it is saved, check the **Check compatibility when saving this workbook** box.

⊟ If there are any problems, click the **Copy to a new workbook** button to create a report of all the problems listed in the relevant spreadsheet. Otherwise, click **OK** to leave the **Compatibility checker** dialog box.

Saving a workbook in Excel 97-2003 format

This task creates a copy of the 2007 workbook that is completely compatible with previous versions of Excel 97-2003.

- In Excel 2007, open the relevant workbook.

- Click the **Microsoft Office** button 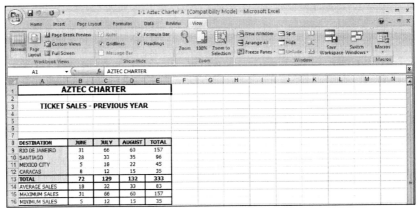, point to the arrow to the right of the **Save as** option, then click **Excel workbook 97-2003**.

  *The **Save as** dialog box opens. Note that the **Excel workbook 97-2003 (*.xls)** workbook is selected in the **Save as type** list.*

- Select the folder in which you want to save the workbook then specify its name in the **File name** box.

  Even if the folder and file name are the same as the Excel 2007 workbook, the latter is not replaced, but duplicated.

- Click **Save**.

To save a workbook in Excel 97-2003 format, you can also click the **Microsoft Office** button , **Save as**, then select **Excel workbook 97-2003 (*.xls)** in the **Save as type** list from the **Save as** dialog box.

Using workbooks from pre-2007 versions of Excel

Working in compatibility mode in Excel 2007

- In Excel 2007, open the workbook created in a previous version.

*The workbook is automatically opened in **compatibility mode**. This term is indicated between brackets next to the file name in the title bar. The file format used is Excel 97-2003 (*.xls).*

The new features of Excel 2007, or those that have been improved, are not available (to ensure that no data or privacy is lost when the workbook is opened in a previous version of Excel).

⊟ You can work and make changes as you normaly would, taking note of the previous comments.

When you save your changes, the file format Excel 97-2003 (*.xls) is maintained.

Converting a workbook to Excel 2007 format

When you decide once and for all to work in the most recent version of Office and take advantage of the new features of Office 2007, you can convert workbooks.

⊟ Open the workbook you want to convert to Office Excel 2007 format.

⊟ Click the **Microsoft Office** button , then **Convert**.

Excel explains the process.

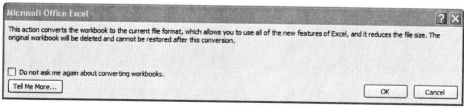

⊟ If you do not want the message to be displayed next time you carry out this task, check **Do not ask me again about converting workbooks**.

⊟ Click **OK**.

The following message appears:

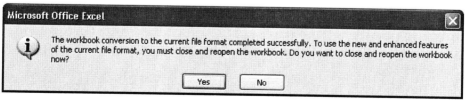

⊟ Click **Yes** to close and reopen the workbook, or **No** to keep the workbook in the old version.

Note that, if you have clicked No, the title bar displays the .xlsx extension, the (compatibility mode) message is still displayed (it will disappear the next time you open the workbook).

Ⓐ Converting a workbook reduces its size.

When you convert a workbook, it is replaced by a copy of the workbook in the current file format (.xlsx). Once the workbook is converted, it is no longer available in the format of the original file. If you want to keep a copy of the workbook in the format of the original file, instead of converting the workbook, you can save it in the format of the current file (.xlsx). Click the **Microsoft Office** button , then **Save as**. If required, change the name of the folder and **File name**, and in the **File type** drop-down list, choose **Excel workbook (*.xlsx)**, then click **Save**. If you do not change either the location or the name of the workbook, two workbooks with the same name will be displayed in the same folder. One will have the **.xls** extension, and the other will have the **.xlsx** extension. If you cannot see these extensions, you can tell the files apart by their icons (and).

Saving a workbook in PDF or XPS format

<u>Installing the Publish in PDF or XPS format add-in</u>

Before saving a file in PDF or XPS format, you must have installed the Publish to PDF or XPS format add-in for Microsoft Office system 2007.

⊟ Click the **Microsoft Office** button , point to **Save as** then click **Find add-ins for other file formats**.

If the add-in is already installed, this option is replaced by PDF or XPS.

⊟ In the help page that opens, click the **Microsoft Save as PDF or XPS Add-in for 2007 Microsoft Office programs** link in the **Install and use the save as PDF or XPS add-in from Microsoft** section.

The Microsoft Office site is displayed in your browser, at the page where you can install the add-in.

⊟ Click **Continue** then, as explained in the page which is displayed, right click on the information bar then click **Install ActiveX control**.

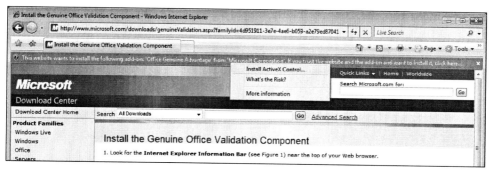

⊡ Click **Install**.

⊡ Click the **Download** button to the left of the **Genuine Microsoft Office Software** then click **Run** from the **Download files** dialog box.

⊡ Click the **Run** button in the **Internet Explorer** dialog box.

The dialog box from the Microsoft add-in installation programme is displayed.

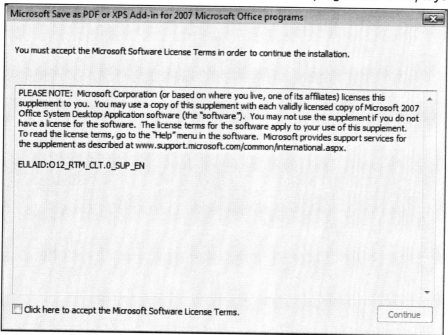

- After reading the terms of the Microsoft software contract licence, and if you accept, check **Click here to accept the Microsoft Software Licence Terms** then click **Continue**.

- Click the **OK** button on the message advising you that the installation is complete.

- Close your browser window then activate the Excel window.

Save as PDF or XPS format

PDF and XPS are file formats that allow documents to be shared electronically (i.e. sent by e-mail). These formats keep a document's fonts, images, graphics and formatting as they appear in the original document. A user can display, share and print PDF files using Acrobat Reader software (available for free from the Adobe web site), and XPS files using Microsoft .NET framework (available for free on the Microsoft site).

- Click the **Microsoft Office** button , point to **Save as**, and click **PDF or XPS**.

  If you cannot see this option, that means the add-in that enables you to save in PDF and XPS format is not installed (cf. previous sub-heading).

- If required, change the folder you are saving to and the **File name** in the corresponding text field.

- Open the **Save as** list then, depending on the type of file you are creating, select either **PDF** or **XPS document**.

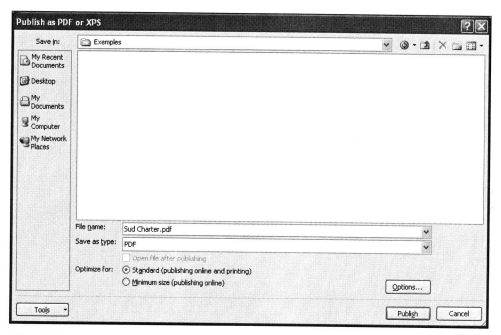

⊟ Check **Open file after publishing** if you want to open it immediately.

⊟ Activate one of the options from the **Optimize for** list:

Standard (publishing online and printing)	for a good quality printed document. This increases the size of the document.
Minimum size (publishing online)	if the file is not for printing. The file size is reduced.

⊟ If required, change the **Options** by clicking the corresponding button.

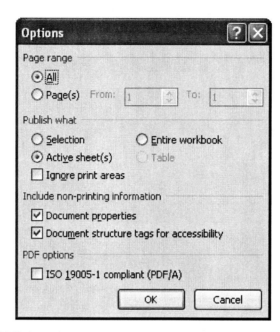

*Here are the **PDF** format options. They are identical to the options in the **XPS** dialog box, except for those under **Options** at the bottom of the box.*

- Specify the part of the workbook to publish by checking one of the following options:

All	To publish every page in the workbook.
Page(s)	To publish the pages specified in the From and To boxes.
Selection	To publish the selected cells.
Active sheet	To publish the selected workbook(s).
Entire workbook	To publish the entire workbook.
Table	To publish the selected table.

- Check **Ignore print areas** to print the entire worksheet, including the existing print areas.

- Check **Document properties** if you want to include the workbook properties (title, subject, author, etc).

◰ Check **Document structure tags for accessibility** to publish a document accessible to disabled users. If you uncheck this option (which is active by default), the published file will be smaller, as it will not contain the information that makes it accessible.

◰ If you are creating a **PDF** document, you can activate the **ISO 19005-1 compliant (PDF/A)** option, if you want the document to be consistent with this format, which is required by some organisations.

◰ Click **OK** in the **Options** dialog box.

◰ Click **Publish** in the **Publish as PDF or XPS** dialog box.

Displaying/editing workbook properties

Properties, also called metadata (i.e. data about other data, for example, the words in a workbook are data, while the number of words in a workbook is metadata) is information relating to a workbook identifying and describing it. They include information such as the title, author name, subject, etc.

◰ Click the **Microsoft Office** button 	, point to the arrow ▸ to the right of **Prepare,** then click **Properties.**

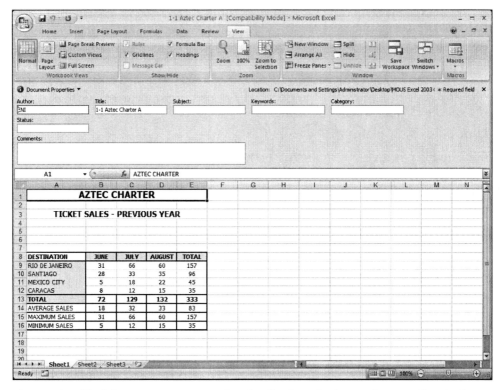

*A panel called **Document properties** is displayed above the workbook, between the ribbon and the formula bar.*

⊟ Enter the information you require in the property fields.

⊟ To access the advanced properties, click the arrow to the right of **Document properties** and click **Advanced properties**.

*The workbook **Properties** dialog box is displayed.*

⊟ Activate the **Summary** tab to fill in additional document properties.

The other tabs in this dialog box, which display general information such as statistics, cannot be modified.

⊟ Click **OK**.

⊟ Save the changes to the workbook ⊟.

Workbooks

⊟ Close the **Document properties** panel by clicking the ☒ button (called **Close document information panel**).

🔄 To display the properties of a workbook when you save or open it, click its name in the **Save as** or **Open** dialog boxes, and click the ▦▾ tool button to choose document properties.

Comparing workbooks side-by-side

⊟ Open the two workbooks you want to compare.

⊟ If necessary, activate one of the two workbooks. In the **View** tab, go to the **Window** group and click **Switch window**, or click the corresponding button in the task bar.

⊟ In the **View** tab, go to the **Window** group and click the **View side by side** button ▥.

*The two workbooks are displayed in separate windows. By default, they scroll simultaneously, ie when you scroll down one workbook, the other scrolls at the same time. This indicates that the **Synchronous scrolling** button ▦↕ is active.*

⊟ To scroll down the two windows independently of each other, click the **Synchronous scrolling** button ▦↕ to deactivate it.

⊟ If you have changed the size or position of the windows, click **Reset window position** ▦ (in the **Window** group).

⊟ When the comparison of the two documents is complete, click the **View side by side** button ▥ in one of the two workbooks to turn off the side-by-side view.

Closing a workbook

⊟ Click the **Microsoft Office** button 🔘, then **Close**, or use the Ctrl F4 shortcut, or click the ☒ button in the top right of the application window.

Remember that if only one workbook is open in the Excel application, the entire application is closed when you close the workbook.

Managing documents

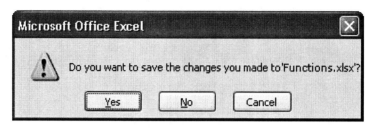

⊟ If the workbook has been modified since it was last saved, Excel prompts you to save it before closing. In this situation, click one of the following buttons:

Yes   to save and close the workbook.

No   to close the workbook without saving the changes made to it.

Cancel   to cancel the closure of the workbook.

Choosing the default working folder

This is the folder that Excel will propose to use when you save or open a workbook.

⊟ Click the **Microsoft Office** button , then **Excel options**, and select the **Save** category.

⊟ Under **Save** workbooks, go to **Default file location** and specify the working folder to use by default.

⊟ Click **OK**.

Managing settings for automatic workbook recovery

Occasionally, Microsoft Excel may stop working (due to power failures or bugs) before you have had a chance to save your work. The automatic recovery program, which is active by default, saves your data as well as the programme status automatically. You can control the settings for this function.

⊟ Click the **Microsoft Office** button , then **Excel options**, and select the **Save** category.

⊟ To activate automatic recovery, check the **Save autorecover information every x minutes** box.

60

⊟ In the **Minutes** box, specify the frequency with which you want the program to save your data.

⊟ You can change the access path in the **Autorecover file location** if you want to change the folder in which the automatic recover program saves a version of your files.

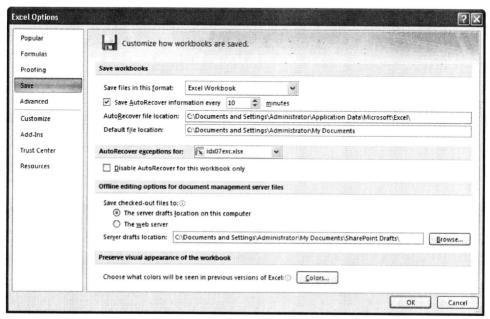

⊟ Click **OK**.

Sending a workbook by e-mail

Microsoft Office Excel 2007 allows you to send workbooks by e-mail (if you have e-mail software and an internet or intranet connection). The message recipients must have Excel to be able to open the workbook.

⊟ Open the workbook you want to send by e-mail.

⊟ Click the **Microsoft Office** button , point to **Send** and click **E-mail**.

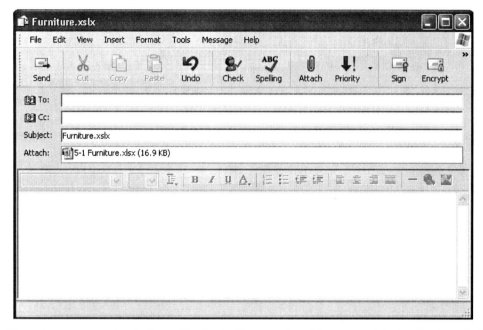

The message send window (Outlook Express in this example) is displayed. The workbook will be sent as an attachment.

- In the **To:** box, enter the address of the message recipient(s) separating their names by a semi-colon or click the **To** button to select addresses from an address book.

- In the **Cc:** box, you can specifiy the address of the message recipients whom you want to copy.

- In the **Subject:** box, enter or edit the message subject.

- Enter the message body in message body field.

- Click **Send**.

To open and modify the sent workbook, the recipient must open the message then double click the workbook name. The workbook will automatically open in the Excel application.

Templates

A template is a document containing worksheets, data, calculations, etc which can be re-used for new documents.

Creating a custom workbook template

⊡ Create the workbook template by including all the common elements of the workbooks that will be created from this template. If required, define the protection for the worksheets or cells (see Protection chapter).

⊡ Click the **Microsoft Office** button 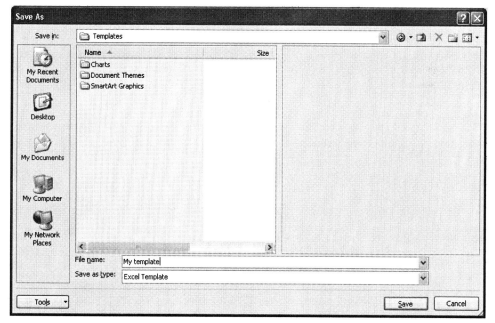, then **Save as**.

⊡ Open the **Save as type** list and select **Excel workbook (*.xltx)**.

*The **Templates** folder on your hard drive (in Window XP) is the default folder location, normally at this address:*

C:/Documents and Settings/username/Application Data/Microsoft/Templates
Note: If you change the default folder location, you will no longer be able to use it as a template. You will only be able to open it.

⊡ Specify the template name in the **File name** box.

63

Click **Save**.

The extension given to templates is XLTX (depending on your Windows settings, this extension may be hidden).

To change a custom template, open it. Proceed as you would for a normal workbook, remembering to select **Templates** in the **File type** box in the **Open** dialog box.

To create a workbook based on a custom template, refer to the relevant heading in the Workbook chapter.

Creating a default workbook or worksheet template

When you start the Excel application, the automatically-generated workbook uses settings (formatting, number of sheets, etc) from a template called **Workbook.xltx**. *The same template is used when you create a blank workbook (see Workbooks chapter).*

When you insert pages into the workbook, you are using a template called **Work-sheet.xltx** *which contains the formatting and contents to create a new sheet.*

 To create your own workbook and or worksheet templates, the idea is to create a template that you call **Workbook.xltx** or **Sheet.xltx** according to the process described in the previous heading (the sheet.xltx template must only contain one worksheet, otherwise all the worksheets will be inserted when you want to insert a sheet).

 Tu use templates automatically, make sure you save them to the following folder:

- C:/documents and settings/username/application data/Microsoft/Excel/XLStart; for the Workbook.xltx template.
- C:/documents and settings/username/application data/Microsoft/Templates, for the Worksheet template.

To restore the original workbook settings, delete the Workbook.xltx template; to restore the worksheets, delete the Sheet.xlts template.

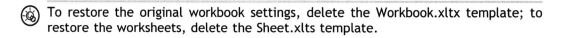

Part 3
Entering/editing data

Moving around in a worksheet

Depending on your preferences, mouse or keyboard, there are several options to navigate within a worksheet.

Use the scroll bars to display the cell you want to activate.

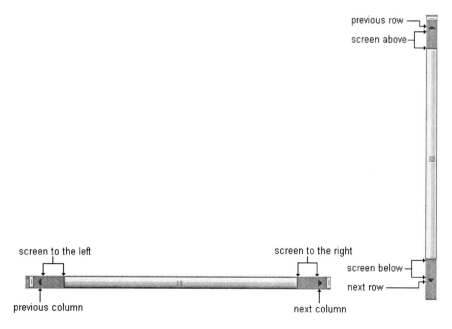

Entering/editing data

 Use the keyboard as follows:

Cell to the right/left	→ or ⇄ / ← or ⇧ Shift ⇄
Cell above/below	↑ or ⇧ Shift Enter / ↓ or Enter
Move one screen to the left/right	Alt Pg Dn / Alt Pg Up
Move up/down one screen	Pg Up / Pg Dn
Column A of the active row	Home
Cell A1	Ctrl Home
Move to the left/right edge of the data region	Ctrl ← / Ctrl →
Move the top/bottom edge of the data region	Ctrl ↑ / Ctrl ↓

*The **data region** is a set of cells containing data surrounded by empty cells or at the edge of the worksheet.*

Accessing a particular cell

Click in the name box (the part of the formula bar displaying the reference of the active cell).

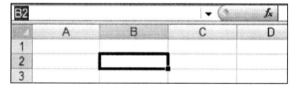

The reference of the active cell is now selected.

Enter the cell reference you want to go to, and press the Enter key to confirm.

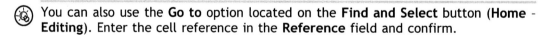

You can also use the **Go to** option located on the **Find and Select** button (**Home – Editing**). Enter the cell reference in the **Reference** field and confirm.

Moving/selecting

Searching for a cell

<u>By contents</u>

⊟ If you want to search the entire worksheet or workbook, activate a cell. If you want to search one part of the active sheet, select the relevant range of cells.

⊟ In the **Home** tab, go to the **Editing** group and click the **Find and select** button, then click **Find**, or use the Ctrl F shortcut.

⊟ Enter the search criteria in the **Find what** box.

⊟ If required, click **Options** to refine the search:

Within	select whether you want to search the active sheet or all pages in the **workbook**.
Search	select whether you want to search by rows or columns.
Look in	select whether you to search **formulas**, **values** or **comments**.
Match case	check this option if you want to distinguish between upper and lower case.
Match entire cell contents	check this option if you want Excel to look for the exact characters displayed in the search field.

⊟ To search cell by cell, click **Find next**. If the search returns the content you were looking for, click **Close**. If not, click **Find next** again.

⊟ To search all cells, click **Find all**; the list of cells found is displayed in the lower part of the dialog box.

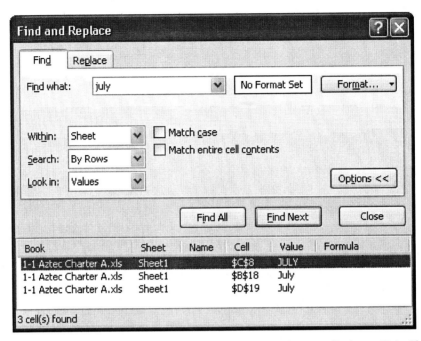

⊡ Click one of the values in the list to select the matching cell then click **Close**.

By format

⊡ Activate a single cell, or select the range of cells to search.

⊡ In the **Home** tab, go to the **Editing** group, click **Find and select**, then click **Find**. You can also use the Ctrl F shortcut.

⊡ Using the Del key, delete the contents of the **Search** field.

⊡ If required, click **Options** to display search options.

⊡ Click the **Format** button and select your search criteria from the **Find format** dialog box.

Choose format from cell selects the format of a cell to search for.

⊡ Click **OK**.

⊡ Click either **Find next** or **Find all**, according to your search choice.

When the **Find and Replace** dialog box is closed, you can press `⬆ Shift` `F4` to continue searching.

You can combine a text and format search by entering text in **Find what**, and using the **Format** button to choose your formatting options.

Selecting cells

Adjacent cells

⊟ Use one of the following techniques:

Drag　　　　Click in the first cell you want to select. Without releasing the mouse button, drag the mouse over the selection. Release the mouse button when you have finished. Note: don't drag using the recopy button (the black square to the right of the active cell).

`⬆ Shift` **click**　　Click in the first cell you want to select. Point to the last cell, press the `⬆ Shift` key, and without releasing it, click. Next, release the mouse button, then the key.

Keyboard　　Press and hold down the `⬆ Shift` key. Make your selection with the relevant arrow keys.

19	Bookshelf small	114
20	*TOTAL*	
21		
22	NUMBER OF PRODUCTS	15
23	AVERAGE PROFIT MADE	58
24	BEST PROFIT MADE	6943
25	LOWEST PROFIT MADE	592
26		

*A **range of cells** is displayed in darker colour with a border.*

Non-adjacent cells

⊟ Select the first cell range.

⊟ Press and hold down the `Ctrl` key and select the other cell ranges. When you have finished, release the `Ctrl` key before the mouse button.

By default, the status bar displays the mean and sum of the selected cells if at least one of the cells has a numerical value. The status bar also displays the number of values (text, numbers, etc) contained in the selected cells.

To select all cells in worksheet, click the 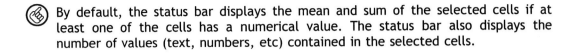 button (situated at the intersection of the row and column headers), or use the `Ctrl` A or `Ctrl` `⇧ Shift` `space` shortcuts.

Selecting rows/columns

Use the following techniques

	Row	Column
	Click the row number to select	Click the column letter to select
	Activate a cell in the row, then use `⇧ Shift` `space`	Activate a cell in the column and use `Ctrl` `space`

When a row or a column is selected, its number or letter is displayed in black against a dark background.

To select several adjacent rows or columns, drag the mouse over the row or column headers. If the rows or columns are not adjacent, hold down the `Ctrl` key as you select each row or column.

You can select rows and columns simultaneously.

70

Selecting cells by content

⊟ In the **Home** tab, go to the **Editing** group, click the **Find and select** button, then click **Go to special**.

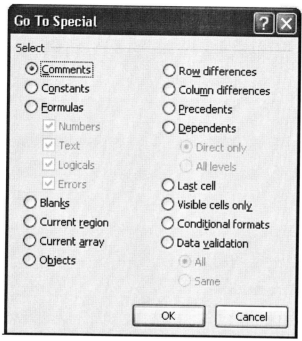

⊟ Click the option that corresponds to the type of cells you want to select.

⊟ Click **OK**.

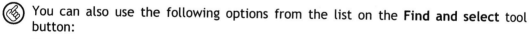 You can also use the following options from the list on the **Find and select** tool button:

Formulas	to search for cells containing formulas.
Comments	to search for cells containing comments.
Conditional formatting	to search for cells with conditional formatting.
Constants	to search for cells with constants.
Data validation	to search for cells with a drop-down list.

When the worksheet does not contain any cells that match the search criteria, Excel displays the following message:

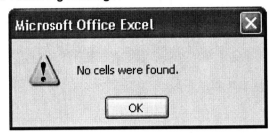

Entering data

Entering constant data (text, values, etc)

⊟ Activate the cell in which you want to data to appear.

Always check the reference of the active cell in the name or formula bar.

⊟ Enter the data.

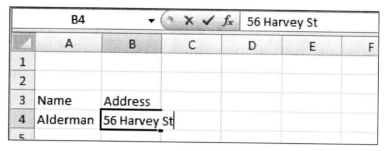

From the moment you enter the first character, two symbols are displayed in the formula bar:

 cancels the data entry (corresponds to the `Esc` key)

 checks the data entry (corresponds to the `Enter` key)

At the same time, the indicator on the status bar indicates that only data entry can currently be performed.

⊟ Confirm the data entry: use the `Enter` or `⇄` keys, or an arrow key or click the ✓ button.

Moving to a new cell confirms the entry in the previous cell. As soon as you have activated a new cell, Excel goes back to Ready mode and the ✗ and ✓ symbols disappear.

After confirmation, text values are aligned to the left of the cells, and date or number values are aligned to the right. Also, date values are automatically formatted (e.g. 31/03 becomes 31 March).

Note the following points relating to data entry:

- for numerical values, make sure you enter 0 (zeroes) instead of O (the letter O).
- For a negative value, place a minus sign before it (-) or put brackets around it.
- To transform 10000 to 10,000€ as you type, enter 10,000€ (the euro sign is often available using the ⌞Alt Gr⌟ **E** key combination, this depends on keyboard types).
- To enter a percentage, enter the % sign just after the number.
- To enter decimals, use the comma or decimal point as a decimal separator (depending on your Windows configuration, either a comma or a decimal point will be displayed in the worksheet).

To enter dates, Excel interprets the year entered based on two figures, as follows:

- From 00 to 29 = from 2000 to 2029.
- From 30 to 99 = from 1930 to 1999.

If you are using Windows XP, the settings for **Date, currency symbols, Time** and the separator can be modified using the Start menu (**Start - Control Panel - Regional and Language Options - Customize**).

 To enter the same content in several worksheets simultaneously, select the relevant worksheets (remember: you are now in a work group) and proceed as you would normally.

Inserting special characters

This technique inserts symbols that do not appear on the keyboard. A special character can be inserted into a blank cell, or within text.

⊡ Activate the **Insert** tab, go to the **Text** group and click the click the **Symbol** button, or use the ⌞Ctrl⌟ **F** shortcut.

*The **Symbol** dialog box is displayed with the **Symbols** tab active.*

⊡ In the **Font** list, select the font containing the character you want to insert.

⊡ To select the character you want to insert, click it.

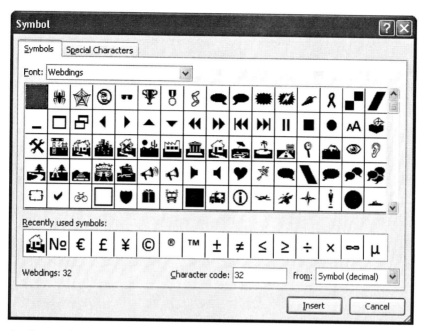

🔲 Click the **Insert** button.

🔲 If required, insert other characters then close the dialog box by clicking the **Close** button.

🔲 Finish entering text, then confirm.

Inserting the current date/time in a cell

🔲 Activate the cell in which you want the current date and/or time to appear.

🔲 To insert a date and/or time, which is updated every time you open the work-book, use one of the following functions:

=TODAY()   To insert the date.
=NOW()   To insert the date and time.

🔲 To insert a static time and/or date, use one of the following shortcuts:

Ctrl ;   To insert the date.
Ctrl :   To insert the time.
Ctrl ; space Ctrl :   To insert the date followed by the time.

Entering/editing data

 If the date displayed is not today's date, correct your computer's date and time (Windows **Control Panel** – **Date and Time**).

Using the AutoComplete feature

When you start entering characters in a cell, Excel may attempt to complete your entry using an existing entry from the same column (providing there is no more than one blank cell above the one in which you are working.

If you want to use the entry proposed by Excel, press `Enter`. Otherwise, to display a list of the entries available, press `Alt` `↓`.

	A	B
1		
2	**NAME**	**FIRST NAME**
3	ARDOUIN	Mathilde
4	BARNET	Linda
5	DA SILVA	Paola
6	EGREFIN	Mélissa
7	QUENTIN	Pierre
8	LILIAN	Paul
9	MARTIN	Romain
10	NAULON	Mathilde
11	POTIER	Linda / Mathilde / Mélissa
12	PULLAN	Paola / Paul
13	ROLIN	Pierre / Romain
14		
15		
16		

*The list of the existing entries in that column appears. You can also display this list by right-clicking the cell and choosing the **Pick From Drop-down List** option.*

Next click the entry you require.

If you do not want to use any of the entries, just type your text as usual.

 This feature is only available if the **Enable AutoComplete for cell values** option in the **Excel Options** dialog box is enabled (**Microsoft Office** button – **Excel Options** – **Advanced** – **Editing Options**).

Entering data

Entering the same data in several cells

⊟ Select the range of cells concerned, they need not be adjacent.

⊟ Enter the formula or text common to all these cells.

If you are entering a formula, enter it as it should appear in the active cell.

⊟ Validate with Ctrl Enter .

This technique enters and copies the data simultaneously.

Entering line breaks in a cell

There are two ways of entering several lines of text in the same cell: by entering it, or by modifying the cell formatting.

Entering a line break

⊟ When you are entering or modifying text, use the Alt Enter keys to create a line break at the required position.

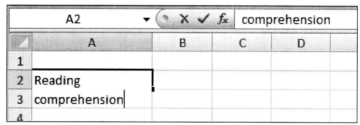

If the height of the formula bar is not changed, you will only see the last line of entered text.

Defining an automatic line break

⊟ Select the cells.

⊟ In the **Home** tab, go to the **Alignment** group and click the **Wrap text** tool button.

The data is wrapped within the cell. If you change the column width, the data is automatically adjusted to the new width.

Creating series of data

A series is a logical pattern of cell values. You can create a series of dates, times, months, days or a combination of text and numerical values. You are using the autofill feature.

Creating a simple series

A simple series shows a list of values, incrementing each time by one value.

- Enter the first value in the series.
- Drag the fill handle from the bottom right of that cell to the last target cell for the series.

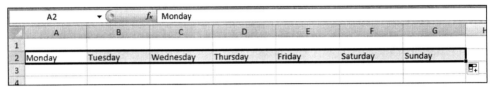

*When you reach the end of your series, the **Auto Fill Options** button appears to the bottom right of the series.*

- If you click this button you can (depending on the type of series, and your needs) choose an option to modify the way the values are copied or incremented.

- Click a suitable option.

Creating a complex series

With this type of series, you can define the interval between each value.

- Enter the first two values, to specify the interval you want to use.
- Select these two cells.

78

Drag the fill handle.

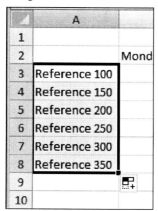

Reference 100 and Reference 150 are the first two values of the series.

Enter the first value in the series then select the cell containing that value.

In the **Home** tab, go to the **Editing** group, click the arrow on the **Fill** tool button and select **Series**.

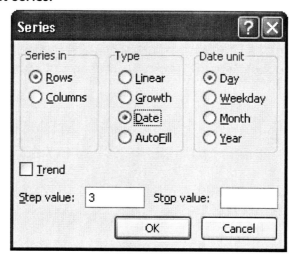

In the **Series in** frame, indicate whether the series should be inserted in **Rows** or **Columns**.

In the **Type** frame, specify the type of series you are creating.

⊟ If you choose a **Date** type, provide the **Date** unit in the right hand frame.

⊟ Modify the **Step value** as required.

⊟ If required, indicate the **Stop value** in the series.

✍ Custom data series are one of the subjects in the Optimizing data entry chapter.

Modifying the contents of a cell

⊟ Double click in the cell you want to modify.

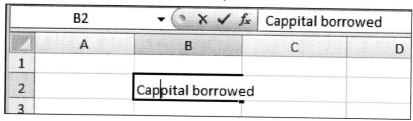

*An insertion point appears in the cell (the small blinking vertical bar) where you clicked, and Excel goes into **Editing** mode.*

⊟ Make your changes.

*When **Insert** mode is active, the new characters are added to the existing characters. If **Overwrite** mode is active, new characters replace the existing characters.*

⊟ To go from **Insert** mode to **Overwrite** mode and vice versa, press Insert.

⊟ Confirm your changes.

You can also click in the cell then in the formula bar to make your changes directly.

Clearing cell contents

⊟ Select the cells to clear then press the Del key.

The cell content is erased, but not the format.

⊟ To delete the content and/or format and/or comments, go to the **Home** tab, **Editing** group and click the tool button.

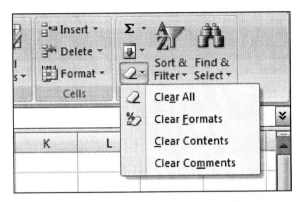

 Click the option corresponding to what you want to clear.

To delete the cell contents, you can also select the relevant cells then drag the fill handle over the same selection.

Replacing the contents/format of one cell with the contents/ format of another

It is possible to replace the text and/or format contained in several cells by another text and/or format. This technique also allows you to change text within formulas.

<u>Replacing text</u>

 If the replacement is to be carried out over the active worksheet or all the worksheets in the workbook, activate a single cell. To make the replacement in a subset of the active sheet, select the relevant range of cells.

 From the **Home** tab, go to the **Editing** group, click the **Find and select** button, then click **Replace**, or use the Ctrl H shortcut.

 Enter the text you wish to replace In **Find what**.

*You can enter letters, numbers, punctuation marks or wildcard characters: ? Replaces one character; * replaces several.*

 Enter the replacement text in **Replace with**.

 As when searching cells (see Finding a cell by its contents), you can click the **Options** button and specify how and where Excel should look for the text you are replacing.

⊟ To make the replacements one by one, click **Find next** to go to the first cell containing the required text then click the **Replace** button (if you want to replace that value) or the **Find next** button (to ignore that text and continue searching).

⊟ To replace all occurences at once, click the **Replace all** button.

⊟ Click the **Close** button.

Replacing formatting

⊟ Activate a cell or select a specific range of cells.

⊟ In the **Home** tab, go to the **Editing** group, click the **Find and select** button, and click **Replace,** or use the Ctrl H shortcut.

⊟ Click the **Options** button to show all the search options.

⊟ Delete any text that may be in **Find what** or **Replace with**.

⊟ Click the first **Format** button and in the **Find format** dialog box, select the required format options.

*The **Choose Format From Cell** button is used to select a cell and retrieve that cell's formatting automatically. You can also access this option by using the **Format** button list.*

⊟ Click **OK**.

⊟ Click the second **Format** button and in the **Replace Format** dialog box, select the required format options and click **OK**.

⊟ Make your replacements one by one using the **Find Next** and **Replace** buttons or use the **Replace all** button to make all the replacements at once.

⊟ Click **Close**.

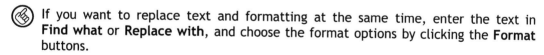 If you want to replace text and formatting at the same time, enter the text in **Find what** or **Replace with**, and choose the format options by clicking the **Format** buttons.

Checking the spelling

The spell checker works in the active worksheet, it checks cell content, cell comments, charts, text boxes, buttons, headers and footers, but it does not check protected sheets, formulas, or text produced by a formula

⊟ To check the whole worksheet, activate any cell. To check part of the text, select that text.

⊡ Activate the **Review** tab, go to the **Proofing** group and click the **Spelling** button, or use the ⌨F7 key.

Excel reads the text, stopping at each unrecognised word. This word may not feature in Excel's dictionary, or it might be entered with an unusual combination of lower case and capital letters (e.g. KingDom).

Spelling is checked against Excel's main dictionary, and against as many personal dictionaries as you wish (by default, the only existing one is CUSTOM.DIC).

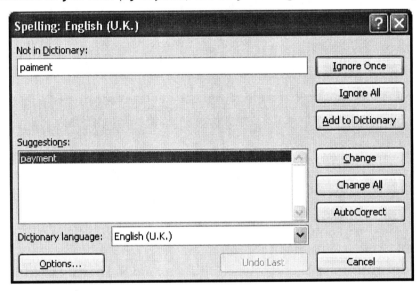

⊡ If the word is correctly spelt, click:

Ignore   to leave the word unchanged and continue the check.

Ignore all   to leave a particular word unchanged each time it occurs in the text.

Add to dictionary to add the word to the current custom dictionary.

⊡ If the word contains a mistake, correct it by selecting one of the suggestions or enter the correct spelling in **Not in Dictionary**, then click:

Change   to replace the incorrect word with the correct one.

Change all   to replace the incorrect word with the correct one each time it occurs.

You can also double-click one of the suggestions.

Excel indicates when the spell check is complete.

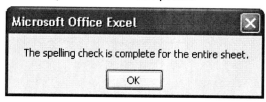

⊡ Click **OK**.

Managing the AutoCorrect function

Excel corrects your recurring errors while you type (e.g. if you always type "magasine" instead of "magazine" using an automatic spell correction feature.

<u>Activating and deactivating AutoCorrect</u>

⊡ Click the **Microsoft Office** button then click **Excel options**.

⊡ Select **Proofing** and click **AutoCorrect options**.

⊡ Deactivate or activate the **Replace text as you type** option depending on whether you want to stop automatic text correction and replacement while you type or let it continue.

This option is checked by default.

⊡ Click **OK**.

<u>Defining automatic correction</u>

Excel puts a comprehensive list of automatic corrections at your disposal. You can add other automatic corrections to this initial list, such as words or abbreviations that Excel will replace while you type.

⊡ Click the **Microsoft Office** button , then click **Excel Options**.

⊡ Select **Proofing** and click the **AutoCorrect Options** button.

⊡ Make sure that **Replace text as you type** is checked.

⊡ Enter the misspelt word or the abbreviation in **Replace**.

⊡ Type the correct spelling in **With**.

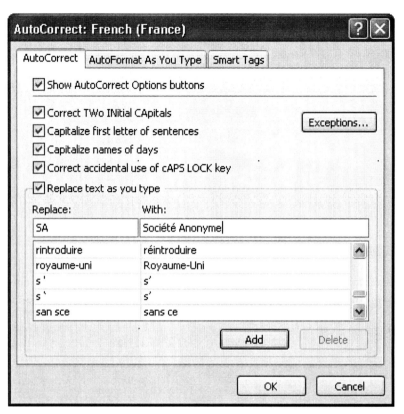

 Click the **Add** button.

 Insert your abbreviations or habitual errors in the same way.

 Close the **AutoCorrect** dialog box using the **OK** button.

 Close the **Excel options** dialog box by clicking **OK**.

Copying and moving

Copying data into adjacent cells

This is a fast way to copy text or formulas.

⊡ Activate the cell you want to copy.

⊡ Point to its fill handle.

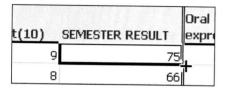

Remember that the fill handle is the small dark square in the bottom right hand corner of the cell. Notice the change in the mouse pointer's shape.

⊡ Drag and drop the fill handle to the last cell for the copy.

The cells over which you drag are enclosed inside a hashed border.

⊡ When you reach the last cell, release the mouse button.

	SEMESTER RESULT	Oral expression (25)	Reading comprehen:
9	75	20	
8	66	16	
9	88	19	
6	58	15	
6	53	11	
7	62	13	
8	81	17	
7	69	17	
9	93	22	
9	86	21	
7	77	19	
7	61	13	
8	48	12	
5	42	10	
6	72	21	
7	69	18	

As soon as you finish copying,

the ⊞ tool button appears on the bottom right of the copied range.

9	93		
5	42		
38	68.75		

⊞ ▾
- ◉ Copy Cells
- ○ Fill Formatting Only
- ○ Fill Without Formatting

Entering/editing data

- ☐ Click the button for copying options: **Fill formatting only** (copy just the format) or **Fill Without Formatting** (copy just the contents).

Copying and moving cells

Use this feature for copying into non-adjacent cells.

First method

This technique is useful when the source cells and the destination cells are visible at the same time.

- ☐ Select the source cells.
- ☐ Point to the edge of the selected range.

	A	
1	1st Year Spanish	
2		
3		SEME
4	STUDENT NAME	Oral expr(
5	ABBOTT, Rebecca	
6	ABBOTT, Rebecca	
7	ABBOTT, Rebecca	
8	ABBOTT, Rebecca	
9	ABBOTT, Rebecca	
10	ABBOTT, Rebecca	
11	ABBOTT, Rebecca	
12	NAUGHTON, Olivia	
13	POTTS, Penelope	

The pointer appears as a white arrow on top of a four-headed arrow. Make sure you do not point to the fill handle.

- ☐ If you are copying, press the ⌨Ctrl key and, without releasing it, drag the cells to their destination.

  If the cells are being moved, just drag the cells to their new position.

  When you drag to copy, a plus sign (+) appears to the right of the mouse pointer.

- ☐ Release the mouse button, then the ⌨Ctrl key.

  The cell contents and their formatting are moved or copied.

Copying and moving

Second method

⊟ Select the source cells.

⊟ Activate the **Home** tab.

⊟ If you are copying, go to the **Clipboard** group and click the **Copy** tool button 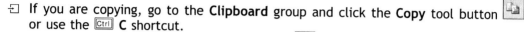 or use the Ctrl C shortcut.

⊟ If you are moving, click the **Cut** tool button ✂ or Ctrl X.

The selected cells are surrounded by a flashing border.

⊟ Activate the first cell of the destination range.

Even when several cells are being copied or moved you should only activate <u>one</u> destination cell.

⊟ Click the **Paste** button or use Ctrl V.

You can change copy options using the 📋 button, which appears at the bottom right of the destination box.

⊟ Click the button and activate the option of your choice.

The original selection remains flashing, and you can paste into other places. When the flashing stops, you can no longer paste your selection.

Copying cells to other sheets

⊟ Select the cells you want to copy.

⊟ Select the other worksheets, by holding down the Ctrl key and clicking their tabs.

⊟ In the **Home** tab, go to the **Editing** group and click the arrow on the **Fill** tool button ⬇▾, then activate **Across all worksheets**.

⊟ Select **All**, **Formats** or **Contents**.

⊟ Click **OK** to confirm.

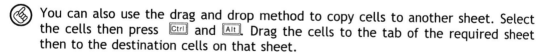 You can also use the drag and drop method to copy cells to another sheet. Select the cells then press Ctrl and Alt. Drag the cells to the tab of the required sheet then to the destination cells on that sheet.

Using the Office Clipboard

The Office clipboard allows you to copy and paste multiple selections.

Displaying and hiding the Clipboard task pane

⊟ To display the **Clipboard** task pane, go to the **Home** tab, **Clipboard** group and click the **dialog initiator** .

⊟ To hide the **Clipboard** task pane, click the ˣ button on the right of the pane's title bar.

Defining Office Clipboard settings

⊟ Open the Office **Clipboard** pane.

⊟ Click the **Options** button at the bottom of the **Clipboard** task pane.

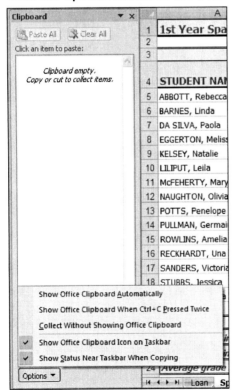

The checked options are enabled.

Copying and moving

🖅 Select your options:

Show Office Clipboard Automatically to display the Clipboard when you copy text.

Show Office Clipboard When Ctrl+C Pressed Twice to display the Clipboard when you use the ⌨Ctrl C (copy) shortcut twice.

Collect Without Showing Office Clipboard to automatically copy items into the Clipboard without displaying the pane.

Show Office Clipboard Icon on Taskbar to display the **Office Clipboard** 📋 icon in the system taskbar's notification area when the Clipboard is active.

Show Status Near Taskbar When Copying to display the message relating to copied items.

🖅 Press Esc to hide the options on the **Options** button.

Copying/moving multiple items

🖅 Display the Office Clipboard task pane.

🖅 Select the relevant cells or objects and transfer them to the Clipboard using **Cut** or **Copy**. Repeat these steps for each item you wish to copy or move.

*A preview of the cut and/or copied items appears in the **Clipboard** task pane. Up to 24 items can be stored there.*

*The **Office Clipboard** contains all the items cut or copied from the various Office applications (Excel, Word, PowerPoint, etc).*

🖅 Activate the first destination cell.

- To paste one of the items from the **Clipboard** task pane, click that item.
- Insert each item from the **Clipboard** task pane in this way, as many times as required.

When you point to an item, an arrow appears on its right. Click this arrow to see options allowing you to Paste or Delete the item;

- Close the Office pane by clicking the ☒ button.

The **Paste all** button from the Office **Clipboard** task pane pastes all the items. They are pasted in a column, from top to bottom. This button is unavailable when there is a picture or object in the list.

To clear the **Clipboard,** click the **Clear all** button on the **Clipboard** task pane.

Copying a format

Use this technique to copy formats from one range of cells to another.

- Select the cell(s) whose format you want to copy.
- From the **Home** tab, go to the **Clipboard** group and click the **Format Painter** tool button 🖌️.

A paintbrush appears next to the pointer.

- Select the cells to which you want to apply the format.

You can also copy formats by making a standard copy/paste operation then clicking the **Paste Options** tool button 📋 at the bottom of the copied cells and choosing the **Formatting only** option.

If the format is to be copied several times, double-click the 🖌️ tool button. Press [Esc] to cancel this function.

Copying and moving

Copying cell content, results and/or formats

⊟ Select the cells containing the results or formats you want to copy.

⊟ From the **Home** tab, go to the **Clipboard** group and click the **Copy** tool button
  .

⊟ Activate the first cell of the destination cell range.

⊟ Open the **Paste** tool button list.

⊟ Choose:

Formulas	to copy the cell contents (formulas or values) without the associated format.
Paste Values	to copy just the results of formulas, without the format.
No Borders	to copy the contents and the formats but not the borders.

These options are also available by activating the **Paste special** function.

Transposing data as you copy

You can transpose, or switch the rows and columns in a table when you copy it to another location.

⊡ Select the data you wish to copy and start the copying process. Next, activate the first destination cell.

⊡ Expand the **Paste** tool button list and choose the **Transpose** option.

When the data is pasted, the rows become columns and vice versa.

Copying Excel data and establishing a link

When a link is in place, any changes made to the data in the original Excel workbook are carried over to the file containing the exported data.

⊡ Select the data you wish to copy.

⊡ Start the copying process by clicking 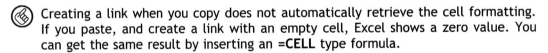.

⊡ Activate the first target cell for the copied data (on the same sheet, another sheet or another book).

⊡ Expand the list on the **Paste** button and choose the **Paste link** option.

The destination cells now contain formulas that show the contents of each source cell. If you modify a source value, it is immediately carried over into the target cell.

⊛ Creating a link when you copy does not automatically retrieve the cell formatting. If you paste, and create a link with an empty cell, Excel shows a zero value. You can get the same result by inserting an **=CELL** type formula.

Making simple calculations while you copy

This is a way of simultaneously copying data and carrying out simple math operations, such as additions or subtractions using the copied data and the existing data in the target cells.

⊡ Select the data you want to copy.

⊡ Start the copying process by clicking .

⊡ Activate the first destination cell (the target cells must contain some data).

⊡ Open the list on the **Paste** button and activate the **Paste special** option.

Copying and moving

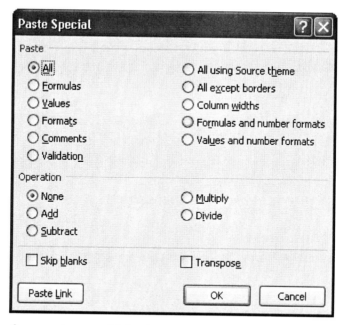

In the **Paste** frame, choose which elements you want to copy.

Next, specify the **Operation** you wish to perform.

If you want to omit any empty cells in the selection, tick the **Skip Blanks** check box.

Click **OK**.

Copying data as a picture

Select the data you want to copy.

Start the copying process by clicking the tool button.

Activate the destination cell for the copy (in the active sheet, a different sheet or another workbook)

Open the list on the **Paste** button, activate the **As picture** option and select **Paste as Picture**, or **Paste Picture Link**, according to your needs.

Part 4
Worksheets

Activating a worksheet

Each workbook consists of worksheets, and each worksheet is represented by a tab.

The worksheet scroll tabs display the name of the tab you want to move to.

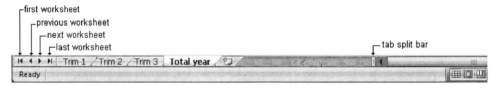

To scroll more quickly through the tabs, hold down the `⇧ Shift` key when you click ◀ or ▶.

Next, click the tab of the worksheet you want to move to.

Use `Ctrl` `Pg Dn` to move to the next worksheet, or `Ctrl` `Pg Up` to move to the previous worksheet.

You can change the spacing allocated to each worksheet tab by dragging the tab split bar located to the left of the horizontal scroll bar.

To change the number of sheets in a new workbook, open the **Excel Options** dialog box (**Microsoft Office** button - **Excel Options** button), then click **Popular**. Under **When creating new workbooks**, specify the number of sheets you want in the **Include this many sheets** box.

Renaming a sheet

⊟ Double click the tab of the worksheet you want to rename.

⊟ Enter the new name over the old name.

This name can be up to 31 characters long, spaces included. It should not be written inside square brackets nor include the following punctuation marks: colon (:), slash (/), backslash (\), question mark (?) or asterisk (*).

⊟ Press Enter to validate.

🖐 You can also use the shortcut menu from the worksheet tab, called **Rename**.

Selecting worksheets

⊟ To select a single worksheet, click its tab (this activates the worksheet).

⊟ To select several adjacent worksheets, click the tab corresponding to the first worksheet, press the ⇧ Shift key, then click the tab of the last sheet you want to select.

⊟ To select several non-adjacent tabs, click the tab corresponding to the first work-sheet, press the Ctrl key and click the tabs of the other worksheets.

⊟ To select all the worksheets, right click one of the tabs and click **Select all work-sheets**.

When several worksheets are selected, the term **(Group)** *appears after the worksheet name on the title bar. It is called group because every change made to the active sheet is carried over to the other sheets in the group.*

⊟ To deactivate the work group and select or activate a single worksheet, click the tab of a worksheet that is not in the work group, or open the tab's shortcut menu and activate **Ungroup sheets**.

If all worksheets are selected, you can deactivate the group by clicking any of the tabs.

Changing the colour of the worksheet tabs

- To change the colour of several tabs, select the corresponding worksheets.

- Open the tab's shortcut menu: right click the worksheet tab to be coloured.

- Move the mouse over the **Tab Color** option.

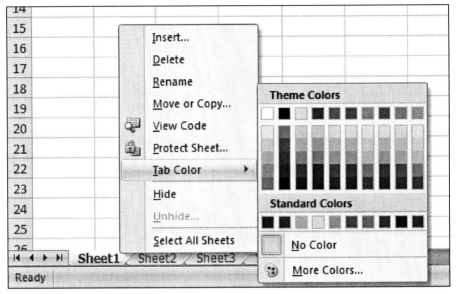

- Click the colour of your choice. The **More colors** option opens a dialog box where you can create a custom colour.

When the sheet is active, only its name is underlined by a coloured line. When the worksheet with the coloured tab is inactive, the entire tab is coloured.

To remove the colour from a tab, open the shortcut menu, move the mouse over the **Tab Color** option and activate the **No Color** option.

Worksheets

Displaying/hiding a worksheet

Hiding one or more worksheets

⊟ Select the worksheet(s).

⊟ Right click one of the selected tabs.

⊟ Activate the **Hide** option.

Displaying a hidden worksheet

⊟ Right click one of the tabs.

⊟ Activate the **Unhide** option.

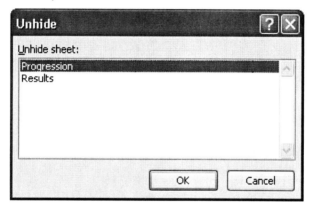

⊟ In the **Unhide** dialog box, double click the name of the worksheet to display, or click its name, then click **OK**.

⊟ Perform the same action for each worksheet you want to display.

Displaying a background picture in the worksheet

With Microsoft Office Excel 2007 you can display a picture in the background of worksheet. This background cannot be printed.

⊟ Activate the relevant worksheet then activate the **Page Layout** tab.

⊟ Go to the **Page Setup** group and click the **Background** button.

The **Sheet background** dialog box opens, similar to the **Open** dialog box. The **My pictures** folder is selected.

- Go to the folder that has the picture you want to display as a background.

- Double click the picture name.

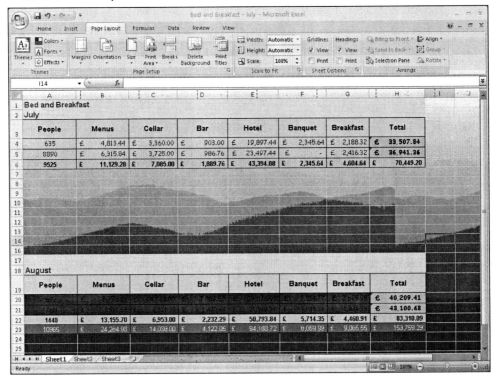

Notice that the **Background** button from the **Page Setup** group has become **Delete background**.

To remove the picture from worksheet background, activate the **Page Layout** tab, go to the **Page Setup** group and click **Delete background**.

Worksheets

Moving/copying one or more sheets in the active workbook

⊟ Select the worksheets you want to move.

⊟ To move the worksheets, point to one of the tabs and drag it to its new position.

The new position is represented by a small black triangle.

⊟ To copy the worksheets, use the same procedure as for moving while holding down the ⌨Ctrl key.

Moving/copying one or more sheets from one workbook to another

⊟ Open the workbook from which you want to copy or move, and the destination workbook.

⊟ Select the worksheet(s) to move.

⊟ Right click one of the selected tabs and active the **Move or copy** option.

⊟ Open the **To book** list and click the name of the destination workbook.

⊟ Indicate the sheet in the destination workbook in front of which you want to insert using the **Before Sheet** list.

⊟ If you are copying, activate **Create a copy**, otherwise leave the check box empty.

▣ Click **OK**.

 The destination workbook becomes active.

Inserting/adding worksheets

▣ To insert a single worksheet, select the sheet in front of which you want to insert. To insert several worksheets at the same time, select as many consecutive tabs as sheets you want to insert.

If you are inserting several sheets at the same time, the sheets will be inserted before the second to last and last sheet selected.

▣ Right click one of the selected tabs and activate the **Insert** option.

▣ In the **Insert** dialog box, make sure the **Worksheet** option is active, and click **OK**.

 To add a worksheet at the end of the list, click the **Insert Worksheet** button or press ⇧ Shift F11 .

Deleting worksheets

⊟ Select the worksheets to delete.

⊟ Right click one of the selected tabs and activate the **Delete** option.

   If any of the worksheets contain data, the following dialog box appears:

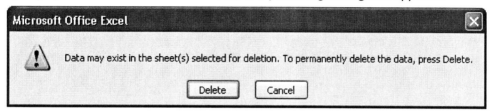

⊟ In this situation, click **Delete**.

Inserting rows/columns

🗗 To insert a single row or column, select the row or column (by clicking the row number or column letter) after the one you want to insert.

To insert several rows or columns, select as many rows and/or columns as you want to insert.

You cannot insert rows and columns at the same time.

🗗 Activate the **Home** tab, go to the **Cells** group and click the **Insert** button, or press Ctrl **+,** or activate the **Insert** option from the selection's shortcut menu.

When you insert a row or column, it has the same format as the previous cell. You can change this option by clicking the 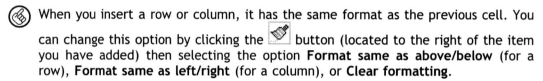 button (located to the right of the item you have added) then selecting the option **Format same as above/below** (for a row), **Format same as left/right** (for a column), or **Clear formatting**.

Deleting rows/columns

🗗 Select the rows or columns you want to delete by selecting the row numbers or column letters.

🗗 Activate the **Home** tab, go to the **Cells** group and click the **Delete** button, or press Ctrl **-** or activate the **Delete** option from the selection's shortcut menu.

Modifying the row height/column width

🗗 Select all columns of the same width or rows of the same height. If you only want to modify one row or column, don't select it.

🗗 Point to the vertical line located to the right of one of the columns, or, horizontal line located below one of the rows:

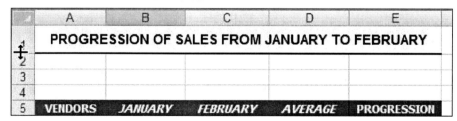

Notice the mouse pointer has a new shape.

🗗 Drag the mouse while holding down the mouse button.

Rows, columns, cells

The new width or height is indicated by a dotted line and the new value is displayed in a ScreenTip.

- Release the mouse button when you are happy with the new row height or column width.

- The width of a column is calculated in number of characters (and pixels); row height is calculated in points (and pixels).

- To reduce computer memory usage, use this method to give your worksheets more space rather than entering new rows or columns.

Adjusting row height and column width

Column widths will be calculated according to the widest cell in the column, and row height will be calculated according to the highest cell in the row

- Select the relevant rows or columns.

- To change column width, double click the vertical line located to the right of the column letter.

  To change row height, double click the horizontal line located below the row number.

Inserting empty cells

The cells will be inserted below or to the left of the selected cell range.

- Select as many cells as you want to insert.

- Activate the **Home** tab, go to the **Cell** group, click **Insert**, then click **Insert cells**. Alternatively, press Ctrl 0 Shift =, or activate the **Insert** option from the selection's shortcut menu.

☐ Activate the first or second option to indicate how to shift the existing cells following the insertion of the new cells.

☐ Click **OK** to confirm.

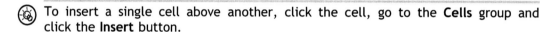

To insert a single cell above another, click the cell, go to the **Cells** group and click the **Insert** button.

Deleting cells

☐ Select the cells you want to delete.

☐ Activate the **Home** tab, go to the **Cells** group, click the arrow on the **Delete** button, then click **Delete cells**. Alternatively, activate the **Delete** option from the selection's shortcut menu.

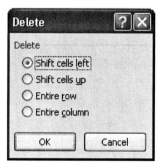

☐ Activate the first or second option to indicate how the existing cells are to be shifted following the deletion of the selected cells.

☐ Click **OK**.

Rows, columns, cells

 To delete cells while shifting the other cells to the left, select the cells you want to delete, go to the **Cells** group and click the **Delete** button.

Moving and inserting cells/rows/columns

Use this feature to move and insert cells, rows or columns between existing cells, rows or columns.

- Select the cells you want to move.
- Point to one of the edges of the selected cells until the point becomes a four-headed arrow.
- Drag the selection while holding down the `⇧ Shift` key.
- Release the mouse button at your insertion point, represented by a bold hashed line.

Holding the `Ctrl` and `⇧ Shift` keys down as you drag the selection copies cells, rows, and columns instead of moving them.

Reproducing the content of one cell in several cells

*This function uses the **Conversion Wizard** to split content from one cell across a number of cells, according to a delimiter such as a space, comma or column break.*

- Prepare one or more empty columns to the right of the cells that contain the data you want to split.

	A	B	C	D
1			ST IGNATIUS SCHOOL Student Results - Se	
2				1st Year Spanis
3				
4	FIRST NAME	SURNAME	BIRTHDAY	Oral expression (25)
5	Rebecca ABBOTT 15/11/1988			18
6	Linda BARNES 14/07/1985			15
7	Paola DASILVA 18/04/1986			22
8	Melissa EGGERTO 04/07/1986			14
9	Natalie KELSEY 17/05/1987			13
10	Leila LILIPUT 04/18/1988			14
11	Mary McFEHERTY 20/03/1984			19
12	Olivia NAUGHTON 15/02/1985			17
13	Penelope POTTS 17/06/1986			23
14	Germaine PULLMAN 16/09/1988			20
15	Amelia ROWLINS 05/11/1988			18
16	Una RECKHARDT 16/12/1987			14

In this example, we are going to split the data from from cells A5 to A16 to cells A5 to C16. The first names in column A (where the actual data is), the surnames in column B and the birth dates in column C.

- Select the relevant range of cells.
- Activate the **Data** tab, go to the **Data Tools** group and click the **Text to columns** tool.

The first step of the **Convert text to columns wizard** appears.

- If required, activate the **Delimited** option, then click **Next**.
- At step two, in the **Delimiters** frame, select the delimiter you want to use.

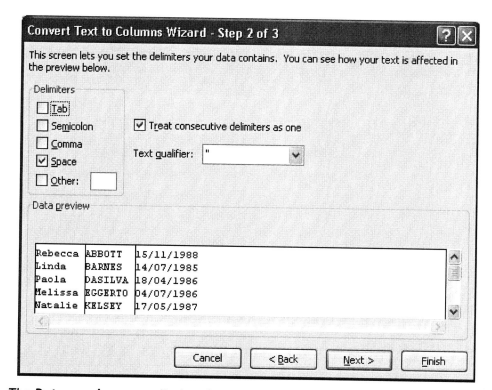

The **Data preview** pane displays how the data will be separated, in columns.

- Click **Next**.

- At step three, specify the format for each column:
    - in the **Data preview** pane, click a column to select it.
    - choose the format you want to apply to it in the **Column data format** frame.

- Specify the place where you want the data to be reproduced. Use the tool button on **Destination** to specify the reference of the first destination cell. In this way, the original cells remain unchanged, and the split data appears next to them.

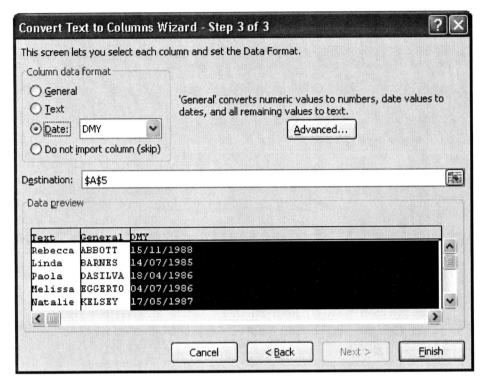

If you do not specify this destination, the original data will be replaced.

Click **Finish**.

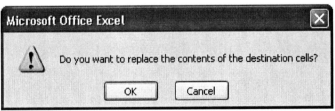

If required, confirm the data replacement by clicking **OK**.

Rows, columns, cells

Removing rows containing duplicates

You can delete rows that contain identical data in several columns.

⊟ Click anywhere in the worksheet.

⊟ Activate the **Data** tab, go to the **Data Tools** group and click the **Remove Duplicates** button.

⊟ In the **Remove duplicates** dialog box, select the columns containing the duplicates you want to delete by unchecking the boxes next to the columns to which this action does not apply. You can also click the **Unselect all** button to uncheck all boxes, then select the columns you want, or click the **Select all** button to activate all the check boxes.

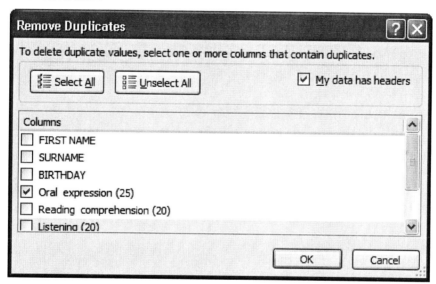

In this example, the rows matching the students with the same marks in Oral expression will be deleted.

⊟ Click **OK**.

Naming cell ranges

You can refer to a cell range by name to select it or to use it in formulas.

*You can create **Defined names,** which represent one cell, a range of cells, a formula, or a constant. Microsoft Office Excel sometimes creates them automatically (for example, when you define a print area). You can also create **Table names** which are lists of data (see Tables).*

First method

⊟ Select the cell or the range of adjacent or non-adjacent cells to which you want to give the same name.

⊟ Click the **Name box,** located on the left of the formula bar.

⊟ Enter the name to use for your selection.

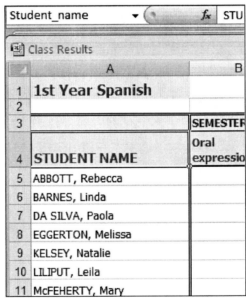

A name can have up to 255 characters. You cannot use spaces. The first character must be a letter, an underscore (_) or a backslash (\). The other characters can be letters, numbers, points and underscores. Names cannot be the same as cell references, and can contain either uppercase or lowercase letters (Excel does not differentiate them).

⊟ Press Enter .

Named ranges

Second method

- Select the cell or the range of adjacent or non-adjacent cells to which you want to give the same name.

- Activate the **Formulas** tab, go to the **Defined names** group and click the **Define name** button.

- In the **New Name** dialog box, enter or modify the name proposed in the **Name box**.

- Open the **Scope** drop-down list to specify the scope of the name. Select **Workbook** or the name of a worksheet in the workbook.

- If required, enter a description of the cell range in **Comment** (up to 255 characters).

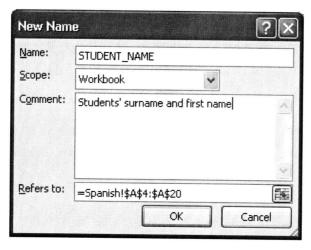

The ▦ *tool button minimizes the dialog box so that you can modify the cell range associated with this name.*

- Click **OK**.

Third method

This method assumes that the names you want to apply exist in the worksheet as column headings or row titles in the cell range.

- Select the cells the contain the names to apply <u>and</u> the cells to name.

- Activate the **Formulas** tab, go to the **Defined Names** group and click the **Create from selection** button.

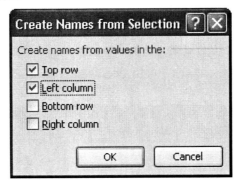

- Indicate the location of the cells that contain the names you want to apply.

- Click **OK**.

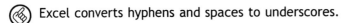 Excel converts hyphens and spaces to underscores.

Managing cell names

Accessing the Name Manager

- Activate the **Formulas** tab, go to the **Defined Names** group and click the **Name Manager** button.

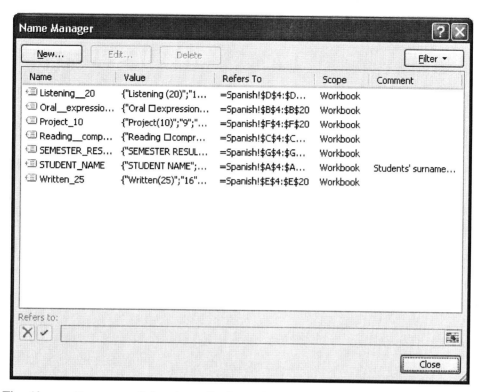

The **Name Manager** dialog box displays the name, value, reference, scope and comments for all existing named cell ranges in the workbook. In this example, they are sorted by name.

- To automatically adjust the column size to its maximum value, double click the right edge of the column header.

- To sort the names in ascending order, click the relevant column header once. To sort in descending order, click the header a second time.

⊟ To filter the displayed names, click the **Filter** button and choose the required filter:

Names scoped to worksheet: to only display names applied to the active worksheet or workbook.

Names with/without errors: to only display names with errors (such as #REF, #VALUE, #NAME, etc), or those without errors.

Defined names: to only display names that have been defined by Excel or yourself.

Table name: to only display the names of data lists.

⊟ Click a name to select it.

Deleting a name

⊟ Access the **Name Manager**.

⊟ Select the name to delete.

⊟ Click the **Delete** button and confirm the deletion by clicking **OK**.

Modifying a name's cell range

⊟ Access the **Name Manager**.

⊟ Select the name to modify.

*The references are displayed in the **Refer to** column.*

⊟ Click the 🔲 tool button to minimise the dialog box so that you can modify the name's cell range.

⊟ Next, click the 🔲 tool button to go back to the **Name Manager** dialog box.

Modifying the name applied to a range of cells

⊟ Access the **Name manager**.

⊟ Select the name to modify.

⊟ Click **Edit**.

*The **Edit name** dialog box opens, similar to the **New name** dialog box.*

⊟ Make your changes in the **Name** and **Comment** fields.

⊟ Click **OK** to go back to the **Name manager** dialog box.

Named ranges

<u>Validating changes made with the Name manager</u>

⊟ When all changes have been made, close the **Name manager** dialog box by clicking the **Close** button or the ✖ button.

Selecting a range of cells by name

⊟ Click the ▼ button located in the **Name box** on the formula bar.

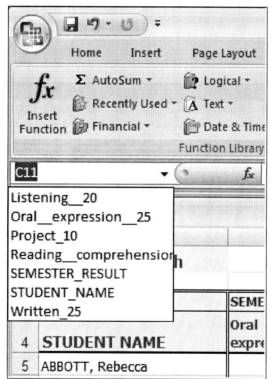

Excel displays all defined name fields in the workbook.

⊟ Click the name of your choice.

117

Displaying a list of names and associated references

This function will paste into the worksheet a list of all the workbook's named ranges (in one column) and the corresponding cell references (in the next column).

🗁 Activate the cell from which the list of names should appear.

🗁 Activate the **Formulas** tab, go to the **Defined names** group, click **Use in formula**, then click **Paste names**.

🗁 Click the **Paste list** button in the **Paste name** dialog box.

Part 5
Calculations

Learning about calculation formulas

🗄 Calculation formulas perform calculations on values within cells.

🗄 A formula starts with the equals (=) sign.

🗄 A formula can contain the following items:
- cell references
- operators, i.e. signs indicating the type of calculation to make. There are four types of operators:

Mathematical operators:

+ for adding

– to subtraction

/ for division

* For multiplication

% for calculating a percentage (e.g. =5% gives 0.05 as a result)

^ for exponentiation (e.g. =2^3 gives 8 as a result)

Comparative operators: the result is a logical value: TRUE or FALSE

= equals to (e.g. =30=40 gives FALSE as a result)

< less than (e.g. =28<35 gives TRUE as a result)

<= less than or equal to

> greater than

>= greater than or equal to

< > different from

Text concatenation operator: uses the & sign to concatenate one or more text strings to produce a single piece of text.

(e.g. ="West"&" and "&"North" gives "West and North" as a result).

Reference operators combine ranges of cells : : (colon) or , (coma)

- Constants, i.e. values which are not calculated and do not change (for example, the number 1210 or the text "Giant wave" are constants).
- Calculation functions are pre-written formulas which take one or more values, execute an operation, then return one or more values.

Creating a basic calculation formula

Use this function to create a calculation comprising cell references, operators and/or constants.

⊟ Click in the cell where you want to enter the formula and display the result.

⊟ Type =.

⊟ Build the formula:

- to include the content of a cell into the formula, i.e. use a cell reference, click the relevant cell or enter its reference.
- to use an operator or a constant, enter the corresponding data.
- if you want to use several operators, define priorities so that you can group values in brackets.

SUM	▼	X ✓ fx	=B5*C5+(0.05*B5*C5)
	A	B	C	D
1	**SUMMARY OF ORDERS FOR 1ST SEMESTER**			
2				
3				
4	**PRODUCT**	**PRICE**	**QUANTITY**	**TOTAL (postage due : 5 %)**
5	Sofa bed	£ 207.00	2	=B5*C5+(0.05*B5*C5)
6	Sofa (3 seater)	£ 449.00	6	
7	Single bed	£ 199.00	9	
8	Double bed	£ 399.00	9	

Calculations

You can follow the development of the formula on the formula bar. The above formula calculates the total cost of sofa bed orders. The unit price is multiplied by the quantity plus 5% of the price by the quantity.

- When you have finished the formula, confirm with Enter or by clicking the 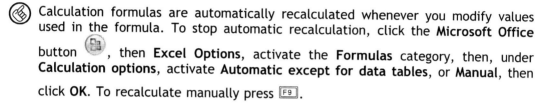 button on the formula bar.

- Calculation formulas are automatically recalculated whenever you modify values used in the formula. To stop automatic recalculation, click the **Microsoft Office** button , then **Excel Options**, activate the **Formulas** category, then, under **Calculation options**, activate **Automatic except for data tables**, or **Manual**, then click **OK**. To recalculate manually press F9.

- When you change a formula, the cell references it includes appear in different colours in the formula bar. In the worksheet, each cell or cell range covered by the formula has a border in the same colour.

- Don't forget that you can use the fill handle in the bottom right corner of the active cell to copy formulas to adjacent cells (see Copying and moving – Copying data into adjacent cells).

Entering a formula from more than one sheet

You can enter a formula into one worksheet that refers to cells on a different worksheet(s) (called a 3-D formula).

- *Activate the cell that is going to display the result.*

- Type =.

- Start the formula and at the appropriate place, click the tab of the required sheet, select the cell(s) you require and finish the formula.

- Confirm.

| B3 | ▼ | fx | =North!B7+South!B7 |

	A	B	C	D	E	F
1						
2		Total				
3	January	3477				
4	February					
5	March					
6	April					

B3 contains the sum of B7 cells of the South and North sector sheets.

 To apply formulas to several workbooks, first open all the revelant worksheets. To access a cell in a worksheet in another workbook, go to the **View** tab, **Window** group and use the **Switch Window** button to go to the corresponding workbook.

Creating a formula with a function

⊟ Activate the cell where you want the result displayed.

⊟ In the **Formula** tab, click the **Insert function** button 🖅 in the formula bar or the **Formulas** tab, or press ⬆ Shift F3 .

⊟ In the **Insert function** dialog box, use the **Or select a category** drop-down list to view functions grouped by category.

*The **Most recently used** category shows a list of the last functions you have used as well as the most frequently used ones. The **All** category shows all available functions.*

⊟ To search for a particular function, you can type its exact name or type a description of what you want the function to do in the **Search for a function** text box. Click **Go** or press Enter to start the search.

⊟ Click the function you are looking for in the **Select a function** box.

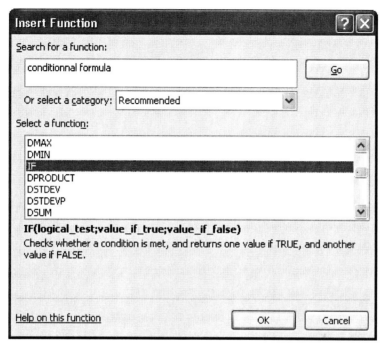

When you select a function, the function's structure and its description show up in the lower part of the frame.

- If you need help, click the **Help on this function** link to display a detailed description of the selected function.

- Click **OK** to activate the **Function Arguments** dialog box.

- To define each argument within the function:

    - click the corresponding text box and click the 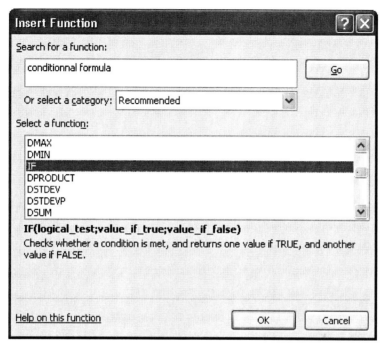 button.

    - on the worksheet, select the cell(s) corresponding to the argument.

    - click the button to return to the dialog box.

You can also enter an argument directly.

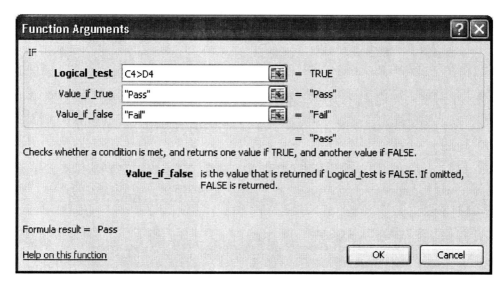

Click **OK** when you have set all the arguments.

You can also insert a function within a formula or within another function. To do this, start the formula, and at the appropriate place, click the ▾ button (located on the left of the formula bar). This displays a list of the last functions used and the **More Functions** option which takes you to a full list of functions. You can also use the **Recently Used** button from the **Function Library** group in the **Formulas** tab.

To insert functions using the Wizard, you can also activate the **Formulas** tab and click one of the button from the **Function Library** group (which lists functions by type), then click the required function.

To find a list of functions that Excel has stored by category, go to the **Microsoft Office Excel Help** function (the 🔵 button), display the **Table of Contents** and click the **Functions Reference** option.

Calculations

Using the semi-automatic entry function

*Use this feature to enter a function yourself, without using the **Function Wizard**. Excel helps you avoid syntax errors and typos.*

⊟ Activate the cell in which you want to enter the formula and display the result.

⊟ Enter the = sign (equals) and the first letters of the function.

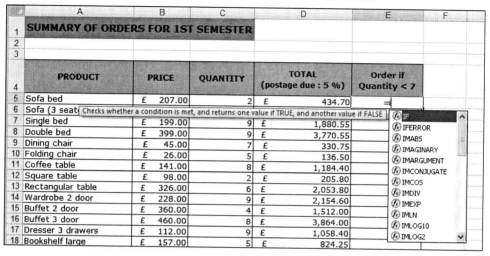

As soon as you start typing, Excel displays a list of functions beginning with that letter.

⊟ Continue entering the name of the function, or double-click the name which appears in the list, then indicate the arguments.

	A	B	C	D	E	F	G
1	SUMMARY OF ORDERS FOR 1ST SEMESTER						
2							
3							
4	PRODUCT	PRICE	QUANTITY	TOTAL (postage due : 5 %)	Order if Quantity < 7		
5	Sofa bed	£ 207.00	2	£ 434.70	=IF(D5< 7,		
6	Sofa (3 seater)	£ 449.00	6	£ 2,828.70	"Order","Wait"		
7	Single bed	£ 199.00	9	£ 1,880.55	IF(logical_test, [value_if_true], [value_if_false])		
8	Double bed	£ 399.00	9	£ 3,770.55			

As you type, ScreenTips provide guidance on how to create the formula.

⊟ Do not forget to complete the formula by entering the) sign.

Summing a group of cells

⊡ Activate the cell which is going to display the result.

⊡ In the **Home** tab, go to the **Editing** group and click the **AutoSum** tool button
Σ ▾ .

You can also find this button in the Formulas tab, in the Function Library group.

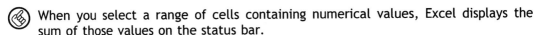

	SUM	▾	× ✓ ƒx	=SUM(D4:D9)	
	A	B	C	D	E
1	**SUMMARY OF ORDERS FOR 1ST SEMESTER**				
2					
3	**PRODUCT**	**PRICE**	**QUANTITY**	**TOTAL (postage due : 5 %)**	
4	Sofa bed	£ 207.00	2	£ 434.70	
5	Sofa (3 seater)	£ 449.00	6	£ 2,828.70	
6	Single bed	£ 199.00	9	£ 1,880.55	
7	Double bed	£ 399.00	9	£ 3,770.55	
8	Dining chair	£ 45.00	7	£ 330.75	
9	Folding chair	£ 26.00	5	£ 136.50	
10	*TOTAL*			=SUM(D4:D9)	
11				SUM(number1, [number2], ...)	
12	NUMBER OF PRODUCTS		6		

Excel displays the SUM() function and proposes cells to sum.

⊡ If you are not happy with this selection, change it by clicking the cells you do not want to select.

⊡ Press the [Enter] key to confirm, or click the **Enter** button ✓ .

(☞) When you select a range of cells containing numerical values, Excel displays the sum of those values on the status bar.

Using simple statistical functions

⊡ Activate the cell where the result will be displayed.

⊡ In the **Home** tab, go to the **Editing** group and open the list of the Σ ▾ tool. You can also use the **AutoSum** tool (**Formulas** tab – **Function Library** group).

Calculations

⊟ Click the required function:

Average	to calculate the average of a set of values.
Count Numbers	to count the number of cells containing numerical values.
Max	to extract the highest value from a group of cells.
Min	to extract the lowest value from a group of cells.

Excel displays the function and selects a group of cells as a suggestion.

⊟ *If the suggested selection is incorrect, modify it by clicking to select individual cells or dragging to select a range.*

⊟ Press the Enter key to confirm the formula, or click ✔.

When you select a range of cells containing numerical values, the status bar displays the average of these values, as well as their sum. It also displays the number of empty cells. To display more function results, right-click the status bar and choose from the functions proposed (**Count Numbers, Minimum** or **Maximum**).

Creating a conditional formula

⊟ Activate the cell in which you want to enter the formula and display the result.

⊟ Use the **IF** function, with the following syntax:

= IF(condition, value if the condition is met, value if the condition is not met).

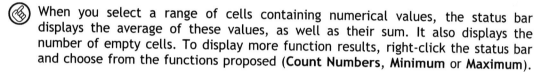

In this example, if the contents of the cell D5 is less than 7, the text "order" is displayed in the results cell; if not, the text "wait" is displayed.

In a conditional formula, you have a choice between several different resulting actions:

Display a number   enter the number.

Display a text   enter the text between quotation marks.

Display the result   enter the formula.
of a calculation

Display the contents   enter the cell reference.
of a cell

No display   type " ".

Several options are available to use in the condition:

>/<   greater than/less than,

< >   different from

>=/<=   greater than or equal to/less than or equal to.

To set multiple conditions, use one of the following functions depending on the result you want to display. If you want several conditions met use the structure: **=IF(AND(cond1, cond2, etc condn), action if all the conditions are met, action if at least one condition is not met).**

If at least one of the conditions must be met: **=IF(OR(cond1, cond2, etc condn), action if at least one condition is met, action if no condition is met).**

If you want to nest conditions: **=IF(cond1, action if met, IF(cond2 action if met, IF(cond3, action if met, action if not met))).**

Creating an absolute cell reference in a formula

This feature lets you set a cell reference in a formula so that the reference does not change when the formula is copied.

🠶 Start entering the formula and stop when you reach the relevant cell.

🠶 Press F4 .

The cell reference now displays the $ sign in front of the column reference and in front of the row reference number.

Calculations

	A	B	C	D	E
SUM	▾ X ✓ fx	=D4+(D4*C12			

	A	B	C	D	E
1	SUMMARY OF ORDERS FOR 1ST SEMESTER				
2					
3	PRODUCT	PRICE	QUANTITY	TOTAL	TOTAL (postage due : 5 %)
4	Sofa bed	£ 207.00	2	£ 414.00	=D4+(D4*C12
5	Sofa (3 seater)	£ 449.00	6	£ 2,694.00	
6	Single bed	£ 199.00	9	£ 1,791.00	
7	Double bed	£ 399.00	9	£ 3,591.00	
8	Dining chair	£ 45.00	7	£ 315.00	
9	Folding chair	£ 26.00	5	£ 130.00	
10	TOTAL				
11					
12		Postage due :	5%		

When you press F4 *, you get an absolute cell reference; if you press* F4 *again, only the row reference becomes absolute; if you press* F4 *a third time, the column reference becomes absolute.*

⊟ Press F4 as many times as required to make your chosen item absolute.

⊟ Finish entering the formula and confirm.

Using named ranges in calculations

This feature lets you replace a cell range reference in a formula with a named range.

⊟ Start entering the formula then stop where the name is required.

⊟ In the **Formulas** tab, go the the **Defined Names** group and click the **Use in Formula** button.

The list of defined name ranges is displayed (see Named ranges – Numbering cell ranges).

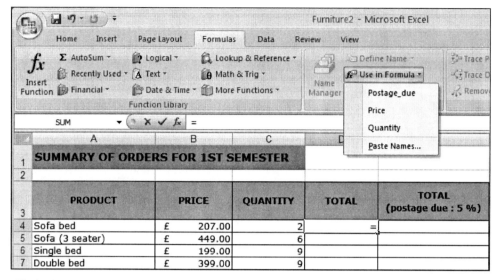

 Click the name of the corresponding cell range to insert in the formula.

 Continue and complete the formula.

You can also enter the name directly in the formula, at the cell reference position.

Using dates in calculations

This section discusses the way Excel calculates dates and gives some examples of certain functions using dates.

Calculating days

 If you are calculating days, proceed as you would for other calculations, since any date you enter is treated as a sequence number. For this reason, dates can be added, subtracted, and included in other calculations.

 Windows Excel uses a calendar beginning in 1900 by default (Excel for Macintosh's calendar begins in 1904). January 1st 1900 thus corresponds to the sequence number 1 (for Windows Excel) and January 1st 2005 equals 38,353, since there are 38,353 days between the two dates.

Calculations

Combining text with a date

⊟ If you want to combine text and a date from different cells in a third cell, use the **TEXT** function, the syntax is =TEXT(value, format_text):

The **value** argument represents a numeric value, a formula with a numeric result or a reference to a cell containing a numeric value.

The **format_text** argument is a number format in text form as defined in the **Category** box of the **Format Cells** dialog box.

Here is an example:

	A5	▾	fx	="Payment date :"&TEXT(B3,"dd-mmm-yyyy")					
	A	B	C	D	E	F	G	
1		Date						
2	Invoice	11/12/2006						
3	Payment	30/12/2006						
4								
5	Payment date :30-Dec-2006							
6								

Calculating the difference between two dates with the DATEDIF function

This is a very useful function for calculating, for example, how long an employee has been working in years and in months. The syntax for **DATEDIF** is **DATEDIF(start_date,end_date,Type)**:

The **Type** argument represents the unit of time used to calculate and can take on the following values:

"y"	to calculate the difference in years.
"m"	to calculate the difference in months.
"d"	to calculate the difference in days.
"ym"	to calculate the difference in months if the two dates are in the same year.
"yd"	to calculate the difference in days if the two dates are in the same year.
"Md"	to calculate the difference in days if the two dates are in the same month.

Here is an example:

	A	B	C
1	Start date	01/02/1994	
2	End date	30/11/2006	
3			
4		**Result**	
5	**Year**	**Month**	**Day**
6			
7	12	153	4685

The formulas used in the example are:

- In A7 =DATEIF(B1,B2,"y")

- In B7 =DATEDIF(B1,B2,"m")

- In C7 =DATEIF(B1,B2,"d")

DATEIF is a "hidden" function in Excel. So, you will not find it in either the help function or the online help function. Hidden functions appear in Excel for compatibility reasons (i.e. with Lotus 123 worksheets). They work perfectly, but are not included in the "official" Excel functions.

Calculating the number of workdays between two dates

Excel can calculate the number of working days (Monday to Friday) between two dates by using the **NETWORKDAYS** function, the syntax is =**NETWORKDAYS** (**start_date,end_date**).

Here is an example:

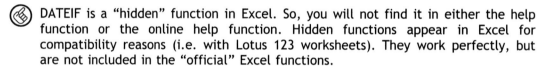

B4		f_x	=NETWORKDAYS(B1,B2)	
	A	B	C	D
1	**Start date**	01/01/2007		
2	**End date**	31/01/2007		
3				
4	**number of networkdays :**	23		

In order for this function to take holidays into account, you need to add a third argument referring to a holiday or a number of days off. The syntax of the function then becomes =**NETWORKDAYS(start_date,end_date,holidays)**.

Calculations

Calculating the date after a number of working days

The **WORKDAY** function returns the date corresponding to a given date (start date) plus or minus a number of working days. Working days exclude Saturdays, Sundays and all holidays.

This is the syntax:

=WORKDAY(start_date,number_of_days,holidays):

start_date   represents the start date.

number_of_days   represents the number of working days before or after the start date. A positive number will give a future date, while a negative number will give a past date (in relation to the start date).

Holidays   represents a list of dates to exclude from the working day calendar (bank holidays, vacations, absences etc). This last argument is optional.

Here is an example:

We want to find the last day of a job starting on 15 October 2006, for 40 working days.

	B8	▾	fx	=WORKDAY(B1,B2,B4:B5)		
	A	B	C	D	E	
1	Start date	15/10/2006				
2	days	40				
3						
4	holidays	01/11/2006				
5		11/11/2006				
6						
7						
8	End date	11/12/2006				

The formula entered in **B8** is **=WORKDAY(B1,B2,B4:B5)** and the **Date** format was applied to the cell, otherwise, Excel gives the date as a number.

If this formula give you an error message, check the following explanations to find out why:

#VALUE!   One of the arguments is not a valid date.

#NUM!   The start date plus the number of days does not give a recognisable date.

Adding months and years

⊟ To add a number of months to a start date, use the following syntax:

=DATE(YEAR(start_date),MONTH(start_date)+period_in_months,DAY(start_date))

For example, to calculate the date two months from now, use:

=DATE(YEAR(NOW)),MONTH(NOW))+2,DAY(NOW)))

⊟ To add a number of years, use:

=DATE(YEAR(start_date)+period_in_years,MONTH(start_date),DAY(start_date))

Calculating using time

In this section, after learning how Excel calculates times, you can see some examples of different methods and formulas using times.

Calculating times

⊟ When you type a time in a cell, Excel records it in decimal number form using a number from 0 to 1 (1 exclusive) for each 24 hour period.

⊟ For Excel to recognise the data as a time and save it as a decimal number, you have to separate the various parts of the time with a colon (:). For instance, you should type 6.30 PM and 43 seconds using the syntax **18:30:43**. If you do not want seconds, type **18:30**.

Entered time	Value recorded by Excel
00:00 (midnight)	0
11:59	0.499305555555556
12:00 (midday)	0.5
15:00 (3 PM)	0.625
18:00 (6 PM)	0.75

This way of defining time, particular to Excel, allows arithmetic calculations on times.

Calculations

For example, to calculate the difference between 18:00 (6 PM) and 15:00 (3 PM), Excel calculates:

=0.75 - 0.625 = 0.125

Excel offers a wide variety of predefined time formats (see Formatting - Formatting dates/times).

Calculating the difference between two times

⊟ To do this and show the result in a standard time format, i.e., hours:minutes:seconds, you need to use the **TEXT** function with this syntax **=TEXT(value, format_text)**

- the **value** argument represents a numeric value, a formula giving a numeric result, or a reference to a cell containing a numeric value.

- the **format_text** argument represents a number format in text form as defined in the **Category** section of the **Format Cells** dialog box (**Home** tab - **Cells** group - **Format** option - **Protection** - **Format Cells** - **Number** tab).

Here is an example of its use:

	A	B	C
1	Start time	08:30:45	
2	End time	15:15:00	
3			
4		Result	Formula
5	Number of hours between two hours times	6	=TEXT(B2-B1,"h")
6	Number of hours and minutes between two times	6:44	=TEXT(B2-B1,"h:mm")
7	Number of hours, minutes end seconds between two times	6:44:15	=TEXT(B2-B1,"h:mm:ss")

Converting times

⊟ If you want to convert time units into another unit of measurement, you can do so using the **CONVERT** function with the syntax **=CONVERT(number,"from_unit", "to_unit")**:

Number	represents the number you want to convert.
"from_unit"	corresponds to the unit of measure of the number that you want to convert from (between quotation marks).
"to_unit"	corresponds to the unit of measure of the result (also between quotation marks).

You can use this function to convert several units of measure (for weight, mass, distance, pressure, force, energy, etc), we will use this function as it applies to converting units of time.

Depending on the units you are converting from and to, use the following arguments:

Year	**"yr"**
Day	**"day"**
Hour	**"hr"**
Minute	**"mn"**
Second	**"sec"**

*For instance, to convert **10 years** into hours, use the following formula:*

=CONVERT(10,"yr","hr")

Result = 87660 (hours)

Using the LOOKUP function

The VLOOKUP function looks for a value in the first column of a table (the V in VLOOKUP refers to vertical) and returns the value found in the cell located on the same row, in the column you have specified.

⊟ Create a table grouping together the data that you will subsequently retrieve during your search, then sort the table in ascending order of the first column. Name this cell range if you do not want to select it when creating your formula.

⊟ Click the cell where the information retrieved from the table should be displayed.

⊟ Create your formula, respecting the following syntax:

=VLOOKUP(lookup_value;table_array;col_index_num;range_lookup)

lookup_value	is the value the function looks for in the first column of the table.
table_array	is the table from which the data is to be retrieved. This argument can be the reference of a range of cells or the name of a range of cells.
col_index_num	is the number of the column in the table (table_array) containing the value that is to be displayed as a result. For example, the first column in the table is column 1.

| range_lookup | is a logical value that looks for an exact or similar match. If the range_lookup is TRUE or is left blank, an equal value or less than the value is returned. If the range_lookup is FALSE, only the exact match will be returned. |

| C9 | ▼ | *fx* | =VLOOKUP(A8,cars,2) |

	A	B	C
1	**MODEL**	**TYPE OF VEHICLE**	**COST PRICE**
2	BAKINI	Mini-hatchback, 3 door	10100.00
3	TAHINI	Hatchback, 3 door	12400.00
4	TAHINI XL	Hatchback, 5 door	12500.00
5	ROTUNDA	Sedan, 5 door	23100.00
6	RELINDO	Sedan, 4 door	16900.00
7	FRACTUS	Station wagon, 5 seater	17100.00
8	GAREDO	Deluxe sedan, 4 door	23580.00
9	GAREDO ESTATE	Deluxe wagon, 4 door	28750.00

In this example, the VLOOKUP function looks for the reference of the car (whose code is contained in A8) in a table called cars and then returns the price of the item located in the second column of that range.

↵ Confirm the formula by pressing Enter .

 The HLOOKUP function is similar except that it searches horizontally along a row and returns the value in the cell located in the same column and the same specific row.

Inserting rows of statistics

Use this function to include sub-totals in a worksheet.

- Sort the table by the column that contains the entries you want to group together, as a first step to producing a subtotal for each group.

- Select the table you want to sub-total, including header cells.

- Activate the **Data** tab, go to the **Outline** group and click the **Sub-total** button.

- In the **At each change in** list, select the column that contains the groups that are to be used for the sub-total.

- Choose the calculation to be made in the **Use function** list.

- Check the columns that contain the values that you want to use in the calculation:

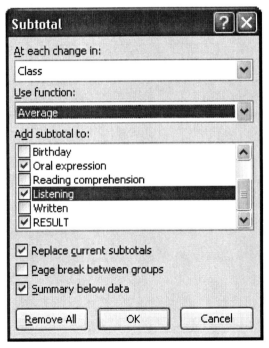

In this example, an average grade will be calculated for Oral expression, Listening and Result.

- Leave the **Replace current subtotals** option active if you want to replace any existing subtotals with those that you are creating.

▱ Check the **Page break between group** box to automatically insert a page break after each group of sub-totals.

▱ Leave the **Summary below data** option active if you want to create subtotals and totals beneath detailed data. If this option is unchecked, only the subtotals will appear below the detailed data.

▱ Click **OK**.

	A	B	C	D	E	F	G	H	J
1	Class	Surname	First name	Birthday	Oral expression	Reading comprehension	Listening	Written	RESULT
2	T101	DUPONT	Paul	17/03/1988	22	19	18	20	79
3	T101	LILIAN	Audrey	02/03/1988	14	15	13	13	55
4	T101	PULLAN	Pierrick	24/04/1988	20	18	17	22	77
5	T101	SOUBIRAN	Julien	31/03/1988	10	11	12	11	44
6	T101 Average				16.5		15		63.75
7	T102	ARDOUIN	Mathilde	10/08/1988	18	17	15	16	66
8	T102 Average				18		15		66
9	T202	ROLLIN	Anne	03/07/1988	19	16	14	13	62
10	T202	BARNET	Linda	05/04/1988	15	16	15	12	58
11	T202	KANTIN	Nathan	01/07/1988	13	12	10	12	47
12	T202	SANDRIN	Victoire	08/12/1988	11	10	10	10	41
13	T202	DUPONT	Michel	12/04/1988	20	17	15	14	66
14	T202 Average				15.6		12.8		54.8
15	T301	ECHARD	Benjamin	21/04/1988	14	13	13	14	54
16	T301 Average				14		13		54
17	T302	DUPONT	Michel	30/11/1988	14	15	11	13	53
18	T302	MARTIN	Marie	15/01/1988	19	19	17	18	73
19	T302	NAULLON	Dominique	15/12/1987	17	16	15	14	62
20	T302	POTIER	Emma	16/08/1988	23	20	19	22	84
21	T302	ROLLIN	Amélie	14/12/1988	18	19	16	17	70
22	T302 Average				18.2		15.6		68.4
23	Grand Average				16.6875		14.375		61.9375
24									
25									

Excel calculates the subtotals that provide the statistics you have requested and creates an outline from them. Here, the average grades appear for each class in Oral expression, Listening and Result.

 The **Remove all** button in the **Subtotal** dialog box removes all the subtotals, plus the outline, from the selected table.

Consolidating data

When you consolidate data, you combine and analyse several separate ranges of data from different worksheets.

▱ Before starting the consolidation, you should check that:

- each range of data to be consolidated is a list, with a label in the first row, with columns containing similar data, and with no empty rows or columns.

- each source range must be on a <u>separate</u> worksheet. None of the source ranges must be on the sheet where you wish to consolidate the data.

- make sure all the ranges are in the same place on the sheet.

- you can name each source range (see Named ranges – naming cells).

☐ Activate the sheet to be used for the consolidation.

☐ Select the first destination cell where you want to display the consolidated data.

☐ Activate the **Data** tab, go to the **Data Tools** group and click the **Consolidate** button.

☐ Choose the **Function** you wish to use for the calculation.

☐ For each range of cells you want to consolidate:

- click the 🔲 tool button to minimize the dialog box,

- go to the worksheet and select the relevant cells, or enter the name of the source range,

- click the 🔲 tool button to display the dialog box again.

- click the **Add** button.

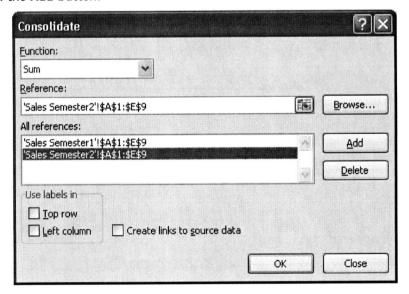

This consolidation will calculate the sum of cells A1 to E9 from the Sales Semester 1 and Sales Semester 2 worksheets.

⇥ Check the **Create links to source data** option if you want to create a permanent link between the source sheets and the consolidation sheet. If there is a link, the consolidated data will be updated each time the source data is changed.

⇥ Activate or deactivate the **Use labels in** options if the copied data contains headings for rows and/or columns.

⇥ Click **OK** to confirm.

When you request a link, Excel produces an outline of the consolidation table as well.

Using the PMT financial function

This function calculates the repayments on a loan, based on constant payments and interest rates.

⇥ Click the cell in which you want to display the result.

⇥ Enter your calculation using this syntax: **=PMT(rate,nper,pv,fv,type)**

Rate refers to the interest rate of the loan. If you are using an annual rate and you want the result to be a monthly payment, you must divide it by 12.

Nper corresponds to the total number of payments. If you calculate this number using years, but pay monthly, multiply by 12.

Pv corresponds to the principal per period.

Fv corresponds to the balance obtained after the last payment (capitalised value). If you leave this argument out, Excel treats it as equal to 0.

Type number between 0 and 1 specifying when payments are due. If the type is 1, payments are due at the beginning of the period. If you leave it out or it is equal to 0, payments are due at the end of the period.

*The **Fv** and **Type** arguments are optional. If you leave them out, the default value is 0 (zero).*

⇥ Confirm by pressing [Enter].

The result only includes the principal and interest, not charges, deposits, etc.

	A	B	C	D
1		Loan details		
2				
3		Size of the swimming pool	5m x 10m	6m x 15m
4		Price	20,000.00 €	29,000.00 €
5		Deposit	5,000.00 €	5,000.00 €
6		Loan	15,000.00 €	24,000.00 €
7		Interest rate	5.50%	5.50%
8		Number of repayments	20	20
9				
10		Monthly payment	-786.62 €	
11				

The repayment amounts are always negative amonts.

- To return a positive value, place a minus (-) sign before the PMT value (=-PMT) or **=ABS(number)** function, which calculates the absolute value of a number or an expression (E.g. =ABS(PMT(C7/12;C8;C6))).

To calculate the total amount paid over the course of the loan, simply multiply the result of the **PMT** formula by the **Nper** value.

Calculating the present value of an investment

- Activate the cell where you want the result displayed.
- Enter the formula, respecting the following syntax:
  =PV(Rate,Name,Pmt,Fv,Type):

Rate	corresponds to the loan's interest rate. If you have an annual rate, but you want to calculate monthly, divide it by 12.
Nper	corresponds to the total number of payments. If you calculate this number using years, but pay monthly, multiply by 12.
Pmt	corresponds to the repayment amount per period.
Fv	corresponds to the balance obtained after the last payment (capitalised value). If you leave this argument out, Excel treats it as equal to 0.

Type   number between 0 and 1 specifying when payments are due. If the type is 1, payments are due at the beginning of the period. If you leave it out or it is equal to zero, payments are due at the end of the period.

Fv and *Type* are optional arguments.

⊡ Confirm by pressing the [Enter] key.

⊛ As with the **PMT** function, the result is negative. To make it positive you can use the **ABS()** function.

Making scenarios

⊡ You can use a scenario to help you solve a problem by considering several possibilities. It is an analysis tool that allows you to simulate results.

Creating scenarios

⊡ Activate the **Data** tab, go to the **Data Tools** group and click the **What-If Analysis** tool.

⊡ Select **Scenario Manager**.

⊡ In the **Scenario Manager** dialog box, click **Add**, then enter the **Scenario name** you want to create.

⊡ In the **Changing cells** box, select the cells containing variable data.

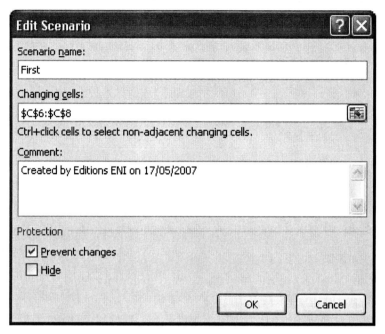

⊟ Click **OK** then type in the value of each changing cell and enter.

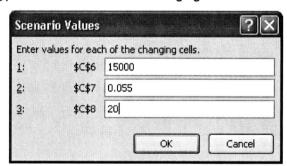

⊟ Create other scenarios in the same way.

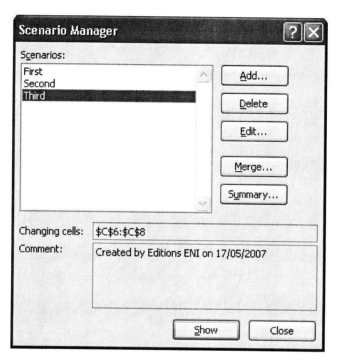

◻ Click the **Close** button.

Running a scenario

◻ Activate the **Data** tab, go to the **Data Tools** group and click the **What-If Scenarios** tool.

◻ Activate the **Scenario Manager**.

◻ If you only want to run one scenario select it. Click **Show** then click the **Close** button. The result replaces the current values on the worksheet (this is why you should start by creating a scenario containing the current values).

If you want to run several scenarios click **Summary** then, in the **Result cells** box, enter the cell references (or select the cells) whose results are of interest.

◻ If you clicked the **Summary** button, Excel offers a choice of two reports. In this case, fill in the **Scenario Summary** dialog box and confirm with **OK**.

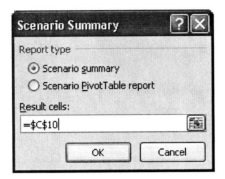

⊟ Click **OK**.

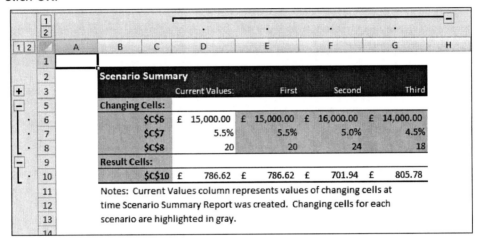

The summary is presented as an outline on a separate worksheet.

 Scenarios and views can be associated in a report.

Creating double input data tables

An example of a double entry table might be to simulate repayments for a fixed loan of 15,000€ and a variable number of repayments and a variable interest rate.

⊟ Enter the initial data for the calculation you want to make, for example, here, the interest rate, the loan duration and the amount being borrowed.

146

Advanced calculations

⊟ Enter the table's column and row headers, which will be the variables.

Make sure that the table which will displays the results is not attached to the initial input data. The variables must be laid out correctly; the row headers must be one row above the column headers and the column headers must be one column to the right of the first row header. There should be a blank cell at the intersection of the two sets of headers.

⊟ In the blank cell at the intersection (A11), enter the formula, then confirm.

	A11		▾	*fx*	=ABS(PMT(D4/12,D5,D6))					
	A	B	C	D	E	F	G	H	I
1									
2									
3									
4		Interest rate		10%					
5		Duration (months)		360					
6		Loan		£ 15,000.00					
7									
8									
9		**Monthly repayment**							
10		**2 years**	**3 years**	**4 years**	**5 years**	**6 years**	**7 years**	**8 years**	**10 years**
11	£ 131.64	24 months	36 months	48 months	60 months	72 months	84 months	96 months	120 months
12	9.00%								
13	9.25%								
14	9.50%								
15	9.75%								
16	10.00%								

⊟ Select the range of cells from the formula down to the last cell in the results table.

⊟ Activate the **Data** tab, go to the **Data Tools** group and click the **What-If Scenarios** tool button.

⊟ Select **Data Table**.

⊟ In the **Row input cell** box, provide the cell reference used in your formula that matches the variables in the first row of the data table.

For example, if the loan duration is in the row, provide the cell that corresponds to the initial loan duration in the formula (Here D5).

⊟ Enter the **Column input cell** with the appropriate cell reference.

147

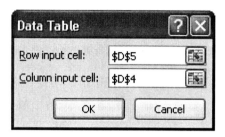

⊟ Click **OK**.

	A	B	C	D	E	F	G	H	I
1									
2									
3									
4		Interest rate		10%					
5		Duration (months)		360					
6		Loan		£ 15,000.00					
7									
8									
9		Monthly repayment							
10		2 years	3 years	4 years	5 years	6 years	7 years	8 years	10 years
11	£ 131.64	24 months	36 months	48 months	60 months	72 months	84 months	96 months	120 months
12	9.00%	£ 685.27	£ 477.00	£ 373.28	£ 311.38	£ 270.38	£ 241.34	£ 219.75	£ 190.01
13	9.25%	£ 686.99	£ 487.74	£ 375.06	£ 313.20	£ 272.25	£ 243.24	£ 221.70	£ 192.05
14	9.50%	£ 988.72	£ 480.49	£ 376.85	£ 315.03	£ 274.12	£ 245.16	£ 223.66	£ 194.10
15	9.75%	£ 690.44	£ 482.25	£ 378.64	£ 316.86	£ 276.00	£ 247.08	£ 225.63	£ 196.16
16	10.00%	£ 962.17	£ 484.01	£ 380.44	£ 318.71	£ 277.89	£ 249.02	£ 227.61	£ 198.23

Excel repeats the calculation for each set of variables and fills in the results table.

Calculating with array formulas

This formula lets you make several calculations giving a single or multiple result(s). An array formula can only apply to two or more groups of values called array arguments. These arguments must have the same number of rows and columns.

⊟ Begin as you would for a normal calculation, but instead of working cell by cell, work with cell ranges, and instead of confirming with Enter or Ctrl Enter, confirm with the Ctrl ⇧ Shift Enter key combination.

Advanced calculations

Here are three different examples of array formulas:

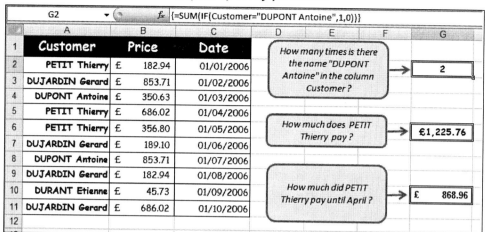

To simplify the formulas, we named the ranges: **Customer** *(A2:A11),* **Amount** *(B2:B11), and* **Date** *(C2:C11).*

We entered the array formulas in cells G2, G6, and G10.

G2   {=SUM(IF(Customer="Dupont Antoine", 1,0))}
This formula runs a search in the **Customer** cell range for the number or times that the name **"Dupont Antoine"** appears. If the condition is met, Excel adds **1**, if not, Excel adds **0**.

G6   {=SUM(Amount*(Customer="Thierry Petit"))}
This formula calculates the sum of the amounts corresponding to the customer Thierry Petit: **SUM(Amount** such that:***(the Customer is Thierry Petit: **Customer="Thierry Petit"**.

G10   {=SUM(Amount*(Customer="Thierry Petit")*(Date<=DATE(2006,4,1)))}
This formula calculates the sum of the amounts corresponding to the customer Thierry Petit and dated before 1/4/2006 inclusive: **SUM(Amount** such that:***(** the customer named Thierry Petit: **Customer="Thierry Petit"** and such that ***(** the date is less than or equal to 1/4/2006: **Date<=DATE(2006,4,1)**.

You can recognise an array formula by the brackets that enclose it.

Setting a value goal

This feature helps you solve the problem of knowing what value one cell must contain to obtain a given value in another cell.

⊡ Activate the cell that needs to obtain a specific value; check that this cell contains a formula.

⊡ If possible, view the cell you want to modify on the screen at the same time.

⊡ Activate the **Data** tab, go to the **Data Tools** group and click the **What-If Scenarios** tool button.

⊡ Select **Goal Seek**.

⊡ Check that the **Set cell** box refers to the cell (or cell name) for which you want to find the goal value (remember this must contain a calculation).

⊡ In the **To value** box, enter the required goal value.

⊡ In the **By changing cell** box, enter or choose the cell reference or name that should be adjusted in order to find the goal value.

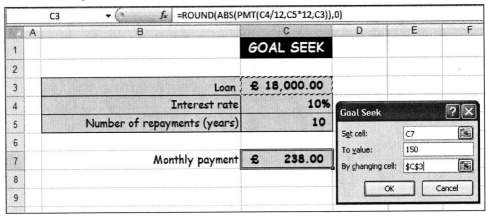

If I repay 150€ per month how much can I borrow?

⊡ Click **OK** to start the search.

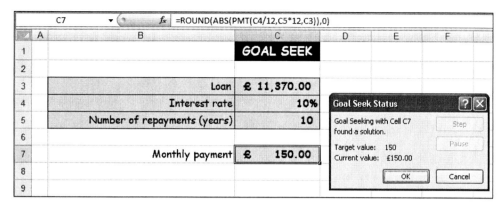

Once Excel has found the answer, it stops and displays its conclusions on the worksheet.

If the proposed solution is satisfactory, click **OK** to keep it in the worksheet. If you want to return to the original values, click **Cancel**.

Displaying formulas instead of results

⊟ Activate the **Formulas** tab, go to the **Formula Auditing** group and click the **Show Formulas** tool button , or press the `Ctrl` " shortcut.

⊟ To hide formulas and display results again, click the tool button or use the same shortcut.

Finding and correcting errors in formulas

Excel can check a certain number of errors made on the worksheet, such as the appearance of an error value (for example, "#NAME?" or "#VALUE!"), numbers stored as text and so on. When Excel finds an error, you can see a little triangle in the upper left corner of the cell containing the formula.

Displaying errors

When a result cell shows an error value such as #NAME?, #N/A, or #DIV/0, it is possible to find all the cells used in the formula.

⊟ Activate the cell containing the error message.

⊟ Activate the **Formulas** tab, go to the **Formula Auditing** group and click the list of the **Error Checking** button .

⊟ Click **Error Checking**.

	A	B	C	D	E
	E6		*fx* =D6/D21		
1	SUMMARY OF ORDERS FOR 1ST SEMESTER				
2					
3					
4	PRODUCT	PRICE	QUANTITY	TOTAL	PERCENTAGE
5	Sofa bed	£ 207.00	2	£ 414.00	1.94%
6	Sofa (3 seater)	£ 449.00	6	£ 2,694.00	#DIV/0!
7	Single bed	£ 199.00	9	£ 1,791.00	#DIV/0!
8	Double bed	£ 399.00	9	£ 3,591.00	#DIV/0!
9	Dining chair	£ 45.00	7	£ 315.00	#DIV/0!

Auditing arrows appear. The red arrows link the error-causing cell to the cells containing references to it, while the blue arrows show the cell's precedents that caused the error to occur.

To remove the arrows, activate the **Formulas** tab, go to the **Formula Auditing** group and click the **Remove Arrows** button.

Analysing errors in one formula

⊟ Activate the cell containing the error, as indicated by the coloured triangle (green by default) in the upper left corner of the cell.

⊟ Click the [⬧] button located to the left of the active cell. If the error indicator does not appear (the green triangle and the button), click the **Microsoft Office** button [⬛], then **Excel Options** then, under the **Formulas** category, check **Enable background error checking**, under **Error Checking**.

A list of options appears, based on the type of error Excel has found (the first option reminds you what type of error has been made).

	E6	▼	f_x	=D6/D21		
	A	B	C	D	E	F
1	SUMMARY OF ORDERS FOR 1ST SEMESTER					
2						
3						
4	PRODUCT	PRICE	QUANTITY	TOTAL	PERCENTAGE	
5	Sofa bed	£ 207.00	2	£ 414.00	1.94%	
6	Sofa (3 seater)	£ 449.00	6	£ 2,69⊕ ▾	#DIV/0!	
7	Single bed	£ 199.00	9	£ 1,79	Divide by Zero Error	
8	Double bed	£ 399.00	9	£ 3,59	Help on this error	
9	Dining chair	£ 45.00	7	£ 31	Show Calculation Steps...	
10	Folding chair	£ 26.00	5	£ 13		
11	Coffee table	£ 141.00	8	£ 1,12	Ignore Error	
12	Square table	£ 98.00	2	£ 19	Edit in Formula Bar	
13	Rectangular table	£ 326.00	6	£ 1,95		
14	Wardrobe 2 door	£ 228.00	9	£ 2,05	Error Checking Options...	
15	Buffet 2 door	£ 360.00	4	£ 1,44		
16	Buffet 3 door	£ 460.00	8	£ 3,680.00	#DIV/0!	

⊟ Click the option of your choice:

Ignore Error   deactivates the error indicator: both the coloured triangle and the tag disappear.

Edit in formula bar   places the insertion point in the formula bar so you can modify the formula.

Error Checking Options   shows the **Options** dialog box so you can choose which **Rules Excel** uses for **Error Checking**.

Depending on the type of error, other options may appear.

 If none of these options are of interest, activate another cell to close this options menu.

Analysing the errors in all formulas

⊟ Open the **Excel Options** dialog box (**Microsoft Office** button , **Excel Options**), activate the **Formulas** category and change the type of error that Excel should find by activating or deactivating the various **Rules**.

⊟ Activate the worksheet that you want to error check.

⊟ Activate the **Formulas** tab, go to the **Formula Auditing** group and click the **Error Checking** button .

*Excel selects the first cell containing a mistake and shows the formula and the error in detail in the **Error Checking** dialog box.*

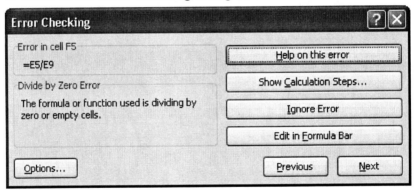

⊟ You can choose to get **Help on this error**, or **Show Calculation Steps**, to **Ignore Error**, or to **Edit in Formula Bar**, by clicking the appropriate button.

*The buttons on the **Error Checking** dialog box may differ depending on the type of error.*

⊟ Depending on the option you choose, the **Restart** button may appear in the **Error Checking** dialog box which enables you to continue checking the worksheet.

⊟ If you want to move to the next or previous error without working on the current one, click the **Next** or **Previous** button.

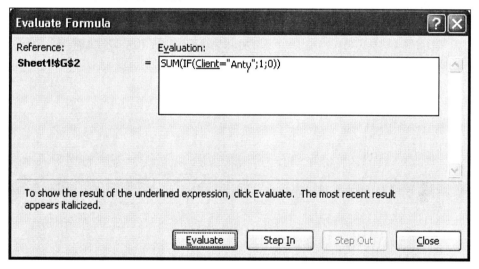

The **Reset Ignored Errors** button (**Excel Options**, **Formulas** category, **Error Checking**) reactivates error indicators in cells where you have chosen the **Ignore Error** option.

Evaluating formulas

This technique can be used to view the result of each part of a nested formula.

🖰 Select the cell you want to evaluate.

🖰 Activate the **Formulas** tab, go to the **Formula Auditing** group and click the **Evaluate Formula** button 🔳.

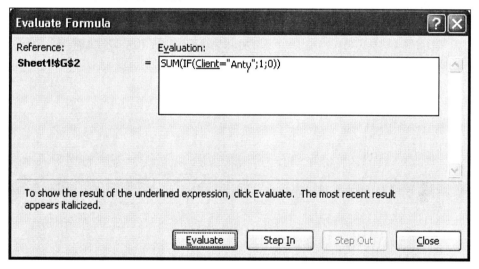

🖰 Click **Evaluate** to see the result of the expression underlined in the **Evaluation** box. The result appears in the formula in italics.

🖰 Click **Evaluate** again to see the result of the next underlined section, and so on.

🖰 When you have evaluated the whole formula, click the **Close** button to end the evaluation or the **Restart** button (that replaces the **Evaluate** button) to evaluate again.

If the formula you are evaluating contains a reference to another formula, the **Step In** button shows the detail of that underlined formula, in a new pane of the evaluation box. The **Step Out** button returns to the initial formula.

Using the Watch Window

The Watch Window lets you see cell contents and formula details.

🔲 Select the cells you wish to watch.

🔲 Activate the **Formulas** tab, go to the **Formulas Auditing** group and click the **Watch Window** button.

*If the **Watch Window** appears on the worksheet, you can anchor it like an ordinary toolbar by double-clicking its title bar.*

🔲 Add the cells you want to watch to the **Watch Window**:

- select the cell(s). To select all the cells in a worksheet containing formulas, activate the **Home** tab, go to the **Editing** group, click the **Find and Select** button, and select **Formulas**.

- click the **Add Watch** button, check the selection in the **Add Watch** dialog box, and click **Add**.

*As long as the **Watch Window** is displayed, you can select a new cell (or range) at any time and add it to the list of watched items.*

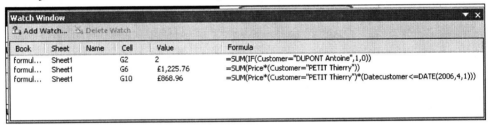

🔲 You can change the column widths on the **Watch Window** by dragging the vertical line between the column headers.

🔲 To go rapidly to a cell listed in the **Watch Window**, double-click that cell's row in the list.

🔲 When you no longer need the **Watch Window**, go to the **Formulas** tab and click the **Watch Window** button again.

Tracing relationships between formulas and cells

Showing precedents

These are the cells which are linked to the formula: they can be found using auditing arrows.

⊟ Select the cell containing the formula.

⊟ Activate the **Formulas** tab, go the the **Formula Auditing** group and click the **Trace Precedents** tool button.

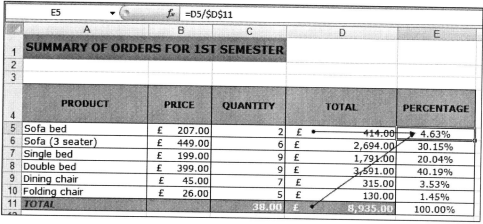

In this example, the blue arrows show the precedents of cell E5.

⊟ To hide the precedent arrows, open the list on the **Remove Arrows** button and click **Remove Precedent Arrows**.

Showing dependent cells

Dependent cells contain formulas that refer to a selected cell. Like precedents, they can be highlighted with arrows.

⊟ Activate the relevant cell.

⊟ Activate the **Formulas** tab, go to the **Formula Auditing** group and click the **Trace Dependants** button.

D11	▼	*fx*	=SUM(D5:D10)	

	A	B	C	D	E
1	SUMMARY OF ORDERS FOR 1ST SEMESTER				
2					
3					
4	PRODUCT	PRICE	QUANTITY	TOTAL	PERCENTAGE
5	Sofa bed	£ 207.00	2	£ 414.00	4.63%
6	Sofa (3 seater)	£ 449.00	6	£ 2,694.00	30.15%
7	Single bed	£ 199.00	9	£ 1,791.00	20.04%
8	Double bed	£ 399.00	9	£ 3,591.00	40.19%
9	Dining chair	£ 45.00	7	£ 315.00	3.53%
10	Folding chair	£ 26.00	5	£ 130.00	1.45%
11	TOTAL		38.00	£ 8,955.00	100.00%

Cell D11 is involved in the formulas in cells E5 to E11.

⊡ To hide the dependent arrows, click the list on the **Remove Arrows** button and select **Remove Dependent** arrows.

To clear the auditing arrows, go to the **Formulas** tab, **Formula Auditing** group and click the **Remove Arrows** tool button.

Part 6
Presenting data

Modifying the font and/or font size

⊟ Select the relevant cells or characters.

⊟ Activate the **Home** tab.

⊟ To change the font, go to the **Font** group and open the **Font** list. To change the font size, open the **Font size** list.

⊟ Move the mouse, <u>without clicking</u>, to the required font and font size.

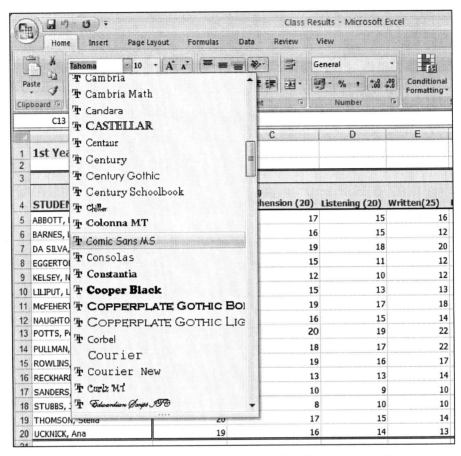

The result is immediately shown in the selected cells in the worksheet.

⊟ Click the font or font size you want.

You can also go to the **Font** group and click the dialog box launcher [⧉] to open the **Format Cells** dialog box (or use [Ctrl] [⇧ Shift] **1**) and make your changes in the **Font** tab.

Characters

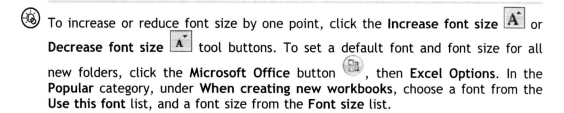

To increase or reduce font size by one point, click the **Increase font size** $\boxed{A}$ or **Decrease font size** $\boxed{A}$ tool buttons. To set a default font and font size for all new folders, click the **Microsoft Office** button , then **Excel Options**. In the **Popular** category, under **When creating new workbooks**, choose a font from the **Use this font** list, and a font size from the **Font size** list.

Adjusting character size

If this function is active, Excel reduces the size of the characters automatically when the cell is not wide enough to display them all.

⊟ Select the relevant cells.

⊟ Activate the **Home** tab, go to the **Alignment** group and click the dialog box initiator ▫.

⊟ If necessary, activate the **Alignment** dialog box launcher tab and check **Shrink to fit**.

⊟ Click **OK**.

If you widen a column, characters which have been reduced in size return to their original size.

Formatting characters

Applying Bold, Underscore and Italics

⊟ Select the relevant cells or characters.

⊟ Activate the **Home** tab and apply the required attributes:

- to apply bold, click the **Bold** tool button $\boxed{B}$, or press ⌈Ctrl⌉ B, or ⌈Ctrl⌉⌈⇧ Shift⌉ 2.
- to apply italics, click the **Italics** tool button $\boxed{I}$, or press ⌈Ctrl⌉ I or ⌈Ctrl⌉⌈⇧ Shift⌉ 3.
- to apply a basic underscore, click the **Underline** tool button 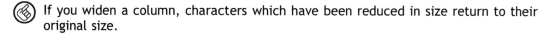, or press ⌈Ctrl⌉ U, or ⌈Ctrl⌉⌈⇧ Shift⌉ 4.
- to apply a double underline, open the list on the **Underline** tool button $\boxed{U}$ and check **Double Underline**.

⊟ To cancel a format, repeat one of the previous commands.

 You can apply several formatting attributes to the same text.

Applying more character formats

*This feature applies **Strikethrough**, **Superscript** or **Subscript** as well as other formatting styles.*

⊟ Select the relevant cells or characters.

⊟ Activate the **Home** tab, go to the **Font** group and click the dialog box launcher
[▣] , or press Ctrl û Shift **1**. If required, activate the **Font** tab.

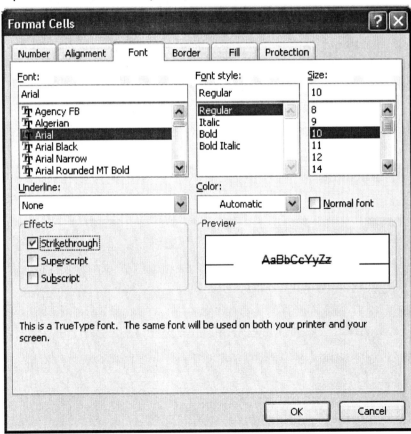

- Under **Effects**, **Strikethrough**, **Superscript** and/or **Subscript**, select all the formats to be applied to the text.

  *You can choose more underline types from the **Underline** list.*

- Click **OK**.

Changing character colour

- Select the relevant cells or characters.

- Activate the **Home** tab, go to the **Font** group and open the list on the **Font Colour** tool button [A ▾].

- Click the colour you want.

⊛ You can also select a colour from the **Format Cells** dialog box, under the **Font** tab.

⊛ The colour you select is displayed on the **Font Colour** tool button [A ▾]. To apply this colour to more text, simply click the tool button without opening the list.

Using the mini-toolbar to format characters

- Activate the cell containing the characters you want to modify.

- Select the relevant characters in the cell (not in the formula bar).

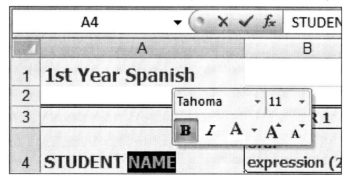

When you move the mouse slightly, a small semi-transparent tool bar, called the
***Mini Toolbar** appears.*

*The mini toolbar helps you define font, font size, **Bold** and **Italic** formatting and*
text colour.

Point to the mini toolbar and click the tool you want to use.

For the mini tool bar to appear, you must check the **Show Mini Toolbar on**
selection option (**Microsoft Office** button 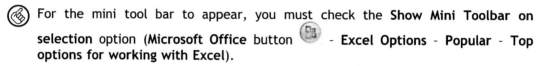 – **Excel Options** – **Popular** – **Top**
options for working with Excel).

Numbers and dates

Formatting numeric data

Applying a preset format

⊟ Select the relevant cells.

⊟ Activate the **Home** tab, go to the **Number** group and click the **Number Format** list.

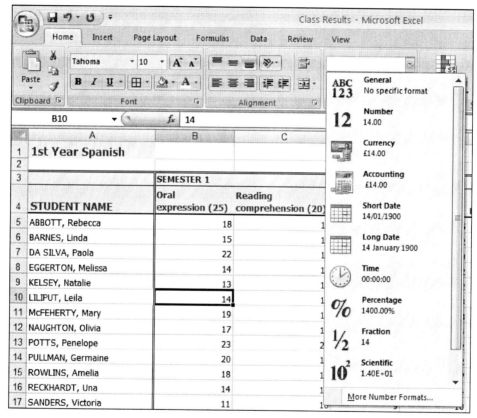

This list of principal Excel formats is displayed.

⊟ Click the format you want: **Number, Currency, Accounting, Percentage, Fraction** or **Text**.

When you apply the **Percentage** option, the relevant numbers are multiplied by 100 to convert them into percentage.

*The **Text** option displays numeric values as text (by default, they are left-justified in the cell).*

⊡ You can increase or decrease the number of decimal places by clicking the **Increase Decimal** ⊞ or **Decrease Decimal** ⊞ tool buttons.

Ⓒ Hash symbols may appear if a cell's width is insufficient for the format. Simply widen the column in this case.

To restore the number format of the selected cells, open the **Number Format** list and click **General**. Cells with **General** formatting do not have a particular format.

Ⓒ For a fast way to apply a currency, percentage or thousand format, click the ⊞, ⊞, or ⊞ tool buttons respectively.

Applying other formats

⊡ Select the cells you want to format.

⊡ Activate the **Home** tab, go to the **Number** group, click the **Number Format** list, then select **More number formats**. Alternatively, click the dialog box launcher ⊞ in the **Number** group, or press Ctrl ⇧ Shift **1** and activate the **Number** tab in the **Format Cells** dialog box.

⊡ Under the **Category** list, select the format you want to use.

⊡ If required, change the number format settings (**number of decimal places**, etc).

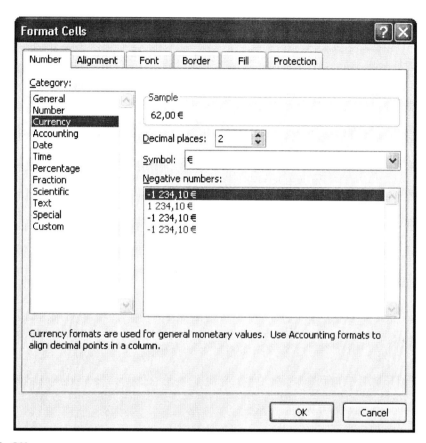

⊟ Click **OK**.

Formatting dates/times

⊟ Select the cells containing the dates or times you want to format.

⊟ Activate the **Home** tab, go to the **Number** group, click the **Number Format** list, and select **Short date**, **Long date** or **Time**.

or

Click the dialog box launcher ☒ (**Home** tab – **Number** group), or press ⌨Ctrl⌨ ⌨⇧ Shift⌨ **1** and activate the **Number** tab. In the **Category** list, select **Date** or **Time**, select the format you want in the list, then click **OK**.

To combine text with a date, you can use the TEXT function (see Calculations –
Calculating with dates and using date functions) or simply customize the format
(see Formatting – Creating a custom format).

Creating a custom format

⊟ Select the cells to which you want to apply the format.

⊟ Activate the **Home** tab, go to the **Number** group, click the **Format Number** list,
then select **More number formats**. Alternatively, click the **Number** group dialog
box launcher ⬚, or press Ctrl ⇧Shift 1 and activate the **Number** tab.

⊟ Activate **Custom** in the **Category** list then use **Type** to enter or modify the custom
format.

- a custom format can contain up to four sections, separated by semi-colons which
define, respectively, the format of positive numbers, negative numbers, null
values, and the format of text.

*For example, 0.00" kg";[red]-0.00" kg";0. This example shows positive values
with two decimal places followed by the text: "kg", negative values in red,
preceded by a minus sign and followed by the text "kg", null values as zero and
any text without formatting.*

- if you define only one section, it is used for all number types.

*For example: #, ##0" net". With this format, whatever the value (positive,
negative or null), the hundreds and thousands are separated by a comma and the
value is followed by the text "net".*

- remember that you can use the following syntaxes when creating a custom
format:

To add text to a custom format: Text added to a format must have quotation
marks. Make sure you do not leave spaces in front of quotation marks. If you do,
Excel will interpret the space as a command to divide by 1,000.

To customise a number format: # ## puts a space between the thousands and
hundreds.

0 shows values without decimals.

0.00 shows two decimal places.

For example # ##0.00" net" displays 2415 as **2 415.00 net**

<u>To customize a date format</u>: For days, use the codes d (1), dd (01), ddd (Sun) or dddd (Sunday),

For months, use m (1), mm (01), mmm (Jan) or mmmm(January),

For years, use yy (04) or yyyy(2004).

Use the character of your choice as the separator.

For example, the format **ddd dd mmm yyyy** displays **25/4/04** as **Sun 25 Apr 2004**.

<u>To include a text entry</u>: to display whatever is entered in the cell, use the @ character. For example, **"State; "@** displays **State: Queensland** when you type **Queensland** into the cell.

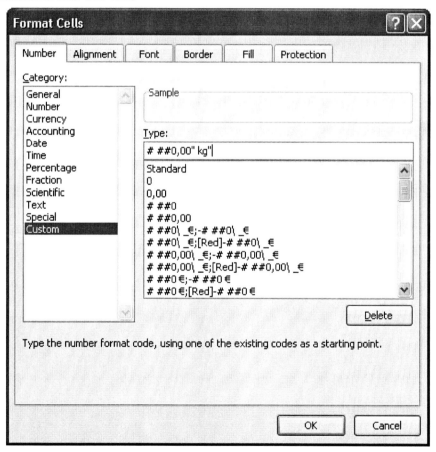

⊐ Click **OK** to confirm.

You can also display data as text using the TEXT function (see Calculations - Calculating with dates and using date functions.).

To hide the contents of a cell, enter the custom format ;;; (three semi-colons) in the **Type** text box.

Aligning data

Modifying the orientation of cell content

⊟ Select the relevant cells.

⊟ Activate the **Home** tab, go to the **alignment** group and click the list on the **Orientation** tool button 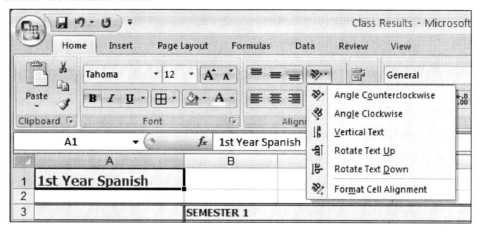.

⊟ Click the orientation you want.

👆 The **Format Cell** – **Alignment** option on the list on the 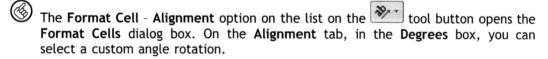 tool button opens the **Format Cells** dialog box. On the **Alignment** tab, in the **Degrees** box, you can select a custom angle rotation.

Aligning cell content

⊟ Select the relevant cells and activate the **Home** tab.

⊟ To modify the vertical alignment of a cell in relation to the height of the row, click one of the following tool buttons, located in the **Alignment** group.

≡ top alignment.

≡ centered.

≡ bottom alignment.

⊡ To modify the horizontal alignment of a cell in relation to the column width, click one of the following tool buttons:

  left alignment.

  centered.

  right alignment.

You can find these options in the **Format Cells** dialog box (**Home** tab – **Alignment** group – dialog box launcher 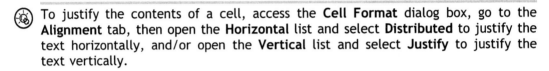), in the **Horizontal** and **Vertical** lists. The **General** option in the **Horizontal** list restores the original alignment.

To justify the contents of a cell, access the **Cell Format** dialog box, go to the **Alignment** tab, then open the **Horizontal** list and select **Distributed** to justify the text horizontally, and/or open the **Vertical** list and select **Justify** to justify the text vertically.

Indenting cell contents

⊡ Select the relevant cells.

⊡ Activate the **Home** tab, go to the **Alignment** group and and click the dialog box launcher. Alternatively, press [Ctrl] [⇧ Shift] **1** and activate the **Alignment** tab.

⊡ Open the **Horizontal** list and select the type of indent you want:

Left (indent)　　　　　to apply left-alignment and a left indent.

Right (indent)　　　　to apply right-alignment and a right indent.

Distributed (indent)　to apply a justified alignment and indent.

⊡ Use **Indent** to specify the required value.

Aligning data

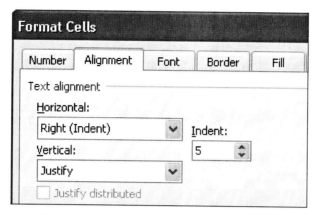

*Each increment in the **Indent** box represents the width of a character.*

Click **OK**.

The [icon] and [icon] tool buttons from the **Alignment** group in the **Home** tab increase or decrease the indent.

Merging cells

This command merges several cells so you can carry over content from the first cell to the others. The merged cells form one cell.

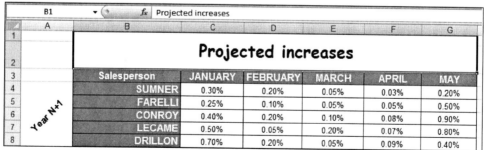

In this example, cell B1 is merged and centre-aligned on cells B1 to G2. Cell A4 is also merged and centered (horizontally and vertically) with cells A4 to A8 (the orientation has also been modified).

⊟ Select the cells containing the data and the adjacent cells where you want the data to appear.

Only data in the first cell of the selection will appear in the merged cells.

⊟ Activate the **Home** tab, go to the **Alignment** group and open the list on the **Merge and Centre** tool button . Choose one of the following options:

Merge and centre	to merge the selection and centre align the contents of the first cell with the merged cells.
Merge across	to merge the selection horizontally, without changing the horizontal alignment of the selection.
Merge cells	to merge the selection horizontally or vertically, without changing the horizontal alignment of the selection.
Unmerge cells	to cancel the merge.

You can also merge cells using the **Format Cells** dialog box, **Alignment** tab and check the **Merge cells** option.

Borders and fill

Applying cell borders

By default, cells are not bordered. The grid does not print unless you specify.

Applying preset borders

⊟ Select the cells to which you want to apply a border.

⊟ Activate the **Home** tab, go to the **Font** group and open the list on the 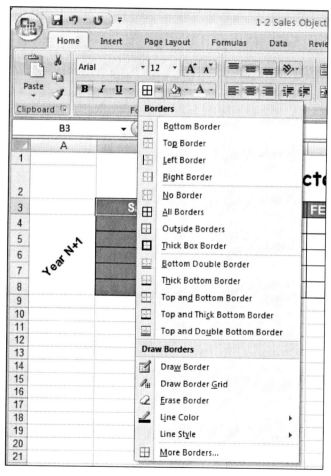 tool button.

⊟ Click the type of border you want.

The ⊞▾ *tool button now displays the last type of border chosen.*

The ⊞▾ displays the last border applied. To apply the same border to another range of cells, simply click the ⊞▾ tool button, without opening the list.

To delete all borders applied to the selection, select **No border** from the list on the ⊞▾ tool button.

Applying more borders

⊟ Select the cells to which you want to apply a border.

⊟ Activate the **Home** tab, go to the **Font** group, open the list of the ⊞▾ tool button and click **More borders**. Alternatively, click the **Font** group dialog box launcher ▣, or press ⌨Ctrl ⌨⇧Shift **1** and activate the **Border** tab.

⊟ To put a precise border around the edges of the selection, select the border **Style** and **Color**, then click the **Outline** button. To apply the border to each cell in the selection, click the **Inside** button.

To place a border along one or more specific edges of the selected range, choose a **Style** and **Colour** then click the corresponding button in the **Border** section to display or hide that border. You can even click an edge in the **Border** preview (this activates the corresponding button). Click the **Inside** button to apply the border to each individual cell in the selection, but not around the outside edges.

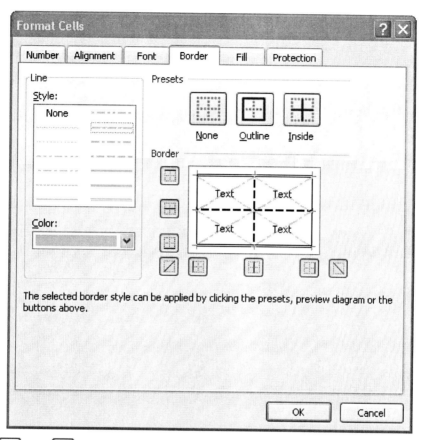

The ⬚ and ⬚ tool buttons draw diagonal lines across individual cells.

- Click **OK** to confirm.
- Click outside the selection to view the final result.

Applying colour to cells

- Select the relevant cells.
- Activate the **Home** tab, go to the **Font** group and open the list on the **Fill Color** tool button ⬚.

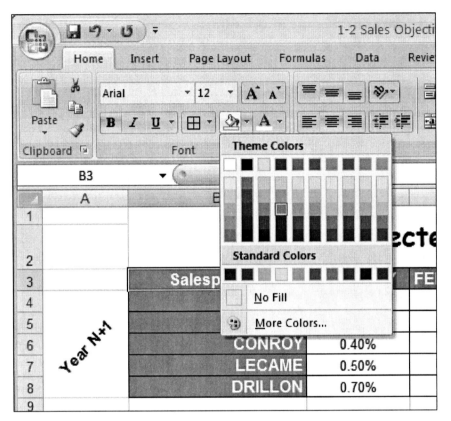

🗗 Click a colour from **Theme Colors** or **Standard Colors**.

🗗 To select another colour, select **More Colors** and in the dialog box that opens, choose one of the two commands:

- in the **Standard** tab, click a colour from the palette to apply it

- in the **Custom** tab, use the colour cursor or the **Red, Green** and **Blue** boxes to create your own colour.

Click **OK** in the **Colors** dialog box.

The last colour applied is displayed on the **Fill Color** tool button. To apply this colour to another selection, simply click the tool button, without opening the list.

The colours selected in the **Colors** dialog box are then displayed in the **Recent colors** box in the list on the **Fill Color** tool button .

The **Format Cells** dialog box, **Fill** tab, applies a background colour to selected cells.

To remove a fill colour from a cell range, select the **No Fill** option from the list on the **Fill Color** tool button.

Applying a pattern to cells

⊟ Select the relevant cells.

⊟ Activate the **Home** tab, go to the **Font** group and click the dialog box launcher ▣. Alternatively, press `Ctrl` `⇧ Shift` **1**.

⊟ Activate the **Fill** tab.

⊟ Open the **Pattern Color** list and select a foreground colour.

⊟ Under **Background Color**, choose a colour for the pattern background.

⊟ Open the **Pattern Style** list and select the pattern you want to apply to the cells.

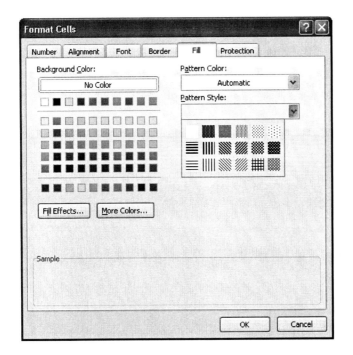

This dialog box also applies a fill colour to the cells.

⤶ Click **OK**.

Applying a fill effect to cells

⤶ Select the relevant cells.

⤶ Activate the **Home** tab, go to the **Font** group and click the dialog box launcher ▣. Alternatively, press `Ctrl` `⇧ Shift` **1**.

⤶ Activate the **Fill** tab and click the **Fill Effects** button.

⤶ Open the **Color 1** and **Color 2** lists to select the shade colour.

⤶ Under **Shading Styles**, choose the one you want then click one of the models from the **Variants** box.

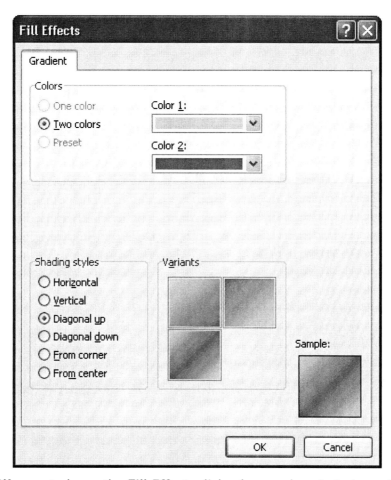

⊟ Click **OK** once to leave the **Fill Effects** dialog box, and again to leave the **Format Cells** dialog box.

Applying preset conditional formatting

Conditional formatting highlights cells containing numeric values, dates, times by showing data using data bars, colour scales and/or icon sets. A condition changes the appearance of cells.

🖻 Select the cells to which you want to apply conditional formatting.

🖻 Activate the **Home** tab, go to the **Styles** group and open the list on the **Conditional Formatting** button.

🖻 Move the mouse over one of the following options:

Data Bars: they let you see the value of a cell relative to other cells, and to spot the highest and lowest values. The length of the data bar represents the value in a cell. A longer bar represents a higher value, a shorter bar represents a lower value

Colour scales: are visual guides that help you understand data distribution and variation. You can apply a two – colour scale (the shade of the colour represents higher or lower values), a three – colour scale (the shade colour represents higher, middle or lower values).

Icon sets: let you annotate and classify data into three to five categories separated by a threshold value. Each icon represents a range of values. For example, in the **3 arrows icon set**, the green up arrow represents higher values, the yellow sideways arrow represents middle values, and the red down arrow represents lower values.

🖻 Click the type of data bar, colour scale or icon set you want to apply.

*When you point (without clicking) to a model, a ScreenTip tells you its name, particularly if it is a two or three colour scale (in the **Color Scales** list).*

	A	B	C	D	E	F
1		January	February	March	April	TOTAL
2	**RICHARD**	£ 1,450.00	£ 1,475.00	£ 1,342.00	£ 1,346.00	£ 5,613.00
3	**ALBAN**	£ 1,320.00	£ 1,120.00	£ 1,500.00	£ 1,512.00	£ 5,452.00
4	**MERCIER**	£ 1,450.00	£ 1,356.00	£ 1,400.00	£ 1,420.00	£ 5,626.00
5	**LECAMA**	£ 1,360.00	£ 1,423.00	£ 1,450.00	£ 1,420.00	£ 5,653.00
6	**DRILLON**	£ 1,420.00	£ 1,523.00	£ 1,475.00	£ 1,389.00	£ 5,807.00

Conditional formatting

In the previous example, **Data bars** have been applied to cells B2 to E6, emphasising the differences between one quarter and the next, particularly in relation to the *ALBAN* row.

	A	B	C	D	E	F
1		January	February	March	April	TOTAL
2	**RICHARD**	£ 1,450.00	£ 1,475.00	£ 1,342.00	£ 1,346.00	£ 5,613.00
3	**ALBAN**	£ 1,320.00	£ 1,120.00	£ 1,500.00	£ 1,512.00	£ 5,452.00
4	**MERCIER**	£ 1,450.00	£ 1,356.00	£ 1,400.00	£ 1,420.00	£ 5,626.00
5	**LECAMA**	£ 1,360.00	£ 1,423.00	£ 1,450.00	£ 1,420.00	£ 5,653.00
6	**DRILLON**	£ 1,420.00	£ 1,523.00	£ 1,475.00	£ 1,389.00	£ 5,807.00

In the above example, a **Three - colour scale** has been applied to cells B2 to E6. Values inferior to a particular value are represented by several colour scales, values between two values are represented by scales in a different colour, and higher values are represented by scales in a third colour.

	A	B	C	D	E	F
1		January	February	March	April	TOTAL
2	**RICHARD**	⬆ £ 1,450.00	⬆ £ 1,475.00	➡ £ 1,342.00	➡ £ 1,346.00	£ 5,613.00
3	**ALBAN**	➡ £ 1,320.00	⬇ £ 1,120.00	⬆ £ 1,500.00	⬆ £ 1,512.00	£ 5,452.00
4	**MERCIER**	⬆ £ 1,450.00	➡ £ 1,356.00	⬆ £ 1,400.00	⬆ £ 1,420.00	£ 5,626.00
5	**LECAMA**	➡ £ 1,360.00	⬆ £ 1,423.00	⬆ £ 1,450.00	⬆ £ 1,420.00	£ 5,653.00
6	**DRILLON**	⬆ £ 1,420.00	⬆ £ 1,523.00	⬆ £ 1,475.00	➡ £ 1,389.00	£ 5,807.00

In this example, a **three - arrow icon set** has been applied to cells B2 to E6. Notice that values less than a certain value are represented by a downward arrow, values between two values are represented by a horizontal arrow and higher values are represented by an upward arrow.

 You can combine three conditional formats on the same cell range.

When you change data, the conditional formatting applied to the cell is immediately updated.

Creating a conditional formatting rule

You can create your own rules to apply to preset conditional formatting, or apply your own custom formatting.

- Select the cells to which you want to apply the conditional formatting.

- Activate the **Home** tab, go to the **Styles** group and open the list on the **Conditional Formatting** button.

- Click **New rule**.

*The **New formatting rule** dialog box opens. You can also access this dialog box by selecting **More Rules** from either the **Data Bars**, **Colour Scales** and **Icon sets** menus.*

Creating a Data Bar

- Under **Select a rule type**, make sure that **Format all cells based on their values** is active.

- Open the Format Style list and choose Data Bar.

- Use one of the following commands:

  - to format lower and higher values, select **Lowest Value** and **Highest Value** in the **Type** lists under **Shortest bar** and **Longest bar**.

  In this case, you cannot specify a value.

  - to format number values, dates or times, select **Number** in the **Type** lists under **Shortest bar** and **Longest bar**, then enter a **Value** in each of the boxes.

  - to format percentages, select **Percent** in the **Type** list under **Shortest bar** and **Longest bar**, then enter a **Value** in each of the boxes.

  Valid values must be between 0 and 100. Do not enter a percentage sign.

  - to format **Percentiles**, select **Percentiles** in the the **Type** lists under **Shortest bar** and **Longest bar**, then enter a **Value** in each of the boxes.

  A percentile lets you view a group of high values (such as the top 20th percentile) in one colour grade proportion, and lower values (such as the bottom 20th percentile) in another colour grade proportion, because they represent extreme values that might skew the view of your data. You cannot use a percentile if the range of cells contains more than 8,191 data points.

  - to format a formula result, select **Formula** from the **Type** lists under **Shortest bar** and **Longest bar**, then enter a **Value** in each of the boxes.

Conditional formatting

The formula must return a number, date, or time value. Start the formula with an equal sign (=). Invalid formulas result in no formatting being applied.

*You can choose a different **Type** for the **Shortest bar** and the **Longest bar** (for example, you can choose **Number** in the **Shortest bar** and **Percent** in the **Longest bar**.*

*Make sure the value in the **Shortest bar** is less than the value in the **Longest bar**.*

⊟ Open the **Bar color** list to choose a colour scale.

*The bar colour that you select is displayed in the **Preview** box.*

⊟ To only display the data bar and not the cell value, check **Show bar only**.

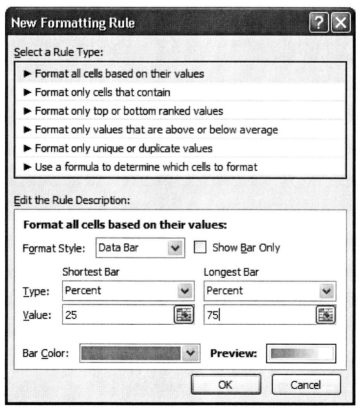

⊟ Click **OK**.

Creating a colour scale format

- In the **New Formatting Rule** dialog box, make sure that **Format all cells based on their values**, under **Select a Rule Type**, is active.

- Open the **Format Style** list and select **2-color scale** or **3-color scale**.

- Carry out the same commands as for the previous sub-title:
  - Under **Minimum**, open the **Type** list and select **Lowest value, number, percent, formula**, or **percentile**.
  - In the **Value** box, enter the number, percent (without the symbol), percentile, or create the formula indicating the condition to display minimal values.
  - Choose a colour from the **Color** list.

- Repeat this action for the **Maximum** box and, for a three-colour scale, in the **Midpoint** box.

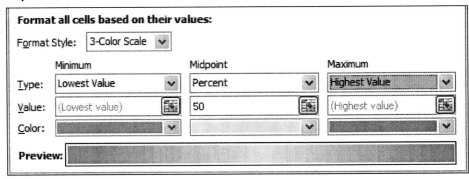

- Click **OK**.

Creating icon set formatting

- In the **New Formatting Rule** dialog box, make sure that the **Format all cells based on their values** option, under **Select a Rule Type**, is active.

- Open the **Format Style** list and select **Icon Sets**.

- Choose an **Icon Style** from the **Icon Style** list.

- Perform the same commands as for the previous tasks:
  - open each of the **Type** lists and choose a **Number, Percent, Formula, Percentile**.
  - in the **Value** boxes, enter the number, percent, percentile, or create a formula.

Conditional formatting

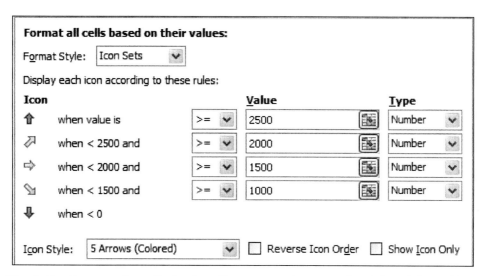

☐ Check the **Reverse Icon Order** box if you want icons to the right of the cells.

☐ Check **Show Icon Only** if you want to only display icons and not cell values.

Icons come in three sizes. The size displayed depends on the size of the font.

☐ Click **OK**.

Formatting cells according to their content

These techniques let you select or create a format based on the contents of a cell.

Applying a preset format

☐ Select the cells to which you want to apply a conditional format.

☐ Activate the **Home** tab, go to the **Styles** group and open the list on the **Conditional Formatting** button.

☐ Select one of the options under **Highlight Cell Rules**, or under **Top/Bottom Rules**.

Depending which option you choose, you can use the dialog box to enter or edit the data for the rule you want to apply. In this example you can edit the first box to apply a format to the first n values.

- Modify or enter data for the rule you want to apply.

- Choose a format to apply from the drop-down list that follows.

- Click **OK**.

Customising a format

- Select the cells to which you want to apply the conditional formatting.

- Activate the **Home** tab, go to the **Styles** group and open the list on the **Conditional Formatting** button.

- Click the **New Rule** option.

- Under **Select a Rule Type**, select the type of rule you want to create from one of the options that starts with **Format only** or **Use a formula to determine which cells to format**.

- Under **Edit Rule Description**, use the list or text boxes to specify the conditions to apply to the rule.

Conditional formatting

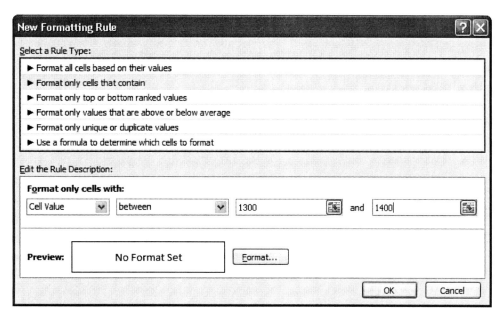

↵ Click the **Format** button. The **Format Cells** dialog box appears. Use the tabs to customize the cell format to apply to the condition and click the **OK** button twice.

Remove all conditional formatting

Use this to remove conditional formats (that apply to rules) from a worksheet or a cell range.

↵ Activate the worksheet containing the conditional formatting to clear, or select the cells to which conditional formatting has been applied.

↵ Activate the **Home** tab, go to the **Styles** group and open the list on the **Conditional Formatting** tool button.

↵ Move the mouse over the **Clear Rules** option and click either **Clear rules from selected cells** or **Clear rules from entire sheet**.

Managing conditional formatting rules

⊟ Select the cells containing the conditional formatting you want to modify.

⊟ Activate the **Home** tab, go to the **Styles** group and open the list on the **Conditional Formatting** button.

⊟ Click **Manage Rules**.

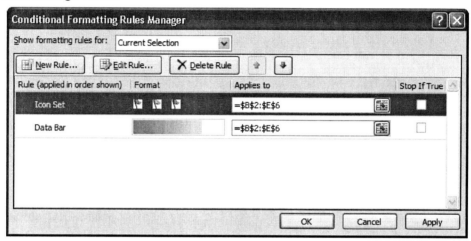

The **Conditional Formatting Rules Manager** dialog box displays the various rules applied to the selection (two rules in this example).

⊟ To select a rule, click the row.

⊟ To modify a rule, select it, click the **Edit Rule** button and make your changes in the **Edit Formatting Rule** dialog box, similar to the **New Rule** dialog box.

⊟ To clear a rule, select it and click **Delete Rule**.

⊟ To modify cells to which a rule is applied, select the rule and use the [img] tool button, under **Applies to**.

⊟ To change the rule priority, select the relevant rules and click the [img] or [img] tool button.

A rule appearing higher in the list has priority over another rule appearing lower down. By default, new rules are always placed at the top of the list and therefore have higher priority.

⊟ To stop rule evaluation, tick the check box under **Stop if true**.

Conditional formatting

*The **Stop if true** check box also simulates how conditional formatting might appear in earlier versions of Microsoft Office Excel that do not support several conditional formatting rules. For example, if you have more than three conditional formatting rules for a range of cells, a version of Excel earlier than Office Excel 2007 applies the last rule in precedence that is true. If you want the second rule to be applied, tick the **Stop if true** check box for that rule.*

⊟ Click **OK** to confirm the changes by closing the **Conditional Formatting Rules Manager** dialog box, or click on the **Close** button.

Applying a cell style

A cell style is a defined set of formatting characteristics that can be applied to any cell. You can create your own cell styles.

⊟ Select the cells to which you want to apply a style.

⊟ Activate the **Home** tab, go to the **Styles** group and click the **Cell Styles** button.

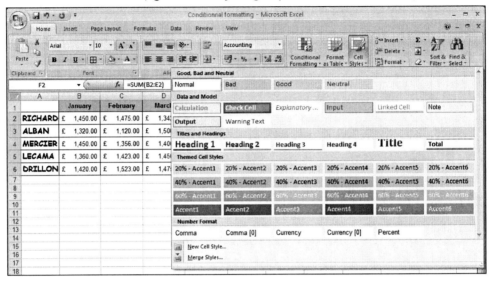

The list of all the styles are displayed in different categories (**Good**, **bad**, **neutral**, **data** and **model**, etc).

⊟ Click the style you want to apply.

To restore the formatting applied before the application of the style, go to the **Styles** group, click the **Cell Styles** button and, under **Good**, **bad**, **neutral** select **Normal**.

Cell styles

Creating a style

Creating a style saves a common presentation so that you can apply it to other cells.

⊟ Activate the cell to which you want to apply an automatic presentation.

⊟ Activate the **Home** tab, go to the **Styles** group, lick the **Cell Styles** button, then click **New Cell Style**.

⊟ Enter the **Style** name in the **Style** dialog box.

*The style is described in the **Style Includes (By Example)** frame.*

⊟ Uncheck the format style you do not want to include in the style.

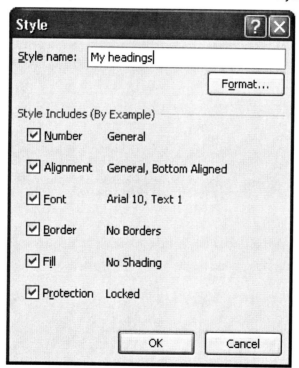

⊟ You can edit formatting characteristics using the **Format** button.

⊟ Click **OK** to confirm.

Notice that the style you have created is not applied to the active cell. This can be done (see previous heading). Styles are only defined for the active workbook.

 The styles you have created appear in the **Cell Styles** list, under the **Custom** category.

Managing existing cell styles

Modifying a cell style

⊟ Activate the **Home** tab, go to the **Styles** group and click the **Cell Styles** button.

⊟ Right click the style you want to modify.

⊟ Click **Modify**.

⊟ The **Style** dialog box appears: click **Format**.

⊟ Make your changes in the **Format Cells** dialog box and click **OK**.

⊟ Click **OK** again.

All cells formatted in that style are immediately modified.

Deleting a cell style

⊟ Activate the **Home** tab, go to the **Styles** group and click the **Cell Styles** button.

⊟ Right click the style you want to delete.

⊟ Click **Delete**.

The deletion is immediate. Cells that are formatted in this style lose their formatting. They return to a standard format.

Be careful: you cannot undo the deletion of a style.

Inserting a list of cell styles from the Quick Access Toolbar

⊟ Activate the **Home** tab, go to the **Styles** group and click the **Cell Styles** button.

⊟ Right click one of the styles.

⊟ Click **Add Gallery to Quick Access Toolbar**.

*The **Cell Styles** tool button now appears on the **Quick Access Toolbar**. Simply click to open the list of existing styles.*

Cell styles

Adding cell styles from different workbooks

⊟ Open the workbook containing the styles you want to add to the active workbook.

⊟ Activate the **Home** tab, go to the **Styles** group and click the **Cell Styles** button.

⊟ Click **Merge Styles**.

⊟ Double-click the workbook which contains the style you want to use.

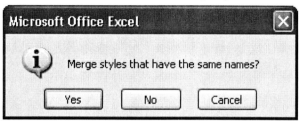

⊟ Click **Yes** to merge the styles and overwrite the styles in the active workbook; otherwise, click **No**.

Applying a theme to a workbook

A theme is a pre-defined set of colours, fonts (including header and body text fonts) and effects (such as line styles and fill effects) which give a uniform look to your workbook. Changing a theme immediately impacts the presentation of cells to which that theme has been applied.

⊟ Activate the worksheet to which you want to apply a theme.

⊟ Activate the **Page Layout** tab, go to the **Themes** group and click the **Themes** button.

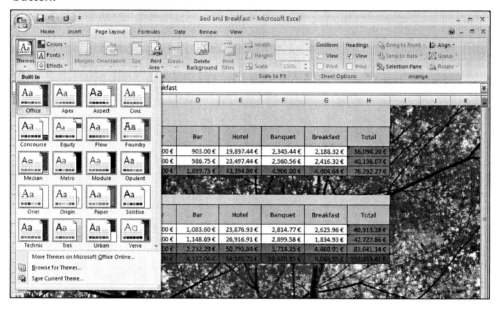

The list of built-in themes is displayed.

⊟ Move the mouse (without clicking!) over the themes to see how your theme would appear in your workbook.

⊟ When you have chosen, click a theme name.

The applied theme changes the presentation of the formatted cells with styles.

The default theme is called **Office**.

If the theme you want to use is not listed, click **Browse for themes** to find it on your computer or a network, or **More themes on Microsoft Online** to find more themes on Office Online.

Customising theme colours

Theme colours contain text colours, two cell fill colours, six highlighting colours and two hyperlink colours.

Modifying all colours associated with a theme

- Activate the **Page Layout** tab, go to the **Themes** group and click the **Colors** button.

- Move the mouse (without clicking!) over the different colours to see how they would appear in your workbook.

  In the list, the four text and fill colours are represented by the ▨ button. The other eight colours appear to the left of the colour name.

- When you have chosen a colour set, click its name.

Creating a colour set

- On the **Page Layout** tab, go to the **Themes** group, click the **Colors** button, go to the end of the list and click **Create New Theme Colors**.

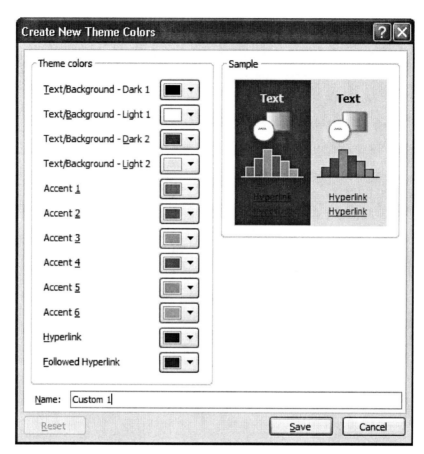

⊟ In the **Theme Colors** list, click the button corresponding to the colour theme item you want to change, then select the colour you want.

*The **Sample** box changes according to what you choose.*

⊟ When all the colour items have been modified, enter an appropriate **Name** for the new theme colours.

*If you want to restore the original colours for each item, click the **Reset** button.*

⊟ Click the **Save** button.

The colour sets you have created appear in the list on the **Colors** button, under **Custom**.

Customising theme fonts

Theme fonts contain a title font and body text font.

Modifying theme font sets

- Activate the **Page Layout** tab, go to the **Themes** group and click the **Fonts** button.

- Move the mouse (without clicking!) over the different fonts to see how they would appear in your worksheet.

  The name of the font set appears in a ScreenTip, along with the name of the title font used for each theme font.

- When you have chosen, click the name of the font you want.

Creating a font set

You can change two fonts to create you own theme font set.

- In the **Page Layout** tab, go to the **Themes** group, click the **Fonts** button then, at the end of the list, click **Create New Theme Fonts**.

- Select the fonts you want to use in the **Heading font** and **Body font** lists.

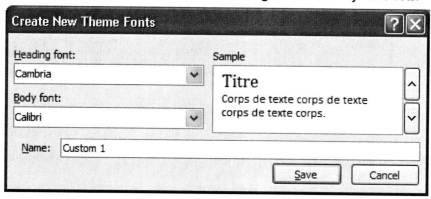

*The selected fonts are previewed in the **Sample** pane.*

- Enter an appropriate **Name**.

- Click **Save**.

- The font sets you create are displayed in the list on the **Fonts** button, under **Custom**.

Customising theme effects

Theme effects are sets of lines and fill effects. Although you can't create your own set of theme effects, you can choose the one you want to use in your own document theme.

⊡ Activate the **Page Layout** tab, go to the **Themes** group and click the **Effects** button.

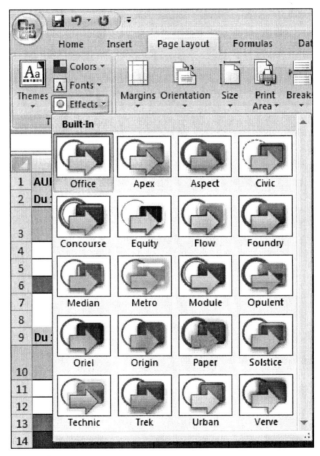

The lines and fill effects used in each theme effect set are displayed in a graphic.

⊡ Move the mouse over the various items then, when you are ready, click the one you want.

Themes

Saving a theme

Any changes that you make to the colours, fonts or the line and fill effects of a document theme can be saved as a custom document theme that you can apply to other documents.

⊟ Make your changes to the active theme (customize the colours, fonts, effects).

⊟ Activate the **Page Layout** tab, go to the **Themes** group and click the **Themes** button.

⊟ Click **Save Current Theme**.

⊟ Enter its **Name**.

The customized document theme save-to folder is active: C:\Documents and Settings\username\Application Data\Microsoft\Templates\Document themes.

⊟ Click **Save**.

 Custom themes are displayed in the list on the **Themes** button, under **Custom**.

Part 7
Organising data

Sorting data in a table by the content of one column

Using Excel 2007 you can quickly sort a table by the values in a column.

⊡ Select the cells you want to sort.

If you want to sort the entire table, and if the table has no blank rows, columns or merged cells, you do not need to select.

⊡ Click one of the cells in the column you want to sort. If you have made a selection, use the ⇄ or ⇧ Shift ⇄ keys to move to that cell.

⊡ In the **Home** tab, go to the **Editing** group, click the **Sort and Filter** button then select ⬆ (Sort A – Z or 0 to 9) to sort the selection so that the lowest values are at the top of the column, or ⬇ (Sort Z – A or 9 to 0) to sort the selection so that the highest values are at the top of the column.

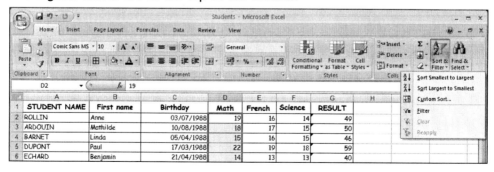

These options have different names depending on the content of the selected cells. **Sort A to Z** *or* **Sort Z to A** *for text,* **Sort Smallest to Largest** *or* **Sort Largest to Smallest** *for numbers, or* **Sort Oldest to Newest** *or* **Sort Newest to Oldest** *for dates. In this example, where the active cell is G2, the table will be sorted by numbers in the* **Results** *column.*

 The and tool buttons are also in the **Sort and Filter** group on the **Data** tab.

To sort table data by several different values, refer to the heading "Sorting table data using several criteria".

To cancel a sort, you can click the **Cancel** button on the **Quick Access Toolbar**, or press Ctrl **Z**.

Sorting data by cell colour, font or icon set

If you have applied a cell or font colour to a cell or range of cells or a table column, you can sort by these values. You can also sort by an icon set created by conditional formatting (see the corresponding chapter).

⊟ If required, activate the cells you want to sort.

⊟ In the **Home** tab, go to the **Editing** group, click the **Sort and Filter** button and select **Custom Sort**.

The **Sort** *dialog box appears.*

⊟ Check **My data has headers** if the first line of the selection contains column titles that must not be sorted.

⊟ Open the **Sort by** list and choose the column that contains the colour or icons by which you want to sort.

⊟ In the **Sort on** list, select one of the following options:

- **Cell color** to sort by cell colour.

- **Font color** to sort by font colour.

- **Cell icon** to sort by icon set.

⊟ Open the first drop-down list under **Order** and select, according to the sort, the cell colour, the colour of the font or icon of the cell by which the data are to be sorted.

◻ Open the second drop-down list under **Order** and select **On Top** to display the rows corresponding to the colour or icon you have chosen or **On Bottom**.

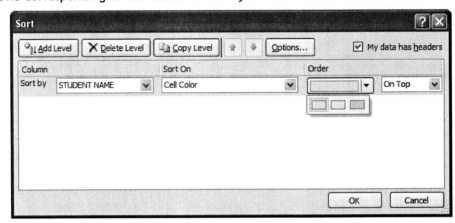

In this example (a table of student grades), the blue rows in the STUDENT NAME column (the first colour in the Order list) will be displayed first.

◻ Click **OK** to start sorting.

Sorting table data using several criteria

With Office Excel 2007, you can combine up to 64 sort criteria.

◻ If required, select the cells you want to sort.

◻ In the **Home** tab, go to the **Editing** group, click to the **Sort and Filter** button and select **Custom Sort**.

◻ Check **My data has headers** if the first row in the selection contains column titles and must not be sorted.

Sorting using several content criteria

You can sort a table by the values of several columns (for example, a table of grades can be sorted by a student's first name, last name, date of birth, grades, etc).

◻ Go to the **Sort** dialog box.

⊡ Specify the first sort criterion:

- open the **Sort by** list and choose the first sort column.

- if required, open the **Sort on** list and select **Values**.

- Open the **Order** list and choose the sort order:

Ascending, with the **A to Z** option if the column contains text, **Smallest to largest** if the column contains numeric values, or **Oldest to newest** if the column contains dates.

Descending, click **Z to A** if the column contains text, **Sort Largest to Smallest** if the column contains numeric values, or **Sort Newest to oldest** if the column contains dates.

⊡ Click the **Add level** button to display a second row of criteria.

⊡ Specify the second sort criterion:

- open the **Sort by** list and choose the second sort column.

- make sure that the **Sort on** list displays **Values**.

- specify the sort **Order**.

⊡ Repeat the last two actions if you want to create more criteria.

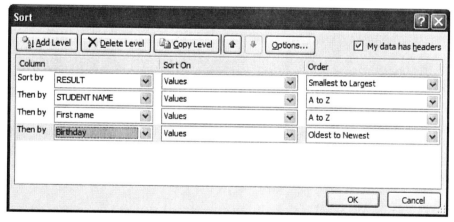

In this example, the table will be sorted by general grades (RESULT column) then, if two students have the same grade, by last name, then first name and finally by date of birth.

⊡ Click **OK** to start sorting.

Sorting using several colour/icon criteria

You can sort a table using several cell and/or font colours and icon sets in the same column.

⊡ In the **Sort** dialog box, specify the first sort criterion:
- open the **Sort by** list and choose the first sort column.
- open the **Sort on** list and select **Cell color, Font color** or **Cell icon**.
- open the first drop-down list under **Order** and select the cell colour, the font colour or cell icon depending on how the data should be sorted.
- open the second drop-down list under **Order** and select **On top** to display rows corresponding to the selected colour or icon from the top, or **On bottom** in the reverse case.

⊡ Click **Add level** to display a second row of criteria.

⊡ Specify the second sort criterion:
- open the **Sort by** list and make sure you select the same column as for the first criteria.
- open the **Sort on** list and choose the sort-by item.
- specify the sort **Order**.

⊡ Repeat the same actions if you want to add more criteria.

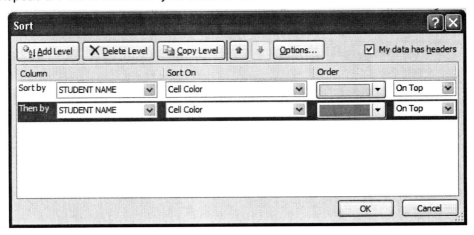

In this example, the table will be sorted using the two fill colours in the **STUDENT LAST NAME** *column.*

⊡ Click **OK** to start sorting.

Sorting data

Combining content and formatting criteria

You can combine several criteria based on cell content or formatting.

⊟ In the **Sort** dialog box, specify the first sort criterion: this can be either a content criterion or a colour/icon criterion (refer to the previous sub-heading).

⊟ Click **Add level** to display a second row of criteria and specify the second sort criterion.

⊟ Repeat this action as many times as you require.

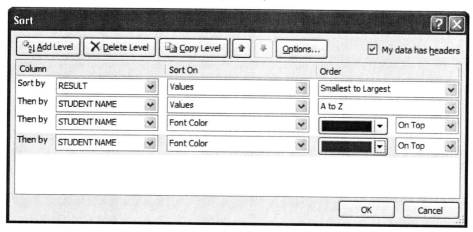

In this example, the table will be sorted by general grades (RESULT column) then, if two students have the same grade, by their last name then, by the font colour on the **STUDENT NAME** column.

⊟ Click **OK** to start sorting.

Managing sort criteria

⊟ Go to the **Sort** dialog box.

⊟ To select a criterion, click at the start of its row (on the heading **Sort by** or **Sort on**), or enter the row options.

⊟ To modify the criteria order, select the row corresponding to the criterion and click the ⬆ tool button to move it up in the list, or the ⬇ tool button to move it down.

⊟ To delete a criterion, select the corresponding row and click **Delete level**.

⊟ To copy a criterion, select it, then click **Copy level**.

 Using the **Options** button in the **Sort** dialog box you can:

- activate the **Case sensitive** option to differentiate upper and lower case.
- modify the **Orientation** so that you can sort columns rather than rows.

Filtering data

Activating automatic filtering

*Using Microsoft Office Excel 2007 you can filter table data to only display rows which match the criteria you have specified, and hide rows you don't want to display. To do this, you must activate the **Autofilter** function.*

⊡ Activate one of the cells in the relevant cell range.

⊡ In the **Home** tab, go to the **Editing** group, click the **Sort and Filter** button, then **Filter**.

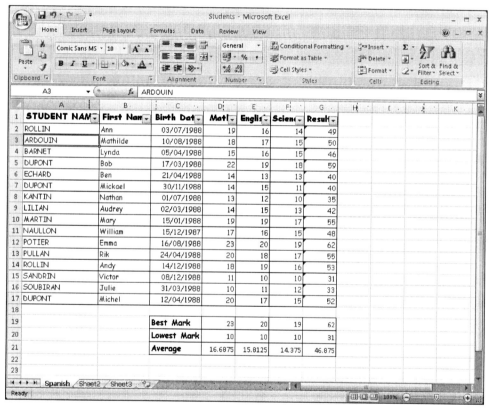

Drop-down list arrows appear in each of the top cells of the columns: this indicates that the filtering is active but not applied.

⊡ Create the filters you require.

You can create three types of filter: by list value, by format or by criteria (see following heading). Once the data is filtered, you can copy it, edit it, format it, turn it into graphics or print it without reorganizing or moving it.

⊟ To deactivate automatic filtering, click the **Sort and Filter** button again (**Home** tab – **Editing** group) then click **Filter**.

Deactivating the Autofilter cancels any filtering and displays all data.

Filtering data by content or formatting

Using Autofilter, you can filter data by cell content, background colour, font colour or icon set formatting.

Filtering by column value

⊟ Activate Autofilter.

⊟ Open the drop-down list on the column.

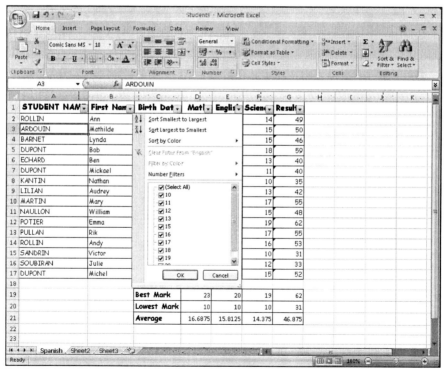

Filtering data

*The **AutoFilter** menu opens and displays a list of values for the column (up to 10,000 values). Each list has all column values. By default, the corresponding check boxes are ticked: you see all column values. The menu also has sort options.*

⊟ To hide certain values, uncheck the corresponding check boxes.

⊟ To display some values, it is quicker to deactivate (**Select all**) then activate the relevant values.

⊟ To filter nonblank cells, in the **AutoFormat** menu at the top of the list of values, select (**Select all**) and then at the bottom of the list of values, clear (**Blanks**). Conversely, to filter for blanks, in the **AutoFilter** menu at the top of the list of values, clear (**Select All**) and then at the bottom of the list of values, select (**Blanks**).

*The (**Blanks**) option is available only if the cell range or table column contains at least one blank cell.*

*To change the size of the **AutoFilter** menu, click and drag the handle at the bottom across or up/down.*

⊟ Click **OK**.

You can only see rows corresponding to the selected values.

When a column is filtered, the arrow on the drop-down list looks like this: 🔽. If you point to this tool button, a ScreenTip displays the filter applied to it.

You can also customize your filter criteria, or use filters specific to the data, such as numeric values, date, etc (see following headings).

Filtering using a cell colour, font colour or icon set

If you have manually or conditionally formatted a range of cells, by cell colour or font colour, you can also filter using these colours. You can also filter using an icon set created through a conditional format.

⊟ Activate automatic filtering and open the drop-down list on the column.

⊟ Select **Filter by color**.

This option is not available if the column does not contain a colour or icon set.

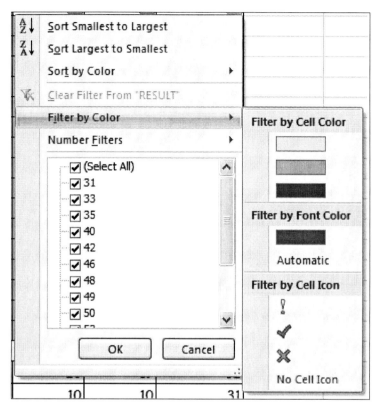

*Depending on the format applied to the column, the options: **Filter by Cell Color**, **Filter by Font Color**, and **Filter by Cell Icon** are displayed.*

Depending on the type of format, click a cell colour, font colour or cell icon.

You cannot combine a cell colour filter with a font colour filter or a cell icon filter.

Filtering by content or cell formatting

You can quickly filter data with criteria that is equal to the contents of the active cell.

⊟ Activate automatic filtering.

⊟ Right-click a cell containing the value, colour, font colour or icon by which you want to filter.

⊟ Click **Filter** and then do one of the following:

Filter by selected cell's value to filter by text, number, date or time.

Filter by selected cell's color to filter by cell colour.

Filter by selected cell's font colour to filter by font colour.

Filter by selected cell's icon to filter by icon.

Filtering using custom criteria

You can sort data by column values. Excel has three types of filter: number (for numeric data), chronological (for date data), or text (for alphanumeric data).

⊟ Activate automatic filtering and open the column drop-down list.

⊟ Depending on the type of data in the column, click **Filter by colour**, **Number filters,** or **Text filters**.

⊟ Click **Custom Filter** or any other option that opens a dialog box (for example, **Equals, Does not equal, Greater than, Before**, etc).

*Whichever option you choose, the **Custom AutoFilter** dialog box opens. If you have selected a different option to **Custom filter**, the first list in the dialog box displays the item matching the chosen option (e.g. **different to** or **before**).*

⊟ Select the comparison operator for the first list.

⊟ Enter the value in the next box. You can use wildcards such as **?** to replace a single character, or ***** to replace a series of characters.

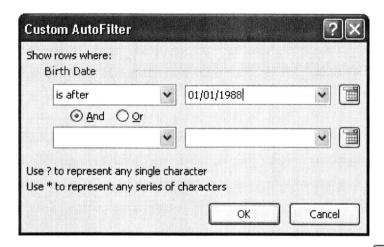

For a chronological filter you can click the **Date Picker** tool button to select a date from a scrolling calendar.

- Click **OK**.

Using data specific filters

Filtering by a data range (numeric or chronological)

- Activate automatic filtering and open the column drop-down list.

- Select **Date Filters** or **Number Filters** then click **Between**.

- In the **Custom AutoFilter** dialog box, specify the lower value in the range opposite the first comparison operator (**before or equal to** or **greater than or equal to**).

- Ensure that the **And** option is active.

- Specify the higher interval value for the second comparison operator (**before** or **equals** or **is less than** or **equal to**).

Filtering by highest and lowest values (numeric filter)

- Activate automatic filtering and open the column drop-down list.

- Select **Number filters**, then **Top 10**.

- Indicate whether you want **Top** or **Bottom** values.

- Specify the number of rows to display.

In the last list in the dialog box, choose **Items** to filter all the records correspon-ding to the criteria (top or bottom) or **Percent** to filter a number or rows corres-ponding to a percentage of the total number of values in the list.

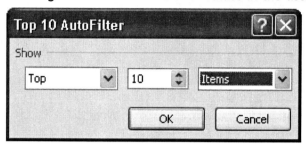

Click **OK**.

Filtering using the average value (number filter)

Activate automatic filtering and open the column drop-down list.

Select **Number filter** then one of the following options:

Above average   to filter data by numbers above the average.

Below average   to filter data by numbers below the average.

Above and below average numbers are based on the original range of cells or table column and not the filtered subset of data.

Using a dynamic filter

With a dynamic filter, you change the criteria when you reapply the filter.

Activate automatic filtering and open the column drop-down list.

Select **Date filters** then click one of the options corresponding to a defined date (**Tomorrow**, **Today**, **Yesterday**, **Next week**, etc).

*The option **All dates in the period** filters by period (for example, **January**, or **Third quarter**).*

*The option **This year** can return dates in the future for the current year, whereas **Year to date** only returns dates up to and including the current date.*

Filtering using several criteria

Two criteria for the same column

⊟ Activate automatic filtering and open the column drop-down list.

⊟ Depending on the type of data you want to sort, select **Number filters**, **Date filters**, or **Text filters**.

⊟ Click **Custom filter**.

⊟ In the first list, specify the first filter criterion: specify the operator and the comparison value.

⊟ Specify how the two criteria should be linked:

  - select **And** for AND logic.

  - select **Or** for OR logic.

⊟ In the second list, specify the second filter criterion: specify the operator and the comparison value.

  Examples:

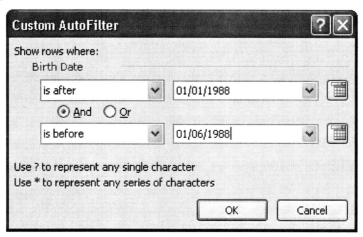

In this example, only the rows where the date of birth is between 01/01/1988 and 01/06/1988 are displayed.

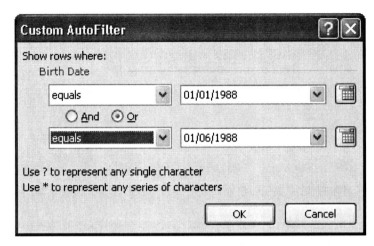

In this example, the rows where the date of birth is equal to 01/01/1988 OR 01/06/1988 are displayed (a person cannot be born on two different dates).

⊟ Click **OK**.

You cannot use content criteria and format criteria on the same column.

Several criteria on different columns

⊟ Activate automatic filtering.

⊟ Define criteria for each column.

Filters are additive; each additional filter is based on the active filter, further reducing the subset of data.

You can use content criteria and format criteria on different columns.

Clearing a filter

This technique simply displays all data.

⊟ To deactivate a filter on a column, open the column's drop-down list and select **Clear filter from**.

⊟ To deactivate all filters, deactivate automatic filtering or click the **Sort and Filter** button (**Home** tab – **Editing** group) then click **Clear**.

Filtering data

Creating a complex filter

To use a complex filter you need to create a criteria range in which you yourself enter the filter criteria. This means you can filter the data directly in the list and copy them elsewhere.

Creating a criteria field

⊟ Locate an empty space of a few columns and a few rows on the sheet, generally next to the list of data.

⊟ In the first empty row, enter or copy the column names that you want to use to define the criteria.

⊟ In the rows below, enter the criteria that should be met, paying attention to the following rules:

- to link criteria by the **OR** combination, enter the criteria on several rows.

- to link criteria by the **AND** combination, enter the criteria on several columns.

- to link criteria by the **AND** and the **OR** combinations, enter the criteria in several rows and several columns.

Examples:

This range of criteria filters students from classes T302 or T101.

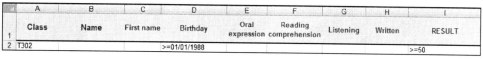

This range of criteria filters students from class T302 who are born after 1st January 1988 and who have a result higher that 50.

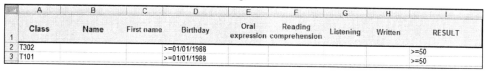

This range of criteria filters students from class T302 and class T101 who are born after 1st January 1988 and who have grades greater than or equal to 50.

Filtering data using a criteria range

⊟ Click one of the cells in the table containing the data to filter.

⊟ Activate the **Data** tab, go the **Sort and Filter** group and click the **Advanced** button.

*The Advanced Filter dialog box is displayed. **Filter the list in place** is preselected.*

⊟ Specify the references of cells containing data to extract in **List Range**.

⊟ Click on **Criteria range**, then click the 🔲 tool button to select the criteria range you created. Next, click the 🔲 tool button to reopen the dialog box.

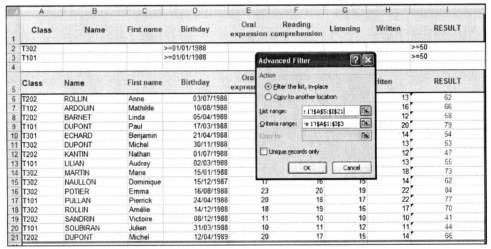

⊟ Check **Unique records only** to filter data by taking out duplicates.

⊟ Click **OK**.

Only the rows matching the criteria are displayed.

⊟ To display all rows again, clear the filter: in the **Data** tab, go to the **Sort and Filter** group and click the **Clear** button.

Copying data from a complex filter

⊟ Find a blank space on the sheet, near the data you wish to filter and extract.

⊟ If required, create a criteria range.

⊟ Click one of the cells from the table containing the data you want to copy.

⊟ In the **Data** tab, go to the **Sort and Filter** group and click the **Advanced** button.

⊟ Select **Copy to another location**.

⊟ If required, specify the table references (**list range**) and the criteria range (**criteria range**).

⊟ Go to **Copy to** and click the ⊞ button to select the upper left cell in the area in which you want to copy the rows. Next, click the ⊞ button to reopen the dialog box.

⊟ Click **OK**.

Creating an outline

An outline is a way of viewing or printing the main results of a table, without showing detail.

Automatically

If you have created your table with formulas (sums, averages and so on) you can create an automatic outline.

⊟ Select the relevant table.

⊟ In the **Data** tab, go to the **Outline** group, open the list on the **Group** button and select **Auto Outline**.

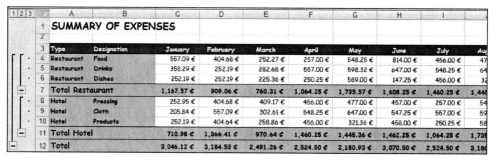

Buttons for managing the various levels of the outline appear to the left of and/or above the worksheet. The outline above is composed of several levels: level 1 shows the most important elements, the grand totals. Level 2 shows type totals, level 3 monthly type totals and so on. All the levels have been expanded in this outline.

If you can't see the ⊟ and ⊞ outline symbols, click the **Microsoft Office** button then **Excel Options**. Scroll down the **Advanced** category until you find **Display options for this worksheet**. Check **Show outline symbols if an outline is applied**.

Manually

⊟ Select the adjacent rows and columns that you want to include in the same level.

Do not include the sub-total row(s) in your selection.

⊟ In the **Data** tab, go to the **Outline** group and click the **Group** button.

⊟ To insert a column or a row into the preceding level, select the column or row then click the **Group** button again.

⊡ To remove a column or row from a group, select it, then click **Ungroup** in the **Outline** group.

⊡ Use the ⊟ and ⊞ buttons to collapse or expand the outline.

Using the outline

⊡ To hide lower-level rows or columns, click the appropriate ⊟ button.

⊡ To hide all the groups of a particular level and all the levels below, click the button with the number corresponding to the level.

	A	B	C	D	E	F	G	H	I
1	SUMMARY OF EXPENSES								
2									
3	Type	Designation	January	February	March	April	May	June	July	Au
7	Total Restaurant		1,167.57 €	909.06 €	760.31 €	1,064.25 €	1,735.57 €	1,608.25 €	1,460.25 €	1,445
8	Hotel	Pressing	252.95 €	404.68 €	409.17 €	456.00 €	477.00 €	457.00 €	257.00 €	54
9	Hotel	Cloth	205.84 €	557.09 €	302.61 €	548.25 €	647.00 €	547.25 €	557.00 €	59
10	Hotel	Products	252.19 €	404.64 €	258.86 €	456.00 €	321.36 €	458.00 €	250.25 €	58
11	Total Hotel		710.98 €	1,366.41 €	970.64 €	1,460.25 €	1,445.36 €	1,462.25 €	1,064.25 €	1,735
12	Total		3,046.12 €	3,184.53 €	2,491.26 €	2,524.50 €	3,180.93 €	3,070.50 €	2,524.50 €	3,180

In this example, the rows and columns from level 3 are not longer visible. The ⊟ *buttons are replaced by* ⊞ *buttons.*

⊡ To show hidden rows or columns, click their ⊞ buttons, or click the button with the number corresponding to the next level.

Removing an outline

⊡ Activate the worksheet containing the outline.

⊡ Activate the **Data** tab, go to the **Outline** group, open the list on the **Ungroup** button and select **Clear outline**.

If you clear an outline with hidden data, you may find that these rows or columns remain hidden. To display hidden data, select the visible row or column headers, and open their shortcut menu and select **Display**.

Part 8
Printing data

Modifying page setup options

Modifying print margins

⊟ Activate the relevant worksheet then the **Page Layout** tab.

⊟ Go to the **Page Setup** group and click the **Margins** button.

⊟ Choose **Normal**, **Wide** or **Narrow**.

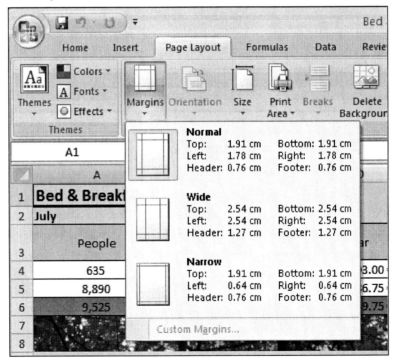

The size of each type of margin is specified.

⊡ To customize the margin size, click the **Margins** button from the **Page Layout** group, then select **Custom Margins**.

*The **Page Setup** dialog box appears, the **Margins** tab is shown.*

Specify the margin values in the **Top**, **Left**, **Right**, or **Bottom** boxes.

Check **Horizontally** or **Vertically** to centre the table according to the width or height of the page.

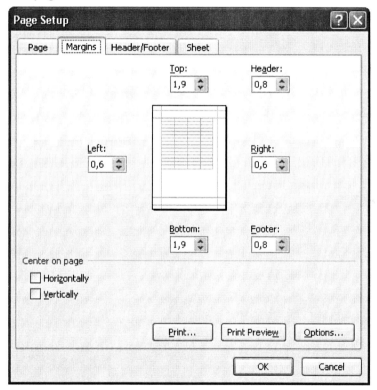

⊡ Click **OK**.

🔍 You can also select **Page Layout** view and point to the border of the margin to modify in the ruler. When the mouse pointer appears as a two-headed arrow, click and drag to set the margin the way you want (a ScreenTip appears and indicates the size of the margin.)

Changing page orientation

⊟ Activate the relevant worksheet then activate the **Page Layout** tab.

⊟ Go to the **Page Setup** group and click the **Orientation** button.

⊟ Select either **Portrait** or **Landscape**.

Defining paper format

⊟ Activate the relevant worksheet then activate the **Page Layout** tab.

⊟ Go to the **Page Setup** group and click the **Size** button.

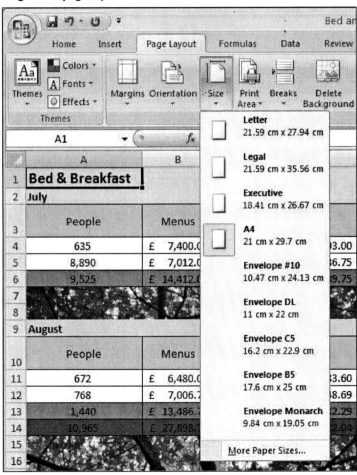

Page setup

- Select an option, or click **More Paper Sizes** to open the **Page Setup** dialog box and choose an option from the **Paper size** list.

Changing the scale of printed pages

- Activate the relevant worksheet then activate the **Page Layout** tab.

- To reduce the width of the printed sheet so that you can include the maximum number of pages, go to the **Scale to fit** group and open the list on the **Width** button, or click the number of pages you want.

- To reduce the height of the printed worksheet so that you can include the maximum number of pages, go to the **Scale to fit** group and open the list on the **Height** button and click the number of pages you require.

- To lengthen or reduce the printed worksheet by a percentage of its size, go to the **Scale to fit** group and select the required percentage from the **Scale** box.

- To restore the original worksheet page settings, go to the **Scale to fit** group and select **Automatic** from the **Width** and **Height** group.

Printing gridlines/row numbers and column letters

- Activate the relevant worksheet then activate the **Page Layout** tab.

- To print the worksheet grid, go to the **Sheet Options** group and check **Print** (under **Gridlines**).

  Even if you have not applied borders to the cells, they will be printed with a basic border.

  The **View** *option in this group is the same as the* **Gridlines** *option (in the* **Show/Hide** *group in the* **View** *tab); it shows the cell gridlines in the worksheet.*

- To print the column letters and row numbers, go to the **Sheet Options** group and check **Print**, in the **Headings** group

  The **View** *option in this group is the same as the* **Headings** *option (in the* **Show/Hide** *group in the* **View** *tab); it shows the row numbers and column letters on the worksheet.*

Creating a print area

If you do not want to print the entire worksheet, you can define a print area. This area is the part of the worksheet that will be printed.

🗗 Select the worksheet you want to print.

🗗 Select the **Page Layout** tab.

🗗 Go to the **Page Setup** group, click the **Print Area** button then **Set print area**.

The print area now defined appears surrounded by dotted lines. When a new print area is defined, Excel replaces the last one.

🗗 To add more cells to the print area, select the print area, click the **Print Area** button then click **Add to print area**.

Different print areas will be printed on different pages.

🗗 To delete the print area, click the **Print Area** button then **Clear Print Area**.

If you have added other areas to the first print area, they will all be deleted.

Inserting/deleting a manual page break

A page break you insert yourself is called a manual page break.

🗗 Activate the cell which is going to be the first on your new page.

The page break will be inserted above and to the left of the active cell.

🗗 Select the **Page Layout** tab, go to the **Page Setup** group, click the **Breaks** button and select **Insert Page Break**.

A dotted line appears representing the page break.

🗗 To delete a page break, activate a cell in the next row or column, click the **Breaks** button then **Remove Page Break**.

🗗 To delete all page breaks, activate any cell in the worksheet, click the **Breaks** button then **Reset All Page Breaks**.

Remember: you can move page breaks using the **View** tab in **Page Break Preview** mode (see Part 1 – Display).

Repeating lines/columns on each page

You can repeat certain rows and/or columns on each printed page.

- Select the **Page Layout** tab, go to the **Page Setup** group and click the **Print Titles** button.

*The **Page Setup** dialog box opens and the **Sheet** tab is active.*

- Click the ⊞ tool button from the **Rows to repeat at top** box and/or the **Columns to repeat at left** box to minimize the dialog box.

- In the worksheet, select at least one cell from the row(s) or column(s) which you want to repeat. The pointer becomes a black arrow.

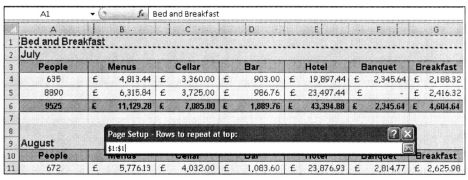

In this example, row 1 will be printed on each page.

- Click the ⊞ button to redisplay the dialog box.
- Click **OK**.

Creating and managing page headers and footers

The header is printed at the top of each page and the footer at the bottom of each page. For each header or footer, you have three text boxes: left, centre and right.

Accessing the create/modify header/footer page

- Activate the relevant worksheet then choose one of the following options:
  - In Normal view, select the **Insert** tab, go to the **Text** group and click the **Header and Footer** button.

*This technique systematically activates **Page Layout** view.*

- in Page Layout view, click the box in the centre of the top margin where it says **Click to add header**.

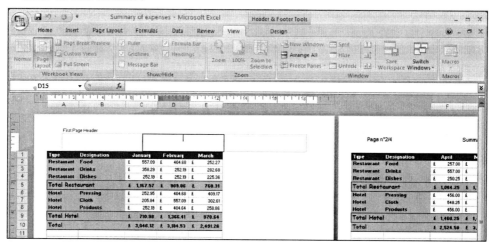

*The insertion point flashes in the central part of the **Header** and the **Design** tab of **Header and Footer Tools** is displayed.*

⮐ To activate one of the other two text areas, click inside them or use the ⮐ key.

⮐ To switch from header to footer, click the **Go to header** or **Go to footer** buttons, and vice versa.

⮐ To leave the header or footer, click in the worksheet or press Esc .

Inserting a predefined page header or footer

You can insert text available in Excel in the page footer or header in preselected areas.

⮐ Go to the page header or footer.

⮐ To insert a header, go to the **Header and Footer Tools** tab open the **Header** list; to insert a footer, open the **Footer** list.

If Excel has only one content, it will appear in the central area. When there are several contents, they are separated by semi-colons and are displayed in the left, centre and right areas.

*The (**none**) option erases the header or footer.*

Page setup

⊡ Click the content you want.

Regardless of where you start, Excel inserts the header or footer in preselected areas.

Inserting a custom page header or footer

⊡ Go to the header or footer area in the page and select the relevant text area by clicking on it.

⊡ Enter the text you want. Use the Enter key to create several rows.

*To insert the & sign (ampersand) in the text of a header of a footer, type it twice. To include "sub contractors & services" in a header, for example, type **Sub-contractors && services**.*

⊡ To insert specific contents, go to the **Header and Footer Elements** group in the **Header and Footer** tab and click one of the buttons: **Page Number**, **Number of Pages**, **Current Date**, **Current Time**, **File Path**, **File Name**, **Sheet Name**, **Picture**, **Format Picture**.

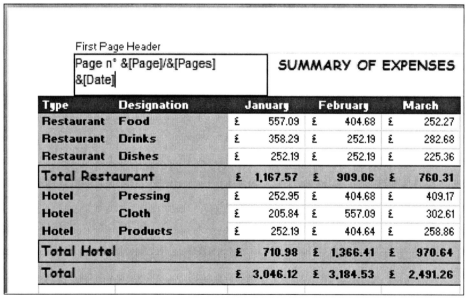

Each content corresponds to a code which appears in brackets.

⊡ To highlight characters, select them and use the tools from the **Home** tab.

Defining page header and footer options

⊟ Go to the relevant header or footer area.

⊟ In the **Header and Footer Tools** tab, go to the **Options** group and select the following options:

Different first page: to use a different header and footer for the first page,
specify the header and/or footer for the first page and for the other pages.

Different Odd & Even Pages to insert a different header or footer for odd pages
and for even pages. In this case create the header/footer on an odd and an even
page.

Scale with Document to use the same font size and scaling as the worksheet.

Align with Page Margins to ensure the header margin or footer margin is aligned
with the left and right margins of the worksheet.

Deleting page headers and footers

⊟ Go to the header or footer area of the relevant worksheet.

⊟ Select the content you want to delete and press ⌨Del.

or

In the **Header and Footer Tools** tab, go to the **Header & Footer** group, open the
list on either the **Header** or **Footer** button and click (**none**).

Creating a watermark

*Although printing backgrounds is not available in Microsoft Office Excel 2007, you
can display a picture on every printed page by inserting a picture in the header
or footer area. The picture appears behind the printed worksheet text.*

⊟ Go to the worksheet page where you are creating or modifying the page header or
footer, then click the text area which is going to contain the picture.

⊟ On the **Header and Footer Tools** tab, go to the **Header and Footer Elements**
group and click the **Picture** button.

The Insert Picture dialog box opens.

⊟ Go to the folder containing the picture you want to use.

⊟ Double-click the picture file name.

⊟ To resize or scale the picture, click the **Format Picture** button (**Header & Footer Elements** group). Choose your options in the **Format Image** dialog box on the **Size** tab, then click **OK**.

Using views

*A **view** is a way of saving certain settings, such as a print area, page setup, filter settings, or hidden rows/columns. When you switch to a view, the saved options are automatically activated.*

Creating a view

⊟ Prepare the sheet for printing (page setup, print area, hidden columns, etc).

⊟ Select the **View** tab, go to the **Workbook Views** group and click the **Custom Views** button.

⊟ Click **Add**.

⊟ Enter the **Name** of the view you are creating.

⊟ Indicate whether the view should include the **Print setting** and **Hidden rows, columns and filter settings** by ticking the options.

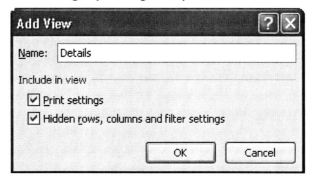

⊟ Confirm.

Using a view

⬎ Select the **View** tab, go to the **Workbook Views** group and click the **Custom Views** button.

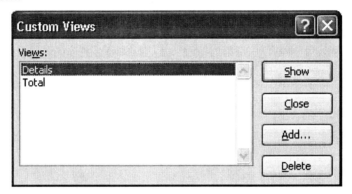

⬎ Click the name of the view you want to use then click the **Show** button.

The **Delete** button removes the view currently selected in the **Views** list.

Using print preview

You can preview worksheets as they would be printed.

⊟ Select the worksheet you want to preview.

⊟ Click the **Microsoft Office** button , move the mouse pointer over the **Print** option and select **Print Preview**. Alternatively, press Ctrl F2 .

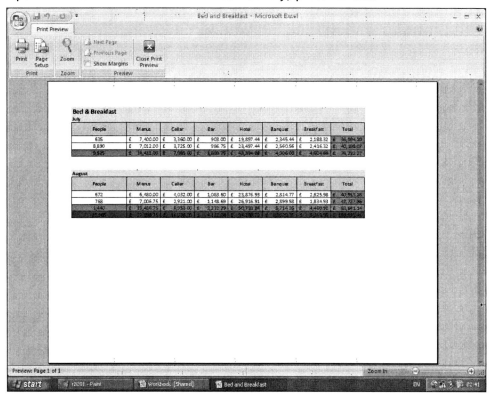

This produces a scaled-down view of the sheet as it will look when printed. On the status bar Excel displays the current page number and the total number of pages to be printed.

⊟ To zoom in on a preview, place the mouse pointer on the item to be magnified and click.

Before you click, the mouse pointer appears as a magnifying glass; afterwards it becomes an arrow.

- To return to the scaled-down preview, click the page again.

- To display another page, use the **Next Page** and **Previous Page** buttons.

In the scaled-down preview, you can also use the vertical scroll bars to change page.

- To change the margins and column widths, click the **Show Margins** button.

Handles appear in the window.

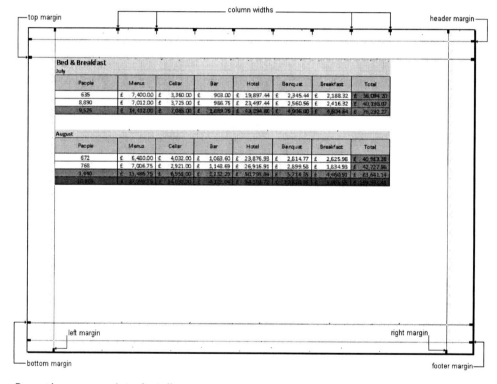

Drag the appropriate handle.

- To start printing, click the **Print** button. When you have checked the print options, click **OK** in the **Print** dialog box.

- To leave the preview, click the **Close Print Preview** button or press the Esc key.

The **Page Setup** button opens the **Page Setup** dialog box in which you can change the page setup options, including orientation, scaling, paper size, etc), margins, page headers and footers and the sheet printing options (titles to repeat, page order, etc).

Printing a worksheet

⊟ Select the worksheet you want to print.

⊟ Click the **Quick Print** button 🖶 on the **Quick Access Toolbar**. If it is not on the toolbar, add it by clicking the **Customize Quick Access Toolbar** button ⊽ and selecting **Quick Print**.

For a moment, Excel gives you a brief opportunity to **Cancel** *the print job. The data is then transmitted to Windows' Print Manager and the pages are printed.*

The 🖶 *tool button prints using the current page setup settings.*

Printing a workbook

⊟ Click the **Microsoft Office** button 🔘 then **Print**, or press ⌷Ctrl⌷ **P**.

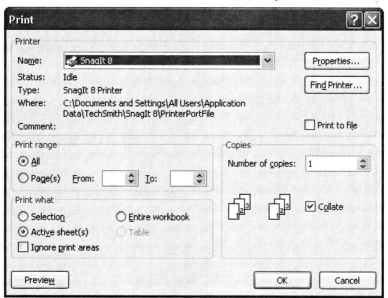

*The **Active Sheet** option, which is active by default, in the **Print what** frame, prints the data from the active worksheet or any other sheets that happen to be selected.*

- To print the selected range of cells in the active worksheet, choose the **Selection** option in the **Print what** frame.

  To print all the worksheets of the active workbook, choose the **Selection** option in the **Print what** frame.

- To print all the worksheets of the active workbook, select the **Entire Workbook** option.

- To print a group of pages, click the **From** box and enter the number of the first page to print, then enter the number of the last page in the **To** box.

- If you want to print several copies of your work, enter the **Number of copies** required in the **Copies** frame.

*If you are printing several copies of a multiple page document, the **Collate** option prints one complete copy of the document after another.*

- Click **OK** to confirm.

You can also access the **Print** dialog box by clicking the **Print** button when you are in the **Print Preview** window.

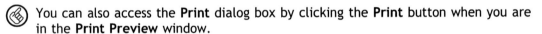

Part 9
Charts and objects

Creating a chart

⊟ Select the data you want in your chart.

- if the data is contained in a continuous block of cells, select that range.

- if the data is in several different ranges, select the nonadjacent ranges with
Ctrl-clicks. So that Excel can analyse the data correctly, make sure the cell
ranges form a rectangular set.

- if the cells are in a range, click one of the cells.

	Semester 1	Semester 2
West	130,000	143,025
South	145,000	142,044
North	142,120	153,000
Center	142,889	140,100
East	139,750	140,800
Total	139,750	140,800

Excel considers the selected ranges as one rectangular block

	Semester 2
West	143,025
South	142,044
Center	140,100
East	140,800

*In the example above, the blank cell in the top left corner was included to ensure
a rectangular selection.*

⊟ Select the **Insert** tab.

⊟ In the **Charts** group, click the button corresponding to the type of chart you want
to insert: **Column**, **Line**, **Pie**, **Bar**, **Area**, **Scatter**, or **Other Charts** (for a **stock**,
surface, **doughnut**, **bubble** or **radar** chart).

*It is very important to choose the right type of chart to represent your data.
Here are some tips on the aim of each chart type.*

- ***Histograms*** *are useful for showing data changes over a period of time or for
illustrating comparisons among data.*

- **Line charts** can display continuous data over a period of time. They are set against a common scale and are therefore ideal for showing trends in data at equal intervals.

- **Pie charts** show the size of items in one single data series proportional to the sum of the items.

- **Bar charts** arrange data so that you can compare among individual items.

- **Area charts** emphasize the magnitude of change over time, and can be used to draw attention to the total value across a trend.

- **Scatter charts** represent the relationship between numerical values and several data series.

- **Stock charts** are used to illustrate fluctuations in stock prices; you can also use them for scientific data.

- **Surface charts** are useful when you want to find the optimum combination between two sets of data.

- Like **Pie** charts, **Doughnut charts** show the relationship of parts to a whole, but can contain more than one data series.

- **Bubble charts** contain data that is arranged in columns on a worksheet so that x values are listed in the first column and corresponding y values and bubble size values are listed in adjacent columns.

- **Radar charts** compare the aggregate values of a number of data series.

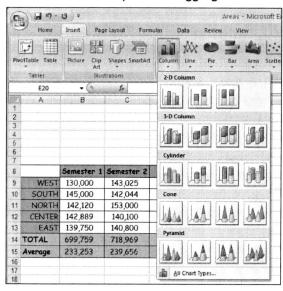

The **All chart types** option that appears at the bottom of each chart list, displays all the chart types available in Excel.

Creating charts

⊡ Click on the type of chart you want to create.

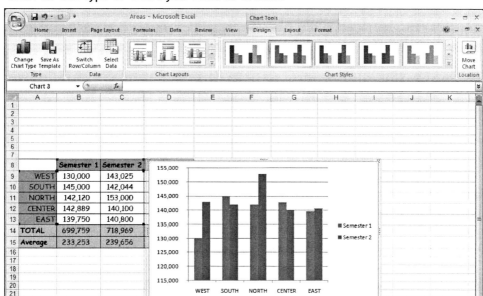

*The chart immediately appears in the worksheet. The **Chart Tools** tab also appears, with **Create**, **Layout** and **Format** tabs.*

When you select an embedded chart made from data adjacent to it on the worksheet, coloured rectangles appear around certain cell ranges. These highlight the data on the sheet that is used in the chart:

- data series are enclosed in a green rectangle;

- categories are enclosed in a purple rectangle;

- data points are enclosed in a blue rectangle.

⊡ If required, move the chart as you would move any other graphic object: point to one of its edges and drag it. You can also reduce the size of the chart by dragging one of the handles.

A chart created on a worksheet is known as an **embedded chart**; it belongs to the graphic objects family.

Unless you change the default, a chart and its source data are linked and any changes to the data are carried over into the chart.

For a quick way of creating a chart that is based on the default chart type, select the data that you want to use for the chart, and then press `Alt` `F1` to display the chart as an embedded chart, and `F11` to display the chart on a separate chart sheet.

Activating/deactivating an embedded chart

⊟ To activate an embedded chart click it once to select the whole chart object, or to select one of the chart items.

*The **Chart tools** tab appears again.*

⊟ To deactivate an embedded chart, click in a cell in the sheet, outside the chart.

Moving a chart

By default, charts are created in worksheets as embedded objects. As an embedded object, you can move a chart to another worksheet.

⊟ If the chart is an embedded object, click it to select it. If the chart is on a chart worksheet, click the worksheet tab to activate it.

⊟ Select the **Chart Tools** tab - **Design,** go to the **Location** group and click the **Move Chart** button.

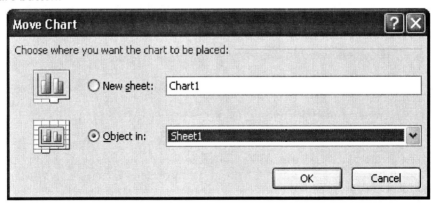

⊟ To move the chart to a new worksheet, click **New Sheet**, and then in the **New sheet** box, type a name for the worksheet.

To move the chart as an object in another worksheet, click **Object in**, and then in the **Object in** box, select the worksheet in which you want to place the chart.

⊡ Click **OK**.

If you have moved the chart to another worksheet, the new sheet is inserted before the active sheet.

Switching chart data

This technique switches series and categories.

⊡ Select the chart.

⊡ Select the **Chart Tool** tab - **Design**, go to the **Data** group and click the **Switch Row/Column** button.

The data on the x and y axes are reversed.

 You can also click the **Select Data** button (**Chart Tool** tab - Design - **Data** group) then, in the **Select Data Source** dialog box, click **Switch Row/Column**.

Changing the chart data source

This technique changes the chart's cell references.

First method

This can only be used on an embedded chart, the series to be added must be next to the series already included in the chart.

⊡ Select the chart area.

On the worksheet, the cells containing the data series are in a blue rectangle.

⊡ Drag the handle of the blue rectangle until it has encompassed the values of the new series.

The series titles (bordered by a green rectangle) and category titles (bordered by a violet rectangle) are adjusted accordingly.

Second method

- Select the chart.

- Select the **Chart Tools** tab - **Design**, go to the **Data Group** and click **Select Data**.

- In the **Select Data Source** dialog box, click the ▦ button to select the sheet containing the new data. Select the data then click the ▣ button to return to the dialog box.

- Click **OK**.

Adding one or more data series to a chart

- Select the chart.

- Select the **Chart Tools** - **Design** tab, go to the **Data** group and click the **Select Data** button.

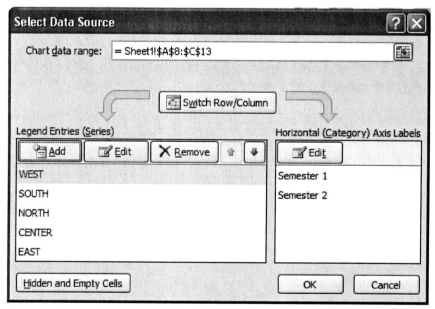

To add several series at once, they must be in adjacent cells.

- In the **Select Data Source** dialog box, click the **Add** button.

Creating charts

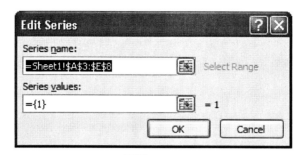

- In the **Series name** box, use the button to select the cell(s) containing the data series labels you want to add.

- In the **Series values** box, use the button to select the cell(s) containing the numeric data series you want to add.

- Click **OK**.

You can also drag the blue rectangle (that appears in the worksheet) to insert cells containing data from the new series.

Deleting a chart data series

- Select the chart and series you want to delete.

- Press the Del key.

You can also delete a data series by clicking the **Delete** button in the **Select Data Source** dialog box in the **Legend Entries (Series)** area.

Changing the order of the chart data series

- Select the chart.

- Select the **Chart Tools** - **Design** tab, go to the **Data** group and click the **Select Data** button.

- Click the series you want to move in the **Legend Entries (Series)** area of the **Select Data Source** dialog box.

- Click the or button as appropriate.

- Click **OK**.

Changing the axes data labels

⊟ Select the chart.

⊟ Select the **Chart Data Tools** - **Design** tab, go to the **Data** group and click the **Select Data** button.

⊟ Under **Horizontal (category) axis labels,** click the **Edit** button.

⊟ Use the  button to select the cells containing the axis labels you want to add.

⊟ Click **OK** in the **Axis Labels** dialog box.

⊟ Click **OK** in the **Select Data Source** dialog box

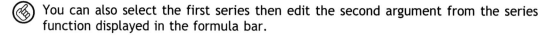 You can also select the first series then edit the second argument from the series function displayed in the formula bar.

Managing chart templates

By creating a chart template you can reuse a chart you have customized.

Saving a chart as a chart template

⊟ Click the chart you want to save as a template.

⊟ Select the **Chart Tools** - **Design** tab, go to the **Type** group and click the **Save as Template** button.

⊟ In the **File name** box, enter the name you want to give to your chart template.

The file extension for chart templates is .crtx and they are saved by default in C:\Documents and Setting\Username\Application Data\Microsoft\Templates\Charts.

⊟ Click the **Save** button.

Applying a chart template

⊟ To create a new chart based on a template, select the **Insert** tab, go to the **Charts** group, click any chart type then click **All Chart Types** or click the dialog box launcher in the **Charts** group.

To change a chart so that it uses a template, go to the **Design** tab, **Type** group and click **Change Chart Type**.

⊟ In the **Change Chart Type** dialog box, click the **Templates** folder from the left frame.

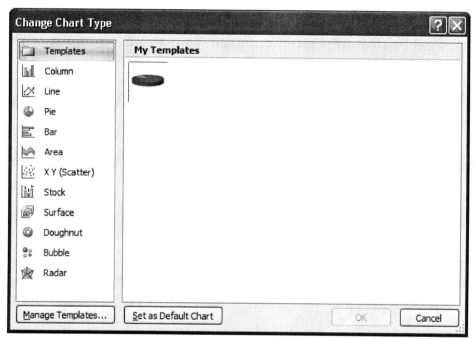

The list of existing templates appears in the right side of the dialog box. When you point to one of the templates, its name appears in a ScreenTip.

⊟ Double-click the name of the template you want to use.

Deleting a chart template

⊟ Go to the **Change Chart Type** dialog box, or **Create chart**.

⊟ Click **Manage Templates**.

A Windows Explorer window appears, the save-to folder is active.

⊟ Click the template you want to delete then press ⌨Del, or use the **Delete** option from the shortcut menu. Confirm the deletion by pressing **Yes**.

⊟ Close the Windows Explorer window to return to the original dialog box.

⊟ Click **OK**.

Selecting elements in a chart

- Select the chart.

- Point to the element you want to select and click it.

  When you point to an element, its name and, depending on the item, its value appear in a ScreenTip.

  When an element is selected, it is surrounded by selection handles.

- To select a single data marker in a series, click the data series, and then click the data marker.

Selecting all the elements of a chart is the same as selecting the element called **Plot Area**.

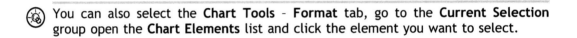

You can also select the **Chart Tools** - **Format** tab, go to the **Current Selection** group open the **Chart Elements** list and click the element you want to select.

Changing the type of chart/data series

- To change the entire chart, simply select the chart. To change a data series in the chart, select that data series.

- Select the **Chart Tools** - **Design** tab, go to the **Type** group and click the **Change Chart Type** button.

- Click the type of chart you want from the left side of the **Change Chart Type** dialog box.

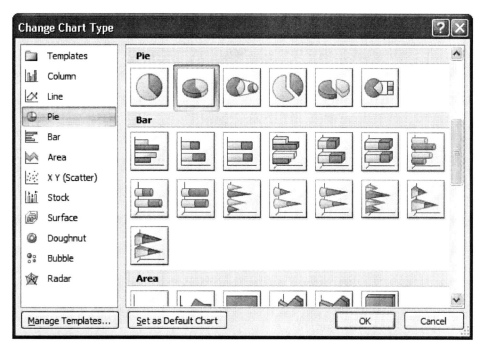

⊟ In the right side of the dialog box, double-click the sub-type of chart you want.

 If you often use the same kind of chart, you should define it as a default chart type: after selecting the type and sub-type from the **Insert chart** dialog box, click the **Set as Default Chart** button.

Applying a predefined chart layout

Different default layouts display a location for the chart title, the legend, data table, etc.

⊟ Activate the chart then the **Chart Tools** – **Design** tab.

⊟ Go to the **Chart Layout** group and click **Chart styles** button.

👉 **Format 5 layout** displays the data table in the chart area.

Displaying/hiding chart elements

You can display (by choosing a predefined location) or hide the chart title, axes labels, legend, data labels, axes, gridlines, etc.

⊟ Select the chart then **Chart tools** – **Layout**.

⊟ To display or change an element, click the button corresponding to the element and choose an option appropriate to the required location:

Chart title	to display a modifiable, centred, overlaid text box in or above the chart (see Changing the content of a modifiable text box).
Axis titles	to display a modifiable text box corresponding to the horizontal and vertical axes (see Changing the content of a modifiable text box).
Legend	to display the data series titles. By default, this element is displayed to the right of the chart.
Data labels	to display the values of selected data series. If no series are selected, Excel displays the labels for all series.
Data tables	to display the table corresponding to the chart source data below it.
Axes	to display the primary horizontal axis with or without labels and/or the primary vertical axis choosing its scale (in thousands, millions, billions).
Gridlines	to display the primary horizontal and/or vertical gridlines.
Plot area	to display the area located between the two axes (active by default).

⊟ To hide an element, click the button corresponding to the element and choose **None**.

By applying certain predefined layouts you can also display or hide certain elements.

To hide an element, you can also select it and press the Del key.

Changing the content of a modifiable text box

You can change the text that appears by default when you display a title.

⊟ Select the chart.

⊟ Click the text box to select it.

⊟ Use the usual methods to edit the text. To carry the text over several lines, use the Enter key to enter line breaks.

Moving/resizing an element

Some elements, such as titles, legends, etc, can be moved anywhere in the chart. These elements and others can be resized.

⊟ Select the chart and the relevant element.

⊟ To move an element, point to the selection and, when the pointer becomes a four-headed arrow, drag it to the required location.

⊟ To resize an item, point to one of the selection handles. When the cursor becomes a two-headed arrow, drag in the required direction.

Changing the category axis

This command changes the position of points, labels, the intersection of the vertical and horizontal axes, etc.

⊟ Select the chart then **Chart Tools** – **Layout**.

⊟ Go to the **Axes** group, click the **Axes** button and select the **Primary Horizontal Axis** option, then **More Primary Horizontal Axis Options**, and **Axis Options**.

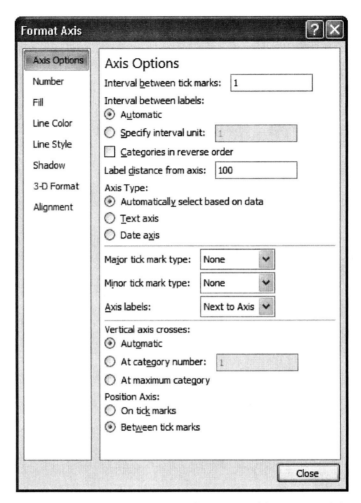

⊟ Specify the space between tick marks in the **Interval between tick marks** box.

⊟ Specify the space between the tick mark labels in the **Interval between labels** box.

⊟ To display the primary tick marks, open the **Major tick mark type** list and choose their position.

⊟ To display the **Minor tick mark type**, open the **Minor tick mark type** list and choose their position.

- To display tick mark labels, open the **Axis labels** list and choose their position.

- In the **Vertical axis crosses** area, change the point of intersection between the value axis and the category axis.

- When your changes are finished, click the **Close** button.

Changing the value axis

This technique changes the chart scale, the position of the tick marks, labels, the intersection of the horizontal and vertical axes, etc.

- Select the chart then the **Chart Tools** – **Layout** tab.

- Go to the **Axes** group, click the **Axes** button, select **Primary Vertical Axis** then **More Primary Vertical Axis** Options.

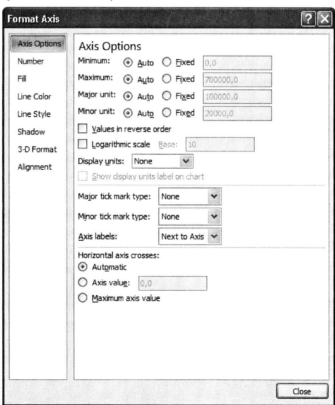

⊡ Use the options in the first part of the dialog box to edit the scale of the chart.

⊡ To display primary tick marks, open the **Major tick mark type** list and choose their position.

⊡ To display secondary tick marks, open the **Minor tick mark type** list and select their position.

⊡ To display tick mark labels, open the **Axis labels** list and select their position.

⊡ Under **Horizontal axis crosses**, change the place where the category axis intersects with the value axis.

⊡ When the changes are complete, click the **Close** button.

Adding a second vertical axis

Use this technique to show two different types of data on the same chart. In this example, the four first series are represented by histogram bars associated to the primary vertical axis, while the second is represented by a line associated with the secondary vertical axis.

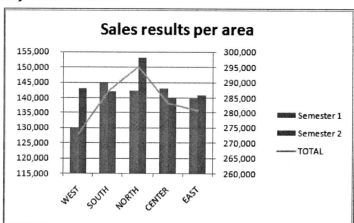

⊡ Select the data series that you want to plot along a secondary vertical axis.

⊡ Select the **Chart tools - Format** tab, go to the **Current Selection** group and click the **Format Selection** button.

⊡ Click **Series Options**, if it is not selected, and then under **Plot Series On**, click secondary axis and then click **Close**.

⊡ Click the **Close** button.

254

Chart options

Editing data labels

You can change the display of values of data from each series.

- In the chart, display the data labels for the relevant series (see Display/hide chart elements).

- Select the **Chart Tools** - **Layout** tab.

- In the **Labels** group, click the **Data Labels** button and select **More Data Label Options**. Then select the **Label Options** category.

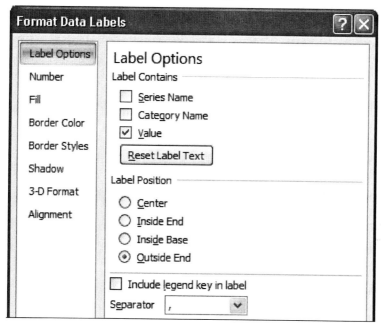

- Under **Label Contains**, specify the label content.

- Choose the **Label Position** in relation to the data series (bars, curves).

- If required, check **Include legend key in label**.

- Click the **Close** button.

Applying a quick style to the chart

A quick style is a set of predefined fill and border colours for the chart elements.

🗗 In the **Chart Tools** – **Design** tab, go to the **Chart Styles** group and choose the style you want. To see all available styles at once, click the **More** button ⬚ in the same group.

You can apply a quick style to a specific chart element (see Managing Objects – Applying a predefined style to an object.)

Changing the format of numeric values in a chart

🗗 Select the chart element containing the numeric values you want to edit.

🗗 Select the **Chart Tools - Format** tab, go to the **Current Selection** group and click the **Format Selection** button.

🗗 Select the **Number** category.

🗗 Choose the **Category** and specify the options.

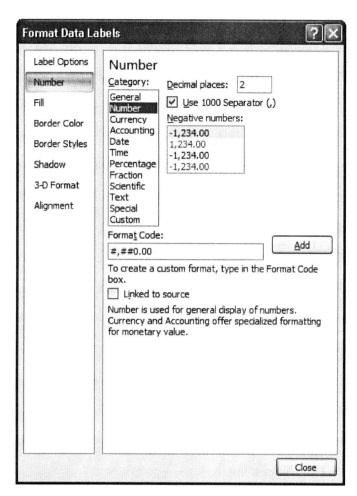

▣ Click **Close**.

Changing the orientation of text in an element

▣ Select the chart element that has the text you want to modify.

▣ Select the **Chart Tools - Format** tab, go to the **Current Selection** group and click the **Format Selection** button.

▣ Select the **Alignment** category.

⊟ Open the **Text direction** list and select **Rotate all text 90°** or **Rotate all text 270°**, or **Stacked** if you want to display the characters one on top of the other.

or

Keep **Horizontal** in the **Text direction** list and specify an angle in the **Custom angle** box.

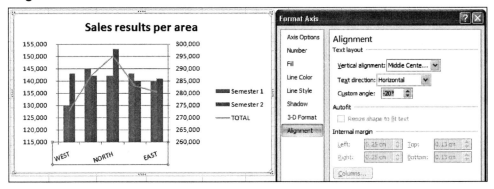

In this example, the category axis labels are set to -20°.

⊟ Click the **Close** button.

 You can also change the presentation of the characters of a chart element (see chapter Managing objects – Formatting object text).

You can also change the fill or border colour of an element, as well as apply a depth effect (see chapter Managing objects – Modifying the fill/border/depth of an object).

Formatting a 3–D chart

These options are used to format the chart element with 3-D effects.

⊟ Select the chart element that you want to format in 3-D.

⊟ Select the **Chart Tools – Format** tab, go to the **Current Selection** group and click the **Format Selection** button.

⊟ Select the **3-D Format** category.

Chart options

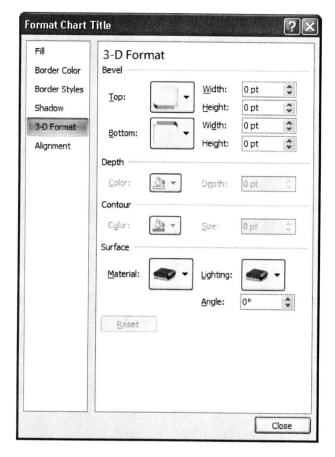

Some 3-D format options are not available for certain charts.

⊟ To apply a 3-D effect to the top border, open the **Top** list under **Bevel** and select the option you want. Next, define the **Width** and **Height** of the top border.

A bevel is a three-dimensional edge effect that is applied to the top or the bottom of a border.

⊟ To apply a 3-D effect to the bottom border of an element, open the **Bottom** list, under **Bevel**, and select the option you want. Next, define the **Width** and the **Height** of the bottom border.

⊟ Chose the **Color** and the **Depth** of the 3-D effect.

⊟ To change the appearance of the element by modifying its highlight, open the **Material** and **Lighting** lists and choose the appropriate option.

*Spectacular highlights make objects look more or less shiny. **Material** can be used to make elements look dull, plastic, metallic or translucent.*

Click **Close**.

 The **Reset** button cancels the 3-D format applied to the element.

Changing the orientation/perspective of a 3-D chart

Select the element in the chart.

Select the **Chart Tools** – **Format** tab, go to the **Current selection** group and click the **Format Selection** button.

Select the **3-D Rotation** category.

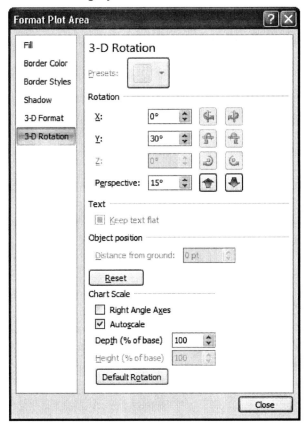

Chart options

- To change the orientation (rotation) and the camera position (view) used to display elements, specify your values in the boxes:

  X to change the orientation of the horizontal axis

  Y to change the orientation of the vertical axis

  Z to change the position of shapes above or below other shapes.

- To change the field of view on the chart, enter the degree of perspective you want in the **Perspective** box.

  The minimum value (0) is the same as having a parallel camera, the maximum value (120) produces the most exaggerated perspective, similar to that generated by a wide-angle camera.

- To prevent text inside a shape from rotating when you rotate the shape, select **Keep text flat**.

  When this option is selected, the text is always on the top of the shape. When it is not selected, the text inside the shape follows the shape's front surface as it rotates.

- To move the shape backward or forward in a 3-D space, enter a number in the **Distance from ground** box.

- Click **Close**.

- The **Reset** button cancels 3-D rotation and perspective effects and restores the default settings.

Modifying a pie chart

You can rotate a pie chart or explode one or more slices.

- Select the chart slice.

- Select the **Chart Tools** - **Format** tab, go to the **Current Selection** group, click the **Format Selection** button and select the **Series Options** category.

- To rotate the chart, drag the cursor under **Angle of first slice**, or enter a value in the box below it.

- To pull out the slices of the chart, drag the cursor under **Pie Explosion** or enter a percentage in the box underneath.

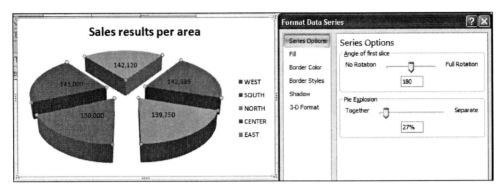

🖅 Click **Close**.

To emphasize the individual elements of a chart, you can change the pie explosion for all slices or individual slices. Click the relevant slice twice to select it, then drag it outside the chart.

Linking the points in a line chart

🖅 Select the Chart Tools – Layout tab.

🖅 To display lines between points, go to the **Analysis** group, click the **Lines** button and choose:

Drop lines to display lines extending from data points to the category axis.

High low lines to display lines extending from the highest value to the lowest value in each category.

🖅 To display bars between the points, go to the **Analysis** group, click the **Up/down bars** button and select the option with the same name.

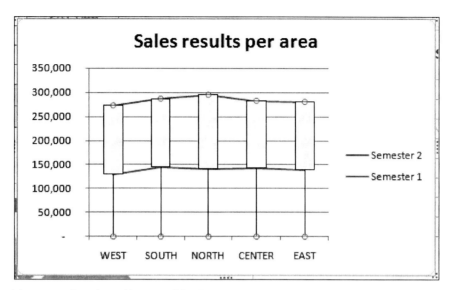

In this example, drop lines and high low bars are displayed.

Part 10
Graphic objects

Drawing a text box

A text box is an object which, by default, does not have a background or border, that is designed to contain text. You can use it to enter text outside a cell.

⊟ Select the **Insert** tab, go to the **Text** group and click the **Text Box** button.

The mouse pointer becomes a vertical black line.

⊟ Click where you want to create the text box.

or

Drag to draw the text box or click the place you wish to start entering the text.

- Use the `Alt` key as you drag if you want to align the text box to the cell gridlines.

- use the `⇧ Shift` key to draw the text box as a square.

⊟ Enter the text you want without worrying about line breaks. Use the `Enter` key when you want to start a new paragraph.

⊟ To format entered text, use the mini-toolbar.

⊟ When the text box is finished, click outside it.

If you want to select a text box, click it and press `Esc`. One single click on the text box selects its content without changing it.

Inserting a WordArt object

A WordArt object is a graphic object which, like a text box, you can use to apply decorative effects to your text. Here is an example:

⊡ Select the **Insert** tab, go to the **Text** group and select the **WordArt** button.

⊡ Click the type of effect you want.

The object is displayed in your worksheet with the following text: ***Your Text Here***.

⊡ Enter the text to which you want to apply the WordArt effect; use the [Enter] key when you want to create a line break.

⊡ Use the mini-toolbar to format the text.

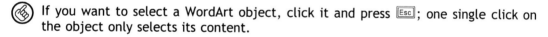 If you want to select a WordArt object, click it and press [Esc]; one single click on the object only selects its content.

Drawing a shape

⊡ Select the **Insert** tab, go to the **Illustrations** group and click the **Shapes** button.

⊡ Click the shape you want to draw.

The mouse pointer becomes a small black cross.

⊡ Click the place in the worksheet where you want to place the shape to draw it with predefined size.

or

Drag to draw the shape.

- Use the [Alt] key as you drag if you want to align the shape to the cell grid.

- use the [⇧ Shift] key to draw the shape as a square, a circle or to limit the size of other shapes.

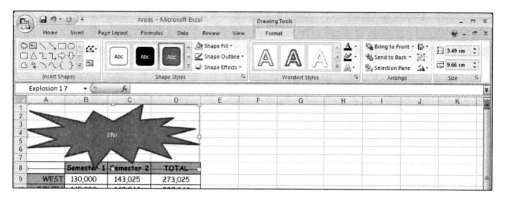

*The shape appears selected and superimposed on the cells. Its name is displayed in the name box on the formula bar. The **Drawing Tools** – **Format** tab appears, starting with the **Insert Shapes** group from which you can add more shapes.*

⊟ If required, enter the text you want to appear in the shape. Use the `Enter` key to move from line to line, and the `Esc` key to finish entering text.

⊟ You can use the mini-toolbar to format entered text.

You can add shapes to a chart or a diagram to customize them.

To add text to a shape you have already created, click to select it then enter your text.

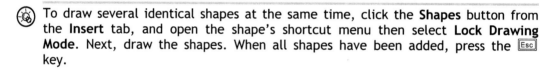

To draw several identical shapes at the same time, click the **Shapes** button from the **Insert** tab, and open the shape's shortcut menu then select **Lock Drawing Mode**. Next, draw the shapes. When all shapes have been added, press the `Esc` key.

Insert a picture file

⊟ Select the **Insert** tab, go to the **Illustrations** group and click the **Picture** button.
*The **Insert Picture** dialog box appears.*

⊟ Go to the drive and the folder containing the picture you want to insert.

⊟ Double-click the name of a picture.

Graphic objects

Inserting a clip

A clip is a picture, a sound, or a video included in the Office media Library.

⊟ Select the **Insert** tab, go to the **Illustrations** group and click the **Clip Art** button.

*The Office **Clip Art** pane immediately opens in the right of the Excel window.*

⊟ Enter one or more words in the **Search for** box.

⊟ To define where the search should be carried out, open the **Search In** list and make a choice, following these guidelines: the plus sign ⊞ expands the hierarchy while the minus sign ⊟ collapses it. Click a check box to select (or deselect) the individual category: double-clicking a category containing other categories selects (or deselects) that category and all its subcategories.

*The **Office Collections** category and its subcategories contain the picture, sound and video elements installed with Office. The **Web Collections** category provides you with elements found on the Web (or more precisely on the Microsoft site). Excel will only take this category into account if you are online.*

⊟ To limit the type of elements being searched for (**Clip Art**, **Photographs**, **Movies** or **Sounds**), open the **Results should be** list and deselect any elements that should be excluded from the search. You can also limit the search to certain file types. To do this, click the plus sign ⊞ on the type of element you want and deselect any file types that should not be included in the search.

⊟ Click the **Go** button.

*If you want to interrupt the search, click the **Stop** button that appears near the bottom of the pane.*

If you have included a Web search in your search, and if you are online, the ◉ *icon on the bottom left of the item indicates that the item has been found online.*

↰ To insert one of the items into your active document, select the cell where you want to place the item, then click the clip in the **Clip Art** task pane.

You can also insert an item by dragging it from the task pane to the active worksheet.

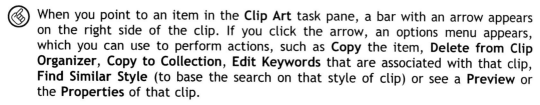

When you point to an item in the **Clip Art** task pane, a bar with an arrow appears on the right side of the clip. If you click the arrow, an options menu appears, which you can use to perform actions, such as **Copy** the item, **Delete from Clip Organizer**, **Copy to Collection**, **Edit Keywords** that are associated with that clip, **Find Similar Style** (to base the search on that style of clip) or see a **Preview** or the **Properties** of that clip.

The **Clip Art on Office Online** at the bottom of the **Clip Art** task pane takes you to the Microsoft site where you can continue searching.

⊟ Close the task pane by clicking the ⊠ button.

Modifying the format of a picture

⊟ Select the picture with a click and with a double-click to display the **Picture Tools** – **Format** tab.

⊟ To apply a predefined style to the picture, click the style you want from the **Picture Styles** group.

⊟ To insert the picture in a predefined shape, go to the **Picture Styles** group, click the **Picture Shape** button and choose the shape in which you want to insert your image.

⊟ To modify the picture border, go to the **Picture Styles** group, click the **Picture Border** button and choose the colour, line weight and style of the border.

⊟ To apply a particular effect to the picture, go to the **Picture Styles** group, click the **Picture Effects** button and choose the kind of effect you want: **Preset** (for a 3-D effect), **Shadow**, **Reflection**, **Glow**, **Soft Edges**, **Bevel**, **3-D Rotation**. Click the style you want.

⊟ To change the picture brightness, go to the **Adjust** group, click the **Brightness** button and choose a suitable percentage.

⊟ To change the picture contrast, go to the **Adjust** group, click the **Contrast** button and choose a suitable percentage.

Graphic objects

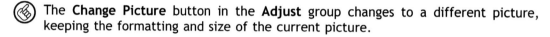 To modify the picture colours, go to the **Adjust** group, click the **Recolor** button and choose from these options:

Color modes   to display the picture in **Grey scale, Sepia, Washout** or **Black and White.**

Dark variations   to display the picture in dark colours.

Light variations   to display the picture in light colours.

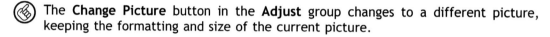 To cancel all picture formatting, go to the **Adjust** group and click the **Reset** button.

The **Change Picture** button in the **Adjust** group changes to a different picture, keeping the formatting and size of the current picture.

To **Crop** an image, i.e. delete parts of the image, go to the **Size** group (**Picture Tools – Format** tab) and click the **Crop** button. Point to the edge or the corner of the image that you want to delete and drag the cursor inwards. Press ⌈Esc⌋ or click the **Crop** button again to end the cropping process.

Inserting a diagram

*A diagram, also called a **SmartArt** graphic is a graphic representation of your data and ideas, such as an organigram.*

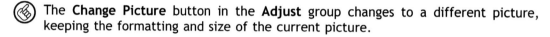 Select the **Insert** tab, go to the **Illustrations** group and click the **SmartArt** button.

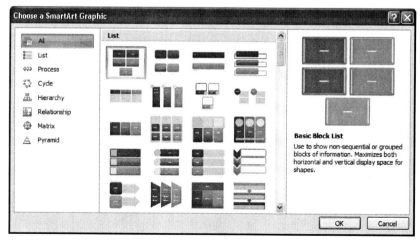

Graphic objects

The left side of the dialog box groups together all the available diagrams. The central part displays all the layouts for the category selected in the left side, and the right side displays a description of the selected layout.

⊟ In the left side of the dialog box, choose the type of diagram you want. The **All** option shows all the layouts for all types of diagrams.

⊟ In the centre of the dialog box, click the layout you want, then click **OK**.

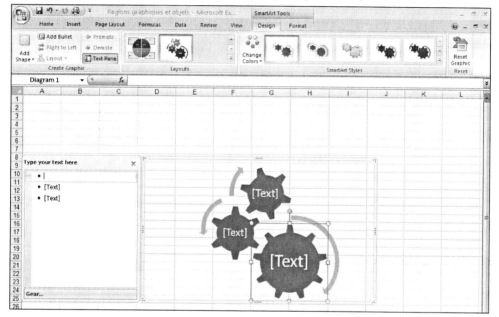

*The diagram appears without any text. You can complete it from the **Text** pane on the left. The insertion point blinks in the first text placeholder, called a bullet, and corresponds to the first shape to complete in the diagram. The **SmartArt Tools** - **Design** and **Format** tabs are displayed.*

⊟ In the Text panes, click the **[Text]** placeholder you want to complete and enter the required text.

The Text pane is like an outline or a bullet list. Each bullet in the Text pane, corresponds to information used to organize the diagram. As you enter text, the diagram is automatically updated. The more text you add, the more the characters get smaller in the active shape as well as in other shapes.

Adding bullets to a shape

*Each bullet in the **Text** pane corresponds to information used to organize a diagram. Each diagram defines its own mapping between the bullets in the Text pane.*

⊟ Click the shape in which you want to add bullets.

⊟ Select the **SmartArt Tools** - **Design** tab, go to the **Create Graphic** group and click the **Add Bullet** button.

Depending on the SmartArt graphic that you choose, each bullet in the Text pane will be represented as either a new shape or a bullet inside a shape. A bullet inside a shape indicates that the corresponding text is at a lower level than the text above it. For example, in the first diagram, a bullet has been added to the first shape. As a result, a new shape is created, with bulleted text inside.

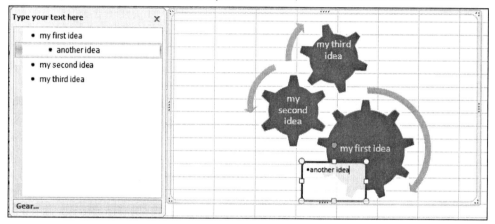

In this diagram, a bullet has also been added to the first shape. Instead of a new shape, a paragraph starting with a bullet has been created.

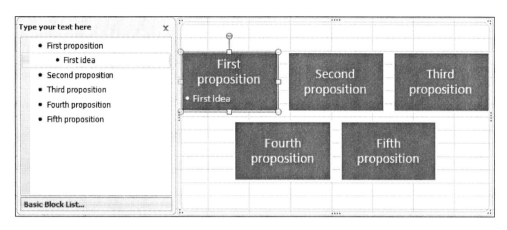

Displaying/hiding the Text pane

▱ To close the Text pane, click its close button ⧄, or the **Text Pane** button from the **Create a graphic** group, from the **SmartArt Tools** – **Design** tab.

▱ To redisplay the Text pane, click the ▮ button.

Managing diagram shapes

You have several options: you can work in the Text pane, using bulleted text, or directly on shapes in the diagram.

Creating a new shape

▱ Select the shape after which you want to add another shape. Under the **SmartArt Tools** – **Design** tab, go to the **Create Graphic** group and click the **Add Shape** button.

or

In the Text pane, click at the end of the bulleted text line after which you want to insert a new line and press Enter .

As a result, a new shape or bullet is created in the diagram. For diagrams containing a constant number of shapes, a red X appears in the Text pane and the shape is not created in the diagram.

To avoid this, switch to a different layout (see next subtitle).

Modifying the level of a shape

- To demote a shape, i.e. indent a bulleted line, select the line that you want to indent in the Text pane, then press the ⮐ key. Alternatively, go to the **SmartArt Tools – Design** tab and, in the **Create Graphic** group, click **Demote**.

- To promote a shape and reduce the indent of a line from the text pane, click that line, then press ⇧ Shift ⮐. Alternatively, go to the **SmartArt Tools – Design** tab and, in the **Create Graphic** group, click **Promote**.

  The diagram is updated. You can not demote text by several levels in relation to the line above, nor demote the first level.

Deleting a shape

- Select the shape you want to delete in the diagram or select its text line in the Text pane, then press the Del key.

Moving shapes in a diagram

- Select the shape you want to move in the diagram. If you want to move several shapes, use the Ctrl key to select them.

- Drag them to the place where you want them in the diagram.

Graphic objects

⊡ To switch the layout of your shapes, select one of them then, in the **SmartArt Tools** – **Design** tab, go to the **Create Graphic** group and click **Right to Left**.

To replace one shape with another, select it, then select the **SmartArt Tools** – **Format** tab, go to the **Shapes** group, click the change shape button and choose a new shape.

Modifying the general layout of a diagram

You can change the layout, type and colours of a diagram, or apply a quick style.

⊡ Click the diagram and select the **SmartArt Tools** – **Design** tab.

⊡ To change the layout of the diagram, go to the **Layouts** group and select the layout.

⊡ To change the type of diagram, go to the **Layouts** group and click the **More** button ⬚ then click **More Layouts**.

In the **Choose a SmartArt Graphic** dialog box, click the type of layout you want and confirm.

⊡ To change diagram colours, go to the **SmartArt Styles** group, click the **Change Colors** button and choose the colour you want.

⊡ To apply a quick style, click the style you want in the **SmartArt Styles** group.

To restore the original presentation, go to the **Reset** group and click the **Reset Graphic** button.

To customize the presentation of each shape in the diagram, you can use the buttons on the **SmartArt Tools** – **Format** tab.

The techniques presented in this chapter apply to graphic objects, but also to charts and chart elements.

Selecting objects

⊟ To select an object, click on it.

Please note to select a text box in WordArt, press Esc *to select the entire object and not its content. For a diagram, press* Esc *twice if you have selected a shape by clicking it.*

*When an object is selected (other than a diagram or a chart), an imaginary frame appears around it containing **selection handles**, represented by small squares on the edges and circles on the angles.*

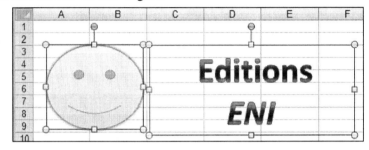

When you point to the handles, the cursor takes the shape of a vertical, horizontal or oblique double-headed arrow, depending on the handle.

*Some objects also display a green dot called a **rotation handle** (see Rotating an object). Diagrams and selected charts are surrounded by a more elaborate frame, but the handles are the same.*

⊟ To select several objects at once, select the first one, then click each object while holding down the ⬆ Shift key.

Deleting objects

⊟ Select the object(s) you want to delete.

⊟ Press the Del key.

Managing objects

Moving objects

⊟ Select the object(s) you want to move.

⊟ Point to one of the edges of the selection until the cursor becomes an arrow with four heads, then drag the object to the new position.

Resizing objects

⊟ Select the object(s) you want to resize.

⊟ Drag one of the selection handles.

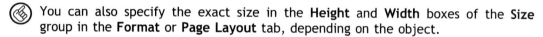 You can also specify the exact size in the **Height** and **Width** boxes of the **Size** group in the **Format** or **Page Layout** tab, depending on the object.

Rotating an object

You can rotate a text box, a shape, a WordArt object, a picture, as well as a shape within a diagram.

⊟ Select the object.

⊟ Point to the green dot at the top of the object, and drag it to rotate the object.

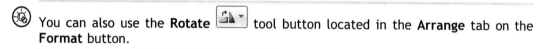 You can also use the **Rotate** tool button located in the **Arrange** tab on the **Format** button.

Grouping/ungrouping objects

When you group objects you can move, resize and format them together.

⊟ Select the objects you want to group.

⊟ Select the **Format or Page Layout** tab (depending on the object).

⊟ Go to the **Arrange** group, click the **Group** tool button and select **Group**.

A single frame now surrounds the objects. Note that the name box in the formula bar now displays the term GroupN.

To ungroup objects, select the group then click the tool button and choose **Ungroup**.

Aligning objects with one another

This command aligns objects in relation to their top, bottom, left or right border, or horizontally or vertically.

- Select the objects.
- Select the **Format** or **Page Layout** tab, depending on the object.
- Go to the **Arrange** group, click the **Align** button and select one of the first six options, depending on the alignment you want.

Distribute horizontally and **Distribute Vertically** justify the space between the selected objects.

Reorganizing overlapping objects

- Select the object.
- Select the **Format** or **Page Layout** tab, depending on the object, and choose one of the following options:
    - Click **Bring to Front** from the **Arrange** group and select the option of the same name to put the object at the very front of all the objects, or **Bring forward** to put it in front of the preceding object.
    - click **Send to back** from the **Arrange** group and select the option of the same name to put the object behind all other objects, or **Send Backward** to put the object behind the one it follows.

Applying a predefined style to an object

You can apply a predefined style to a text box, a shape, a WordArt object, and a shape inside a diagram and a chart element.

⊟ Select the object(s) and select the **Format** or **Page Layout** tab.

⊟ Go to the **Shape Styles** group and click the style you want.

Modifying the fill/border or depth effect of an object

Use this on text boxes, shapes, WordArt objects, shapes inside diagrams, diagrams themselves or chart elements. For pictures, refer to the title: "Modifying picture format" in the previous chapter.

⊟ Select the object(s) and select the **Format** or **Page Layout** tab.

⊟ To modify the background, go to the **Shape Styles** group and click the **Shape Fill** button:

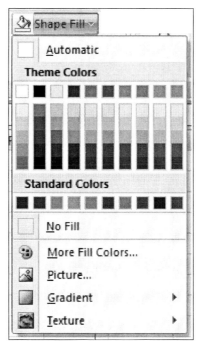

Do one of the following:

Click one of the **Theme colors** or the **Standard colors** to fill the object.

*You can create your own colours using the **More fill colors** option.*

Click **Picture** to fill the object with an **picture** file that you select in the **Insert a picture** dialog box.

Click **Gradient** to apply a higher gradient of the chosen colour.

Click **Texture** to apply a particular texture as an object background.

⊟ To change the border of the selection, go to the **Shape Styles** group and click the **Shape Outline** button:

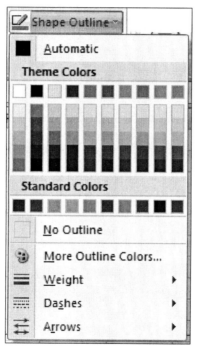

Do one of the following:

Click one of the **Theme Colors** or **Standard Colors** to apply the colour to the border.

*You can create your own colours with the **More outline colors** option.*

Click **Weight** to change the size of the object border.

Click **Dashes** to change the style of the object border.

To apply a depth effect to an object, go to the **Shape Styles** group, click the **Shape Effects** button and select one of the options to see its sub-menu and click the option you want:

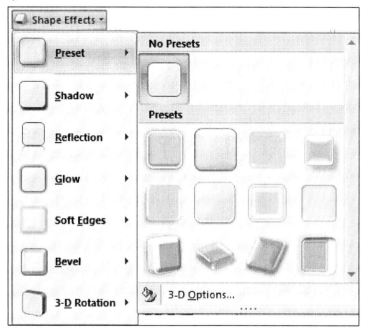

You will find these options in the **Format Shape** dialog box which you can open by clicking the **Shape Styles** group dialog box launcher .

The **No fill** option (**Shape Styles** group - **Shape Fill** button) removes the fill colour from the selected object. The **No Outline** option (**Shape Outline** button) removes a border from an object. Finally, every sub-menu from the **Shape Effects** button includes a **No** option (**No shadow**, **No reflection**) which removes an effect.

Formatting object text

These techniques let you change the appearance of text in a text box, a shape, a WordArt object, a shape within a diagram or a chart element.

⊟ Select the object(s) containing text.

⊟ Use the mini toolbar or the tool buttons from the **Font** group on the **Home** tab to change the font, size, formatting and the colour of the text.

⊟ To apply special effects, select the **Format** or the **Page Layout** tab and use the following buttons from the **WordArt Styles** group:

WordArt Style to apply a WordArt character effect.

to apply a fill colour.

to apply an outline.

to apply a special effect (shadow, glow, etc).

Part 11
Excel tables and pivot tables

Creating an Excel table

A data table, also called a data list (in previous versions of Excel), is made up of a set of rows and columns containing interconnected data that you can manage and analyse independently of data outside the table. You can manage and analyse the data more easily.

⊟ Select the range of cells you want to define as a table.

⊟ Select the **Insert** tab, go to the **Tables** group and click the **Table** button.

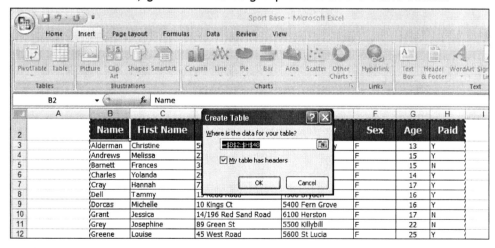

⊟ If the selected range contains data that you want to display as table headers, select **My table has headers** check box.

⊟ Click **OK**.

*Table headers are displayed automatically with drop-down list arrows. A new tab, called the **Table Tools - Design** tab appears. You can use the tools on this tab to customize or edit the table.*

 You can sort or filter data using the header drop-down lists.

 To create a table, you can also select the relevant cells and apply a table style to them using the **Format as Table** option (**Home** tab – **Styles** group – **Table Styles** button).

Resizing an Excel table

⊟ Click anywhere in the table.

⊟ On the **Table Tools - Design** tab, go to the **Properties** group and click the **Resize Table** button.

⊟ Change the selection then confirm.

 You can also point to the resize handle (the small triangle in the lower right of the table) and drag it to select the cell range.

Deleting an Excel table

When you no longer need an Excel table, you can delete it by reconverting it to a data range.

⊟ Click anywhere in the table.

⊟ On the **Table Tools - Design** tab, go to the **Tools** group and click the **Convert to Range** button.

⊟ Confirm the deletion by clicking **Yes**.

Hiding/displaying table headers

⊟ Click anywhere in the table.

⊟ Select the **Table Tools - Design** tab.

To display or hide table headers, go to the **Table Style Options** group and check or uncheck the **Header Row** check box.

 When you turn the table headers off, the AutoFilters and any applied filters are removed.

Adding a row/column to an Excel table

 To add a row to the table, type a value or text in a cell that is directly below the table.

 To include a worksheet column, type a value or text in a cell that is directly to the right of the table.

 You can also drag the resize handle at the lower-right corner of the table down to select rows and to the right to select columns.

 To add a blank row at the bottom of the table, click in the last cell in the table and press the ⇄ key.

If a total row is displayed in the table, go to the last cell in the preceding row.

 To insert and/or delete rows/columns in an Excel table, proceed as you would in a normal worksheet (see Rows, columns, cells chapter).

Selecting rows/columns in an Excel table

 To select data in a table column, point to the upper header border of the table column (the cursor becomes a ⬇). Alternatively, select one of the cells in the column and press Ctrl space.

To select the entire column (with its header), double-click or press Ctrl space twice.

 To select a table row, point to the left border of the table row (the cursor becomes a ➡) and click. Alternatively, click a cell in the row and press ⇧ Shift space.

 To select a table, point to the top edge of the left column (the cursor becomes a ↖ and click). Alternatively, click a cell in the table and press Ctrl ⇧ Shift space or Ctrl A.

To select the entire table (with headers) double-click it or use a shortcut twice.

Displaying a totals row in an Excel table

You can quickly total the data in an Excel table by displaying a totals row at the end of the table and then by using the functions that are provided in drop-down lists for each totals row.

▤ Click anywhere in the table.

▤ Select the **Table Tools - Design** tab, go to the **Table Style Options** group and select the **Total Row** check box.

*The total row appears as the last row in the table and displays the word **Total** in the leftmost cell.*

▤ To display the result of another calculation or another column, click the cell of the relevant column in the **Total Row**, then click the drop-down list arrow:

	A	Name	First Name	Address	PC/City	Sex	Age	Paid
37		Layton	Campbell	16 Jules Road	4100 Tewesbury	M	23	Y
38		Lincoln	James	"One Tree", Devlin Ct	5300 Emerald Bay	M	25	N
39		Lindell	Norman	75 West Bay Road	5000 Gunston	M	19	Y
40		Lindstrom	Ian	86 Clarence St	6200 Ipswich	M	26	Y
41		Michaels	Brett	52 Brittany Close	4400 Mt Gladstone	M	19	Y
42		O Brian	Sean	45 Lincoln St	4100 Tewesbury	M	19	N
43		Pratt	Michael	278 Westport Road	6300 Stoughton	M	24	Y
44		Richards	Brendan	32 Yarmouth Ave	4000 Westport	M	25	Y
45		Salakis	Alex	85 Kessler Ave	6200 Ipswich	M	15	N
46		Stoll	Anthony	34 Barns Drive	4500 Greerton	M	12	Y
47		Townsend	Ken	8 Waterford Dr	4000 Westport	M	15	Y
48		Underwood	Eric	7/19 Clarks Road	6200 Ipswich	M	12	Y
49		Total						46
50								None
51								Average
52								Count
53								Count Numbers
54								Max
55								Min
56								Sum
57								StdDev
								Var
								More Functions.

Excel has most common formulas. You can also enter any formula that you want in any total row cell.

Click the function you want to use.

▤ To hide the totals row, go to the **Table Style Options** group and uncheck the **Total Row** check box.

Creating a calculated column in an Excel table

⊟ Click a cell in a blank table column that you want to use as a calculated column.

⊟ Type the formula that you want to use.

The formula that you type is automatically inserted into all cells of the column.

To delete a calculated column, proceed as you would for an ordinary column.

To edit a calculated column, simply edit the formula in that column; the other cells will be automatically updated.

Apply a table style to an existing table

⊟ Click anywhere in the table.

⊟ Select the **Table Tools - Design** tab, go to the **Table Styles** group and choose a style.

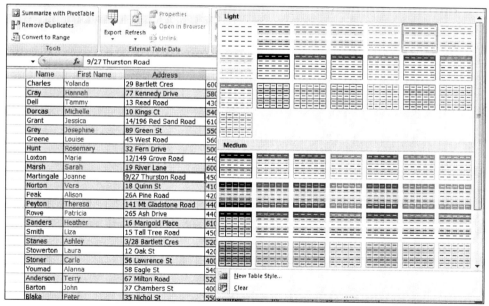

⊟ Click the table style you want to use.

Creating a pivot table

You can use a Pivot Table to summarise, analyse, explore and present summary data.

↵ If the relevant cell range contains column headers or is already an Excel table, click one of the cells. If not, select the cell range *you want to use in the Pivot Table.*

↵ Select the **Insert** tab, go to the **Tables** group, click **Pivot Table**, and then click **PivotTable**.

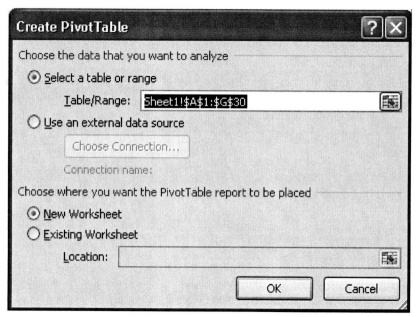

↵ Make sure that **Select a table or range** field contains the data used to fill the table. If not, use the [icon] button to select them.

↵ Choose the location for the Pivot Table: a **New Worksheet** or an **Existing Work-sheet**. For the latter, use the [icon] button to select the first destination cell of the report.

↵ Click **OK**.

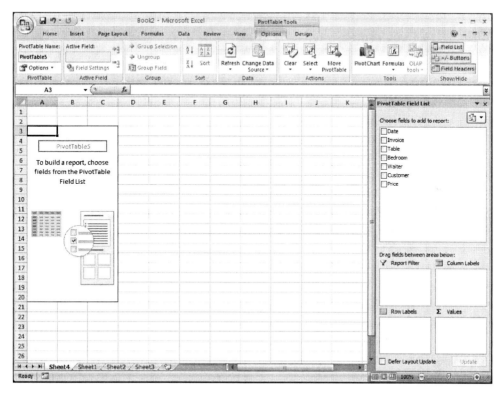

An empty Pivot Table report is inserted at the location that you entered (in this example, at cell **A3** in **worksheet 3**) and the **PivotTable Field List** is displayed to that you can start adding fields, creating a layout, and customizing the Pivot Table report. The **PivotTable Field List** has two sections: a field section at the top for adding and removing fields, and a layout section at the bottom for rearranging and repositioning fields.

The **PivotTable Tools** - **Design** and **Options** tab appear.

Add fields to create the Pivot Table (see next heading).

By default, the **Field** and **Layout** sections are displayed one over the other. If you want to change this layout, choose one of the options on the [icon] tool button.

Deleting a Pivot Table

⮡ Click in the Pivot Table.

⮡ Select the **PivotTable Tools - Options** tab.

⮡ Go to the **Actions** group, click **Clear**, then **Clear all**.

Managing fields in a Pivot Table

Adding/deleting fields

⮡ Right-click the name of a field in the **Field** section of the **PivotTable Field List**, then select the appropriate command:

Add to Report Filter   to filter the table using the field you add.

Add to Row Label   to display fields as rows on the side of the report. A row lower in position is nested within another row immediately above it.

Add to Column Label   to display fields as columns at the top of the report. A column lower in position is nested within another column immediately above it.

Add to Values   to display summary numeric data.

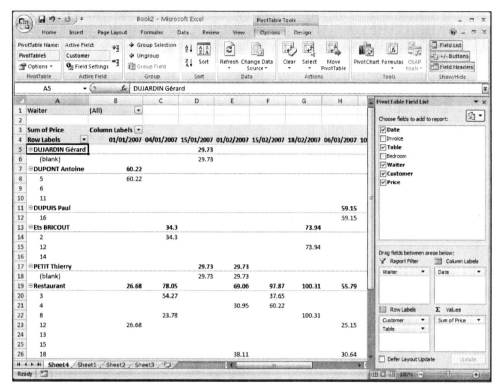

This Pivot Table displays server turnover by date, table and client.

You can also check the check box next to each field name in the **Field** section. The field is placed in a default area of the layout section, but you can rearrange it if you want. By default, non-numeric fields are added to the **Row Labels** area, numeric fields are added to the **Values** area, and OLAP date and time are added to the **Column Labels** area.

To delete a Pivot Table field, uncheck its check box in the **Field** section.

Rearranging fields

Click the name of the field you want to rearrange in one of the four areas of the **Layout** section, then select one of the following options:

Move up   moves the field up one position in the area.

Move down   moves the field down one position in the area.

Move to beginning	moves the field to the beginning of the area.
Move to end	moves the field to the end of the area.
Move to Report Filter	moves the field to the Report Filter area.
Move to Row Labels	moves the field to the Row Labels area.
Move to Column Labels	moves the field to the Column Labels area.
Move to Values	moves the field to the Values area.
Field Settings	displays the **Field Settings** or **Value Field Settings** dialog boxes, which define settings for formatting, printing, sub totals and filters that apply to a Pivot Table report field.

Changing the type of calculation on field

🖘 Click the field in the **Values** area of the **Layout** section, then select **Field Settings**.

🖘 Click the function you want to use.

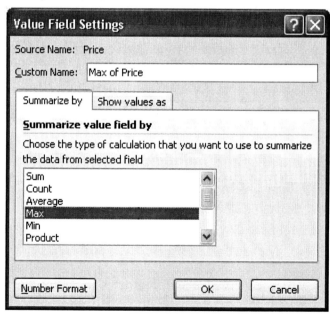

*The **Number format** button lets you change the way that numbers are formatted.*

🖘 Click **OK**.

To add a field or change its position, you can also drag its name from the **Choose fields to include in Report (Field)** section to one of the four layout boxes.

Filtering a Pivot Table

When the Pivot Table has a field in the **Report Filter** section, open the drop-down list which displays, the **All** option by default to filter the information.

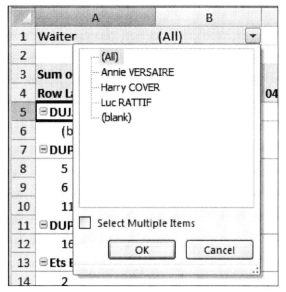

Click the entry corresponding to the information you want to display. To display information for several entries, check the **Select multiple items** check box then check the entries you want. Click **OK**.

To filter information from the **Row labels** and/or **Column labels** section open the drop-down list displayed in the cell at the top of the column and select the entries corresponding to the information you want to display.

When several fields have been added as columns and rows, the higher level fields can be expanded by clicking the ⊞ sign or collapsed by clicking the ⊟ sign.

Grouping elements in a Pivot Table

⊟ Click the Pivot Table field you want to group.

⊟ Select the **PivotTable Tools** - **Options** tab, go to the **Group** group and click **Group Field**.

⊟ Enter the first value to group (a number, date or time) in the **Starting at** box, and enter the last value in the **Ending at** box.

⊟ In the **By** box, do one of the following:

- to group number values, enter the number that represents the interval between each group.

- to group dates or times, enter the time measurement unit to apply to the groups.

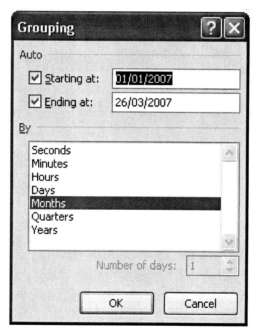

In this example, the Pivot Table columns are grouped by month between 01/01/2007 and 26/03/2007.

⊟ Click **OK**.

Pivot tables

 To cancel the grouping, ungroup the elements: select the elements you want to ungroup and click the **Group** button then **Ungroup**.

Modifying the layout/presentation of a Pivot Table

⊟ Click on the Pivot Table.

⊟ Select the **PivotTable Tools** - **Design** tab.

⊟ To change the layout of the table, use the buttons from the **Layout** group and select the option you want to use.

⊟ To change the table presentation, select or unselect the options from the **PivotTable Style Options** group.

⊟ To apply or change the table style, select it in the **PivotTable Styles** group.

Refreshing Pivot Tables

Changes to the cell range, which is the Pivot Table source, are not carried over to the table. You must update the table.

⊟ Click on the Pivot Table.

⊟ Select the **PivotTable Tools** - **Options** tab.

⊟ Go to the **Data** group and click **Refresh**.

Creating a PivotChart

A PivotChart provides a graphical representation of the data in a Pivot Table. When you create a PivotChart, you also create a Pivot Table.

⤵ If the range of cells has column headings, or is already an Excel table, click one of the cells. If not, select the cell range you want to use in the Pivot Table.

⤵ Select the **Insert** tab, go to the **Tables** group and open the list on the **Pivot Table** button, then click **PivotChart**.

The dialog box that appears is similar to the one used to create a Pivot Table.

⤵ Make sure the **Select a table or a range** contains data to analyse. If not, use the 🔳 button to select them.

⤵ Choose where you want to put your PivotChart; in a **New Worksheet** or in an **Existing Worksheet**. For the latter, use the 🔳 button to activate the first destination cell in the chart.

⤵ Click **OK**.

*An empty PivotChart is inserted at the location that you entered, with an associated empty Pivot Table created directly beside it. As for Pivot Tables, a **PivotTable Field List** pane is displayed in right side of the window. The **Legend Fields (Series)** section replaces the **Column Labels** section while **Axis Fields (Categories)** replaces the **Row Labels** section.*

PivotChart

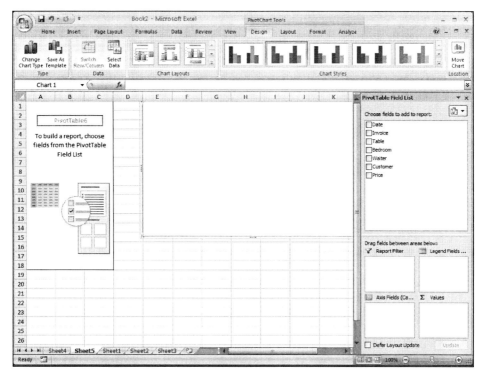

*The **PivotChart Tools** – **Design**, **Layout**, **Format**, **Analyze** tabs appear.*

⊟ Build the PivotChart in the same way as a Pivot Table (see Previous Chapter).

To change the chart type, layout, and formatting applied to a PivotChart, refer to the previous chapters on charts.

To create a PivotChart from an existing Pivot Table, click the Pivot Table, select the **Insert** tab, go to the **Charts** group and click a chart type.

Deleting a PivotChart

⊟ Click on the PivotChart.

⊟ Activate the **PivotChart Tools - Analyze** tab, go to the **Data** group, click the **Clear** button, then **Clear All**.

Filtering a PivotChart

⊟ Click on the PivotChart.

⊟ Activate the **PivotChart Tools - Analyze** tab, go to the **Show/Hide** group and click the **PivotChart Filter** button.

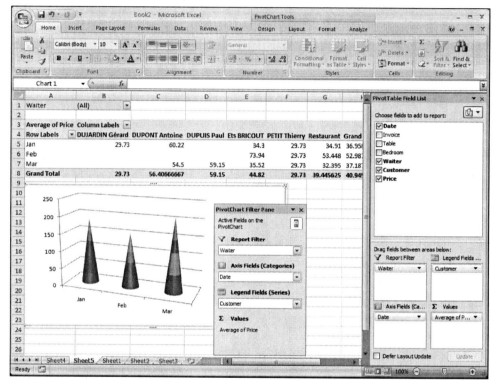

*The **PivotChart Filter Pane** is displayed in the middle of the window.*

⊟ Use the different list boxes in the pane to display or hide the chart data.

⊟ To close the pane, click the close button ⊠.

Part 12
Group work

Protecting a workbook with a password

To allow only authorised users to view or modify your content, you can secure your workbook with a password.

- Access the **Save as** dialog box (Click the **Microsoft Office** button , then **Save as**).

- Click the **Tools** button, then **General Options**.

- To protect the workbook as read-only, i.e. prompt the user for a password to open the document, enter a password in the **Password to open** box.

  By default, this feature uses advanced encryption, a standard method used to secure your files.

- To write-protect the workbook, i.e. prompt the user for a password before they can save changes to the document, type a password in the **Password to modify** box.

  This is not a watertight security feature, but a simple protection device as there is no encryption of data involved. While another user cannot alter the contents of your original file, he/she can make changes to it then save those under another file name.

Use strong passwords that combine uppercase and lowercase letters, numbers, and symbols. Passwords should contain at least eight characters.

To increase protection, select **Read-only recommended**. When opening the file, users are asked whether or not they want to open the file as read-only.

*You can combine this option with a password to open. In this case, the procedure for opening a workbook is slightly different. Even if you know the password, Excel will still ask for the password when you try to open the workbook. Click **Yes** to open the workbook as read-only. Otherwise, click **No**.*

Click **OK**.

When prompted, retype your passwords to confirm them, and then click **OK**.

Click **Save**.

If prompted, click **Yes** to replace the existing document.

Important: you must remember your passwords. Microsoft cannot retrieve them if you lose them. Store the passwords in a secure place far away from the information that they protect.

To remove a password, select the content in the **Password to open** and **Password to modify** boxes and press Del.

Protecting workbook elements

To protect changes to the structure of worksheets as well as their size and position.

- Select the **Review** tab, go to the **Changes** group, click **Protect Workbook** then select the **Windows** check box.

- To prevent users from viewing hidden worksheets, from moving or copying worksheets, inserting new worksheets, check the **Structure** option.

- To prevent other users from changing the size and position of the windows for the worksheet, check the **Windows** option.

- To prevent non-authorised users from removing workbook protection, type a password in the **Password (optional)** box.

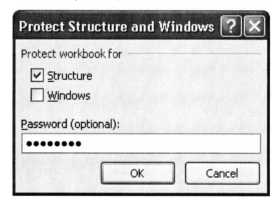

- Click **OK**.

- If required, retype the password to confirm it.

To remove workbook protection, click the **Protect Workbook** button again (**Review** tab – **Changes** group) and uncheck **Structure and Windows**. Enter the password in the **Remove protection** dialog box and confirm.

Protecting worksheet cells

To enable editing on a certain range of cells in a worksheet, you must first unlock the cells (active by default) then protect the worksheet.

Unlocking a cell range

⊟ Select the cells in which you want to allow editing.

⊟ Activate the **Home** tab, go to the **Cells** group, click the **Format** button, and then click **Format Cells**.

⊟ In the **Format Cells** dialog box, select the **Protection** tab.

⊟ Uncheck **Locked**.

⊟ Click **OK**.

Activating worksheet protection

⊟ Activate the **Review** tab, go to the **Changes** group and click **Protect Sheet**.

⊟ Make sure that **Protect workbook and contents of locked cells** is checked.

⊟ Check or uncheck the options corresponding to the actions that could be taken by users in the **Allow all users of this worksheet to** list.

▣ To allow authorised users to deactivate worksheet protection, enter a password in the **Password to unprotect sheet** box.

▣ Click **OK**.

▣ If required, enter the password again to confirm, then click **OK**.

If you try to type in a protected cell, the following message is displayed:

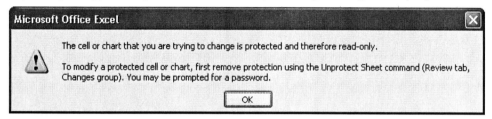

▣ Click **OK** to close the dialog box.

Depending on the authorisation given to users, some options on certain tabs are no longer available on the protected sheet (the corresponding buttons are greyed out).

To cancel worksheet protection, activate the **Review** tab, go to the **Changes** group and click **Unprotect Sheet**. Enter the password and confirm.

Authorising cell access for certain users

This feature protects cells in a worksheet and authorises access to different cell ranges either by different passwords or by selecting usernames (in this case your PC must be part of a domain).

▣ On the **Review** tab, go to the **Changes** group and click **Allow Users to Edit Ranges**.

▣ Click the **New** button.

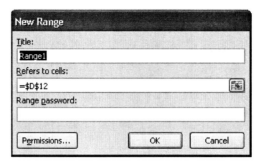

⊟ Edit the **Title** of the range.

⊟ Click the [⊞] button in the **Refers to cells** box, select the relevant cell range, then click [⊞] to return to the **New Range** dialog box.

You can use the Ctrl *key to select discontinuous cell ranges.*

⊟ Type a **Range password** that will allow users to modify the range. Confirm, then confirm a second time with the same password.

If you do not create a password, any user can edit the cells.

⊟ To create a list of users to whom you want to grant access rights, click the **Permissions** button in the **New Range** dialog box or, if you have typed and confirmed a password, click the **Permissions** button in the **Allow users to edit range** dialog box. In the **Permissions for range x** dialog box, click **Add**.

⊟ Enter the usernames or computers or groups separated by semi-colons (;).

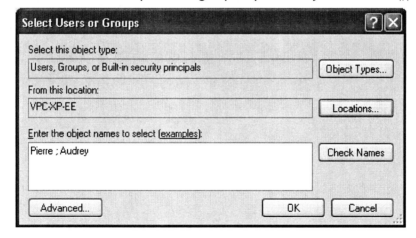

*The **examples** link shows several syntax options.*

- Click **Check Names** to ensure the data is entered correctly.

- When all the names have been entered and confirmed, click the **OK** button once to leave the **Select users, computers or groups** dialog box, and again to leave the **Permissions for range x** dialog box.

- If you need to define a new cell range for another password, click the **New Range** button again in the **Allow Users to Edit Ranges** dialog box, then repeat the actions described above.

*The **Paste permissions into a new workbook** option summarises the permissions in a new workbook.*

- Click the **Protect sheet** button and make sure that **Protect worksheet and contents of locked cells** is checked. Enter a **Password to unprotect sheet** and, if required, check or uncheck the options in the **Allow all users of this worksheet to** list.

- Click **OK**.

- If required, enter the sheet protection password again to confirm.

- Click **OK**.

If you try to type in a cell belonging to a password-protected range, Excel prompts you to type the password:

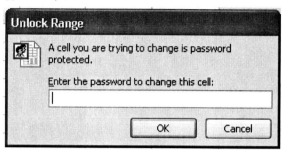

⊟ Enter the password and click **OK**.

There are many ways to share, analyse and communicate information and data in Microsoft Office Excel 2007. One of these, discussed in this chapter, consists of allowing multiple users to edit a workbook simultaneously.

The idea is to set up and save the workbook as "shared" and then make it available on a network. Note that when a workbook is shared, the following features cannot be modified: merged cells, conditional formats, data validation, charts, pictures, objects, hyperlinks, scenarios, outlines, subtotals, data tables, Pivot Tables, workbook and worksheet protection, and macros.

Allowing several users to edit a workbook simultaneously

This must be performed by the workbook owner, who intends to let others use the workbook.

Saving the workbook in a shared folder

- Open or create the workbook.

- Save the workbook to a network drive that is accessible to all users: click the

  Microsoft Office button, then click **Save as**. Click **My network places** on the **My places** bar and select the **Shared documents folder**.

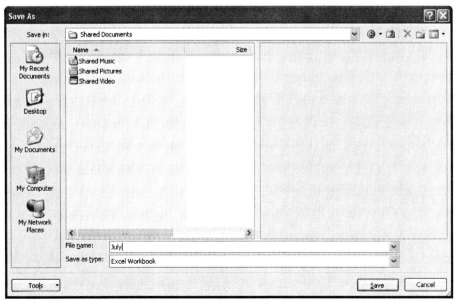

⏎ Click **Save**.

Sharing a workbook

⏎ Under the **Review** tab, go to the **Changes** group and click the **Share Workbook** button.

⏎ Check **Allow changes by more than one user at the same time.**

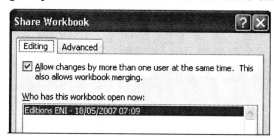

⏎ Click the **Advanced** tab.

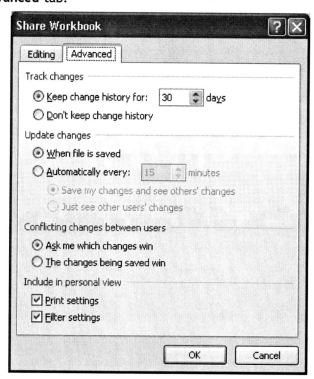

⊟ Select the options you want to use to track and make changes.

Track changes: specify the change history duration, or select **Don't keep change history**.

Update changes: specify whether changes to the workbook should be updated **When file is saved** or **Automatically every n minutes**.

Conflicting changes between users: select **The changes being saved win** if you do not want to display the **Resolve Conflicts** dialog box and have priority in an eventual conflict.

Include in personal view: leave **Print Settings** and **Filter Settings** checked if you want to use your filter or print settings.

⊟ Click **OK**.

⊟ Click **OK** again on the message prompting you to save the workbook.

The name of the workbook, followed by the term [Saved] appears in the title bar.

Protecting a shared workbook

Every user that has access to the network drive has complete access to the shared workbook unless you lock cells and protect the worksheet to restrict access. Protecting a shared workbook is recommended.

⊟ Select the **Review** tab, go to the **Changes** group and click the **Protect and Share Workbook** button.

⊟ Check **Sharing with track changes**.

⊟ Click **OK**.

To remove protection from a shared workbook, click **Unprotect Shared Workbook** (**Review** tab - **Changes** group).

Modifying a shared workbook

After you open a shared workbook, you can enter and change data as you do in a regular workbook.

⊟ Open the shared workbook. Use the normal command to open a workbook, but locate it on the network drive to which it has been saved.

The name of the workbook followed by the term [Shared] in the title bar indicates that you are going to work on a shared workbook.

⊟ Click the **Microsoft Office** button, then **Excel Options**.

⊟ In the **Popular** category, under **Personalize your copy of Office**, in the **User Name** box, enter the username that you want to use to identify your work in the shared workbook.

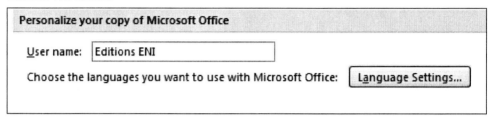

⊟ Click **OK**.

⊟ Enter and edit data on the worksheets as usual.

Note that you will not be able to change all items (see Introduction to chapter).

⊟ Define any filter and print settings that you want for your personal use. Each user's settings are saved individually by default.

*To use the original filter and print settings, go to the **Changes** group, click **Share Workbook** then, on the **Advanced** tab, under **Include in personal view**, clear the **Print settings** or **Filter settings** check box, and then click **OK**.*

⊟ To save your changes to the workbook, click **Save** on the **Quick Access Toolbar** or press Ctrl S.

*If the **Resolve Conflicts** dialog box appears, resolve the conflicts.*

✍ You can see who else has the workbook open on the **Editing** tab of the **Share Workbook** dialog box (**Review** tab - **Changes** group - **Share Workbook** button).

You can choose to get automatic updates of the other users' changes periodically, with or without saving, under **Update changes** on the **Advanced** tab of the **Shared Workbook** dialog box.

Group work

Resolving conflicting changes

A conflict happens when two users are both editing the same shared workbook and try to save changes that affect the same cell. Excel displays a dialog box to let you choose which changes to keep.

⊟ Click **Accept Mine** or **Accept Other** to keep your change or the other person's change and to go to the next conflicting change.

⊟ To keep all your changes or all of the other user's changes, click **Accept All Mine** or **Accept All Others**.

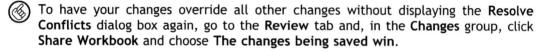 To have your changes override all other changes without displaying the **Resolve Conflicts** dialog box again, go to the **Review** tab and, in the **Changes** group, click **Share Workbook** and choose **The changes being saved win**.

Tracking changes

⊟ Open the shared workbook that has been modified.

⊟ Select the **Review** tab, go to the **Changes** group and click the **Track Changes** button.

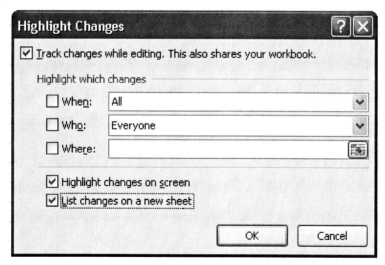

⊟ To display changes made during a specific period, check the **When** check box and select the relevant period in the following list:

Since I last saved   highlights only the changes made since the last time the workbook was saved.

All   highlights all the changes made.

Not yet reviewed   highlights just those changes which have not been accepted or rejected.

Since date   highlights the changes made after the date entered in the **When** text box.

⊟ Activate the **Who** option to choose whose changes should be highlighted (yours or those of another user), using the names in the list box.

⊟ If you wish to highlight the changes in a specific range of cells, activate the **Where** option and select the cells in the workbook.

*If none of the three **Highlight changes** options are active, Excel will highlight all the changes made by all the users of the shared workbook, including your own.*

⊟ Check the **Highlight changes on screen** check box to see the changes directly highlighted in the cells.

When you choose this option, Excel highlights the modified area with a triangle, using a different colour for each user, in the top left corner of each modified cell.

If you point to one of these triangles, details of the changes and the username appear in a ScreenTip.

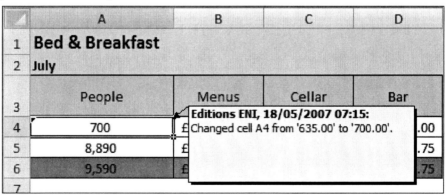

⊟ Select the **List changes on a new sheet** check box to display the changes in a sheet called **History**.

*This sheet displays all changes in a list, in columns. The list can be filtered. The conflicting changes that have been saved are called **Won** in the **Action Type** column. The row numbers in the **Losing Action** column identify the rows with information about the conflicting changes that were not kept, including any deleted data.*

⊡ Click **OK**.

 By default, the history of tracked changes is kept for 30 days. You can alter this value by changing the number of days in the **Keep change history for** option (**Review** tab – **Changes** group - **Share Workbook** button – **Advanced** tab - **Keep change history for**).

Accepting or rejecting changes

⊡ Open the modified shared workbook.

⊡ Select the **Review** tab, go to the **Changes** group, click **Track Changes** then **Accept/Reject Changes**.

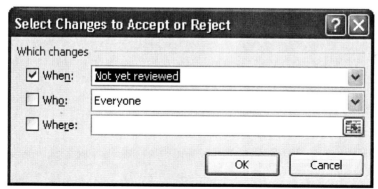

⊡ If necessary, modify the interval in the **When** list box:

Not yet reviewed selects all the changes you have not examined yet.

Since date reviews the changes made to the workbook since the date you specify in the **When** box.

⊡ Activate the **Who** option to choose whose changes should be reviewed, selecting their names in the list box.

⊡ Check **Where** to review changes made to a specific range of cells.

If none of these three options are active, Excel reviews all the changes made to the shared workbook.

⊟ Click **OK**.

The modification details appear in the Accept or Reject Changes dialog box and the first modification is highlighted in the workbook.

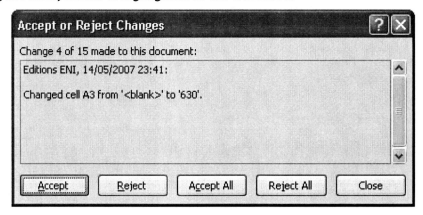

⊟ To review the changes one at a time, choose **Accept** or **Reject** with the appropriate buttons. Excel will go on to the next change.

If several changes have been made to the same cell, Excel will ask you to choose a value. If this happens, choose the correct value and click Accept.

⊟ To do all the changes at once, use the **Accept All** or **Reject All** buttons.

Remove a user from a shared workbook

If needed, you can disconnect users from a shared workbook. Before doing this, make sure they have completed their work on the workbook. If you remove an active user, any unsaved work will be lost.

⊟ On the **Review** tab, in the **Changes** group, click **Share Workbook**.

⊟ On the **Editing** tab, in the **Who has this workbook open now** list, select the name of the user to disconnect.

⊟ Click **Remove User**.

⊟ To delete any personal view settings of the removed user, select the **View** tab, go to the **Workbook Views** group and click **Custom Views**. In the **Views** list, select the view of another user, and then click **Delete**.

Stop sharing a workbook

First check whether you are the only user working on the workbook (see previous heading). Otherwise, any unsaved work by other users will be lost.

- Remove protection from the shared workbook by clicking **Unprotect Shared Workbook** (**Review** tab - **Changes** tab).

- On the **Review** tab, go to the **Changes** group and click **Share Workbook**.

- On the **Editing** tab, uncheck **Allow changes by more than one user at the same time**.

- Click **OK**. Confirm your choice by clicking **Yes** in the dialog box that appears.

Part 13
Various advanced features

Creating a custom lists

Entering a new list

- Click the **Microsoft Office** button then **Excel Options**.
- Select **Popular**, and click **Edit Custom Lists**.
- In the **Custom Lists** box, click **New List**, even if this option is already selected.
  The insertion point appears in the List Entries box.
- In the **List Entries** box, enter your data, separating each one with the Enter key.

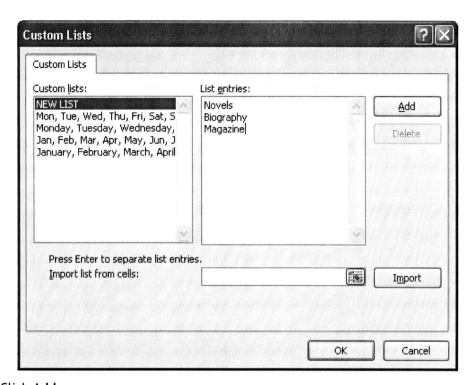

◻ Click **Add.**

The new list appears at the end of the existing series, with each item separated by a comma.

◻ Click **OK** once to close the **Custom Lists** dialog box; a second time to close the **Excel Options** dialog box.

Importing a new series

If the new data series has already been entered on a worksheet, you can create a new custom list from that data.

◻ Click the **Microsoft Office** button then **Excel Options.**

◻ Select the **Popular** category and click **Edit Custom Lists.**

◻ Click the button located at the far right of the **Import List From Cells** box.

The dialog box is minimized.

⊟ Select the cells containing the series you want to retrieve.

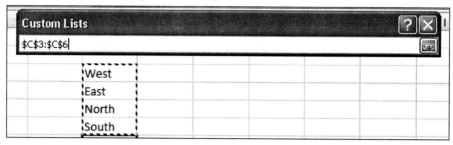

⊟ When you are happy with the selection, click the ⊡ button to confirm your selection and return to the **Options** dialog box.

⊟ Click the **Import** button to add the new list after the **Custom lists**.

⊟ Click **OK** once to close the **Custom Lists** dialog box; a second time to close the **Excel Options** dialog box.

A custom data series is used in the same way as any other data series. Type the first value of the series in a cell and drag that cell's copy handle.

Modifying/deleting custom data series

⊟ Go to the **Custom Lists** dialog box: click the **Microsoft Office** button ⊙ , then click **Excel Options**. Under **Popular**, click **Edit Custom Lists**.

⊟ To modify a custom series, click the series under **Custom Lists**.

⊟ Make your changes in the **List Entries** box: add or remove characters or entries.

⊟ To delete a custom series, select the series you want to delete in the **Custom Lists** box and click **Delete**. Confirm the deletion by clicking **OK** on the **Microsoft Office Excel** dialog box that appears.

⊟ Click **OK** once to close the **Custom Lists** dialog box; a second time to close the **Excel Options** dialog box.

Creating a drop-down list

You can create a drop-down list of entries that are compiled from cells elsewhere in the workbook. When you create a drop-down list for a cell, it displays an arrow in that cell. To enter information in that cell, click the arrow, and then click the entry that you want.

- Type the entries in a single column or row ending with a blank cell.

  You can sort the data in the order that you want it to appear in the drop-down list.

- If you want to use another worksheet, type the list on that worksheet, and then define a name (see Named ranges).

- Select the cell(s) in which you want a drop-down list.

- Under the **Data** tab, go to the **Data Tools** group and click **Data Validation**.

  *The **Data Validation** dialog box appears.*

- Under the **Settings** tab, open the **Allow** list and click **List**.

- If the list is in another worksheet, enter the name you defined for your list in the **source** box and type the equals (=) sign followed by the name given to the cells.

  To select list entries in the current worksheet, click the ⊞ button in the **Source** box.

  *The **Data Validation** dialog box shrinks to enable you to access the worksheet.*

Select the cells containing the drop-down list entries then click the 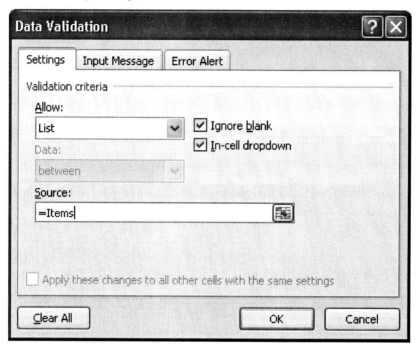 button to maximise the dialog box again.

Whichever solution you choose, the name or selection is preceded by the equals (=) sign.

⊟ To specify whether the cell can be left blank, select the **Ignore blank** check box.

Click the **Input Message** tab and make sure the **Show input message when cell is selected** check box is selected.

Type the title and text for the message (up to 225 characters) in the **Input Message** box.

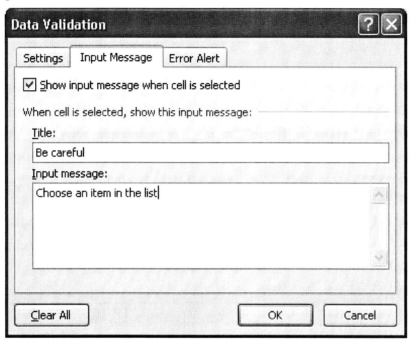

⊟ Specify how you want Excel to respond when invalid data is entered:

Click the **Error Alert** tab, and make sure that the **Show error alert after invalid data is entered** check box is selected.

Select one of the following options from the **Style** box:

Stop	to prevent entry of invalid data and display a message.
Warning	to display a warning message that does not prevent entry of invalid data.
Information	to display an information message that does not prevent entry of invalid data.

Type the title of the message in the **Title** box, and the text in the **Error message** box.

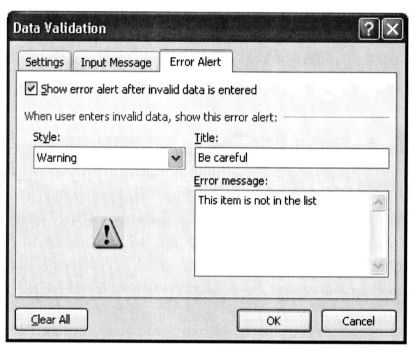

If you don't enter a title or text, the following message appears:

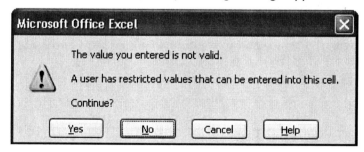

You cannot enter data which is not in the list.

Optimising data entry

 The width of the drop-down list is determined by the width of the cell that contains the data.

The maximum number of entries that you can have in a drop-down list is 32,767.

If the validation list is on another worksheet and you want to prevent users from seeing it or making changes, consider hiding and protecting that worksheet.

 To delete a drop-down list, select the **Data Validation** dialog box (**Data** tab – **Data Tools** group – **Data Validation** button) for the cell containing the drop-down list you want to delete, and click the **Delete All** button from any tab in the dialog box.

Defining acceptable data

With this setting you can limit the type of data allowed in one or more cells by defining validation criteria.

Defining validation criteria

⊟ Select the cells whose data you want to restrict.

⊟ Select the **Data** tab, go to the **Data Tools** group and click the **Data Validation** button.

*The **Data Validation** dialog box appears.*

⊟ Under the **Settings** tab, open the **Allow** list and select an option based on the type of data you want to allow in the cell:

Any value	no restrictions.
Whole number	data must be a whole number.
Decimal	data must be a whole number or a fraction.
List	this option allows you to restrict data to that contained in drop-down list (see previous paragraphs).
Date	data should be a date.
Time	data should be a time.
Text length	this option allows you to define how many characters a cell can contain.
Custom	this option allows you to enter a formula to define acceptable data.

⊟ If you choose **Whole number, Decimal, Date, Time** or **Text Length** you will also have to select an operator in the **Data** list. Then, fill in the other options depending on the operator you have chosen.

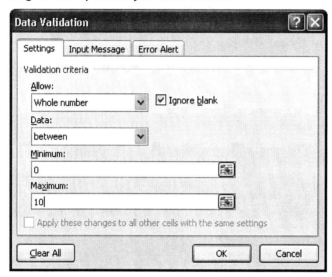

These validation criteria allow data in whole number or decimal form between 0 and 10 inclusive.

⊟ If you choose the **Custom** option, enter the formula in the **Formula** text box starting with an equal sign (=). The formula must be of the logical type giving a TRUE or FALSE result.

⊟ Whatever the type of data you allow, select the **Ignore blank** option if you accept blank cells.

⊟ Optionally specify a message to appear in a ScreenTip when you activate the relevant cell:

Click the **Input Message** tab and make sure that **Show input message when cell is selected** is checked.

Type a message title in the **Title** box, and the message text in the **Input message** box.

⊟ Indicate what Excel should do when invalid data is entered: click the **Error Alert** tab and make sure that **Show error alert after invalid data is entered** is checked.

Select one of the following options in the **Style** list:

Stop   to display a message and prevent input of invalid data.

Warning   to display a warning message that does not prevent the entry of invalid data.

Information   to display an information message that does not prevent the entry of invalid data.

Enter the message title in the **Title** box, and the message text in the **Error message** box.

The buttons that appear in the error message change according to the style you have chosen, providing you with the option to allow or prevent the entry.

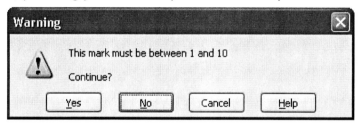

*This example features a **Warning message**: the user can enter the data by clicking **Yes**.*

Circling invalid data

This function allows you to circle cells containing data that does not satisfy the validation criteria.

⊟ Select the **Data** tab, go to the **Data Tools** group and click the button on the **Data Validation** button.

⊟ Click **Circle Invalid Data**.

STUDENT NAME	Oral expression (25)	Reading comprehension (20)	Listening (20)	Written(25)	Project(10)	S
ABBOTT, Rebecca	18	17	15	16	9	
BARNES, Linda	15	16	15	12	8	
DA SILVA, Paola	22	19	18	20	9	
EGGERTON, Melissa	14	15	11	13	11	
KELSEY, Natalie	13	12	10	12	6	
LILIPUT, Leila	14	15	13	13	14	
McFEHERTY, Mary	19	19	17	18	8	
NAUGHTON, Olivia	17	16	15	14	7	
POTTS, Penelope	23	20	19	22	9	
PULLMAN, Germaine	20	18	17	22	9	
ROWLINS, Amelia	18	19	16	17	7	

In this example, grades must be between 0 and 10.

🗗 To hide the red circles, select the **Data** tab, go to the **Data Tools** group, click the **Data Validation** button and click **Clear Validation Circles**.

Adding comments to cells

This feature adds a comment to cells.

Creating a comment

🗗 Select the cell where you want to start.

🗗 Select the **Review** tab, go to the **Comments** group and click **New Comment**.

STUDENT NAME	Oral expression (25)	Reading comprehension (20)	Lis
ABBOTT, Rebecca	18		
BARNES, Linda	20	Teacher: This is the best mark	
DA SILVA, Paola	22		
EGGERTON, Melissa	14		
KELSEY, Natalie	13		12

A ScreenTip appears with the name of the user.

🗗 Enter the comment text.

The comment is entered directly into a ScreenTip. Use Enter *to change lines.*

🗗 Press Esc or click outside the box to stop entering text.

Optimising data entry

By default, a red triangle marks the top right corner of a cell that contains a comment.

Displaying comments

- To display a comment, simply point to the cell that contains the red triangle.

- To display comments one after another, click the **Previous** and **Next** buttons (**Review** tab – **Comments** group).

- To display all comments at once, click **Show All Comments** (**Review** tab – **Comments** group).

- To modify the general display of the comments, click the **Microsoft Office** button , then **Excel Options**. In the **Advanced** category, under **Display**, select either **No comments or indicators**, **Indicators only**, **Comments on hover**, or **Comments and indicators**. Confirm.

To edit a comment, click the cell containing the comment to edit, click the **Edit Comment** button (**Review** tab – **Comments** group). Make your changes then press Esc .

To delete a comment, click the cell containing the comment to delete, then click the **Delete** button (**Review** tab – **Comments** group).

Creating a hyperlink

For quick access to related information in another file or on a Web page, you can insert a hyperlink in a cell or a graphic object.

🖆 Click the cell or select the graphic object you want to represent the hyperlink.

If it is a cell, it can contain data and formatting.

🖆 On the **Insert** tab, in the **Links** group, click **Hyperlink**, or press Ctrl **K**.

Creating a link to a new file

🖆 Click the **Create New Document** option located in the **Link to** frame on the left of the dialog box.

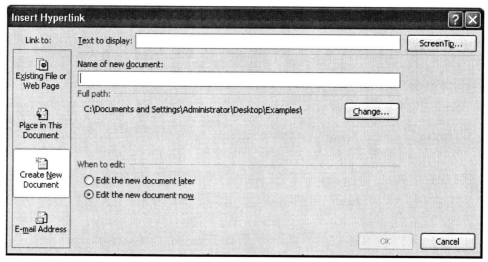

🖆 Enter the **Name of the new document** using its complete address (location + name) if the suggested **Full Path** is not what you require. You can also type only the name of the new document if you are happy with the path.

*The **Change** button allows you to type the name of the new document and to choose a new location for it without having to type in the path.*

🖆 Depending on whether you wish to edit the new document, now or later, you should activate the corresponding option in the **When to edit** section.

🖆 If you need to, click the **ScreenTip** button, and type the text you would like displayed in a ScreenTip when the pointer passes over the hyperlink. Confirm with **OK**.

If you do not give any text for the ScreenTip, Excel will automatically display the full path of the new document.

◰ Click **OK** to confirm setting up the link and the new document.

If you choose to edit the new document now, the workbook containing the new hyperlink will remain open (you will notice its button in the task bar), and your screen will immediately display the new workbook's worksheet.

◰ In this case, make your changes, closing the workbook in the normal way.

Creating a link to an existing file or to a web page

◰ Click the **Existing File or Web Page** button in the **List in** frame on the left side of the dialog box.

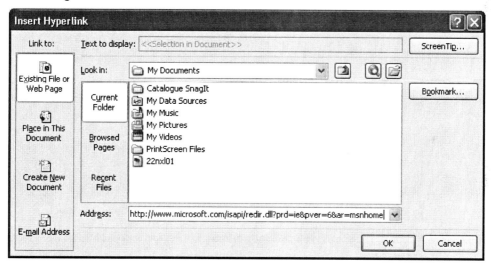

◰ Depending on the document you want to link to, click one of the following:

Current Folder to select a file in the current folder.

Browsed Pages to select a web page from browsed web pages.

Recent Files to select a file that you recently used.

◰ If you know the exact address of the file you want to link to, type it in the **Address** box.

◰ To display helpful information when you move the pointer on the hyperlink, click **ScreenTip**, type the text you want in the **ScreenTip** text box, and then click **OK**.

If you do not enter any text in the ScreenTip, Excel will show the full file address, by default.

⊟ Click **OK** to confirm the creation of the link.

Creating a link to a specific location in a workbook

⊟ Click the **Place in This Document** shortcut, located in **Link to** bar (on the left of the dialog box).

The list of existing worksheets and the names of the active workbook appear in the central part of the dialog box.

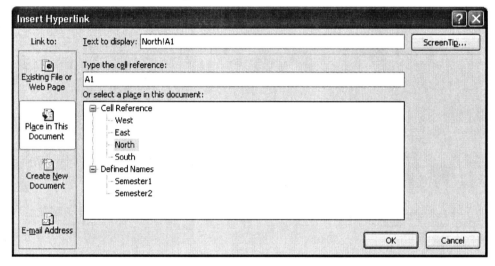

⊟ In the **Or select a place in this document**, click the worksheet you want to link to, or the name range of the worksheet you want to link to.

⊟ Edit the cell reference in the **Type the cell reference** box to specify the cell containing the link.

⊟ If required, click the **ScreenTip** button then enter text to display when the link is pointed to. Confirm the text with the **OK** button.

⊟ Click **OK** in the **Insert Hyperlink** dialog box to confirm the creation of the link.

Hyperlinks

Creating a link to an email address

⊟ Click **E-mail Address** under **Link to** (on the left of the dialog box).

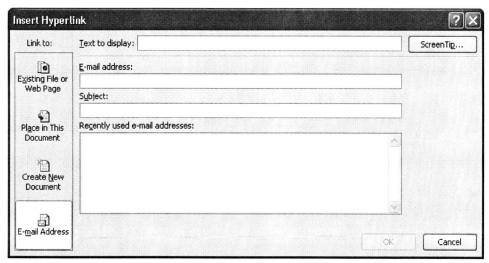

⊟ In the **Email address** box, type the email address and the **Subject** of the message in the **Subject** box.

⊟ In the **Insert Hyperlink** dialog box, click **OK**.

When you click a hyperlink to an e-mail address, your e-mail programme automatically starts and creates an email message with the address pre-filled.

If you have inserted a hyperlink in an empty cell, the text corresponding to the link content (the file pathway or place in the workbook) is inserted in that cell.

You can also create a hyperlink to an email address in a cell by directly entering the address in the cell.

Activating a hyperlink

How to activate the hyperlink destination, i.e. open the corresponding file or go to the location defined by the link.

⊡ Point to the hyperlink you want to activate.

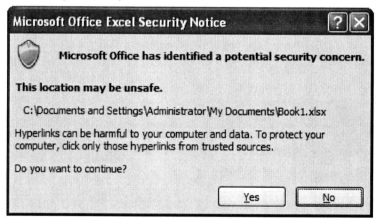

8		Semester 1	Semester 2	TOTAL	
9	WEST	130,000	143,0	file:///C:\Documents and	
10	SOUTH	145,000	142,0	Settings\Administrator\Desktop\Examples\	
11	NORTH	142,120	153,0	1-2 Sales Objectives.xlsx - Click once to	
12	CENTER	142,889	140,100	follow. Click and hold to select this cell.	
13	EAST	139,750	140,800	280,550	

When you point to the link inserted in a cell or in a graphic object, the pointer becomes a hand; if you have no text for the ScreenTip when you created the hyperlink, the ScreenTip displays the complete document address or the name of the active workbook followed by the location to go to.

⊡ When you see the hand, click to activate the hyperlink.

If the hyperlink opens a file, a warning message may appear, prompting you to be careful about using certain files:

Microsoft Office Excel Security Notice [?][X]

Microsoft Office has identified a potential security concern.

This location may be unsafe.

C:\Documents and Settings\Administrator\My Documents\Book1.xlsx

Hyperlinks can be harmful to your computer and data. To protect your computer, click only those hyperlinks from trusted sources.

Do you want to continue?

[Yes] [No]

⊡ If the file you want to open is reliable, click **Yes** to open; otherwise, click **No**.

(☞) When the hyperlink has been activated at least once, it changes colour and goes purple.

Modifying/deleting a hyperlink

Selecting a cell/object without activating the hyperlink

⊟ To select a cell containing a hyperlink, point to it and click while holding down the mouse button. When the cursor becomes a white cross, release the mouse.

You can also use the arrow keys to activate the cell.

⊟ To select a hyperlinked object, press the Ctrl key, hold it down and click the object.

Changing the hyperlink destination

⊟ Select the cell or graphic object containing the hyperlink.

⊟ On the **Insert** tab, in the **Links** group, click the **Hyperlink** button, or press Ctrl K.

*You can also open the shortcut menu of the cell or object and activate **Edit hyperlink**.*

⊟ Make your changes and confirm.

Changing the text or graphic object of a hyperlink

⊟ To edit the text of a cell containing a hyperlink, select the cell and enter the new text, or make your changes directly in the formula bar, then confirm.

⊟ To edit a graphic object, select it then double-click it to display the dedicated editing tab.

Deleting a hyperlink

⊟ Select the cell or graphic object containing the hyperlink you want to delete.

⊟ Right-click the cell or object to display its shortcut menu.

⊟ Click **Delete Hyperlink**.

To change the appearance of hyperlinks, change the **Hyperlink** and **Hyperlink visited** styles (see Cell styles – Managing the styles of existing cells).

To avoid turning an email address into a hyperlink, click the **Microsoft Office** button , **Excel Options**, select the **Proofing** category, then click the **Auto-Correct options** button. Select the **AutoFormat as you type** tab and, to finish, uncheck **Internet and network paths with hyperlinks**.

Importing data from an Access database

This technique imports updateable data from an Access database into Excel by creating a connection to the database. Once the data is imported, you can update it.

↵ Open the workbook that you want to import the data into and activate the first destination cell.

↵ On the **Data** tab, in the **Get External Data** group, click the **From Access** button.

↵ In the **Select data source** dialog box, go to the folder containing the data you want to import and double-click it.

↵ In the **Select Table** dialog box, click the object (table or request) from the database that you want to import.

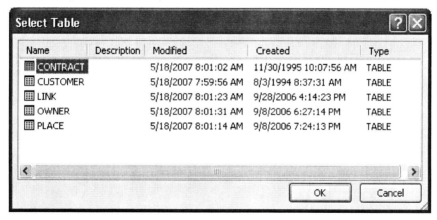

↵ Click **OK**.

Choose how you want to import the data: as a **Table**, **Pivot Table** or as a **Pivot-Chart**.

Specify where you want to put the data: in an **Existing worksheet** or in a **New worksheet**. For an existing worksheet, use the ▦ tool button to activate the first destination cell of the imported data.

*You can define the refresh, format and layout options for the imported data (see. Changing refresh options) using the **Properties** button.*

Click **OK**.

Excel puts the external data range at the location you have specified.

The connection is stored in an Office Data Connection file (.odc) in the following folder: C:|Documents and Settings\username\My documents\My data sources.

Importing/exporting

Importing data from a web page

With this technique you can import refreshable data from a web page into Excel by establishing a connection to the web page. Once the data is imported, you can refresh it.

- Make sure you are online.

- Open the workbook that you want to import the data to and activate the first destination cell.

- On the **Data** tab, in the **Get External Data** group, click the **From Web** button.

- In the **New Web Query** dialog box, enter the URL or web address of the page with the data you want to import in the **Address** box, then click **Go**.

  *You can also open the list on the **Address** box to use a recently entered address.*

- If the tool buttons are not visible in the page, click the tool button to display them.

- Select the data you want to import: click the tool button located on the top left:

  - from the table(s) (if you are importing table data)
  - from the page, to import all the data from a page.

The  tool button becomes a ▓.

⊟ Click the **Options** button to modify the formatting and import options.

Importing/exporting

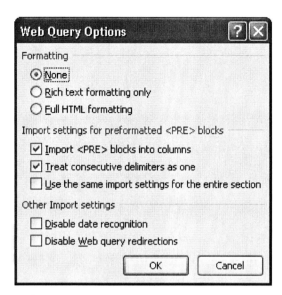

Note that imported data is not formatted, by default.

▣ Modify any options you need and click **OK**.

▣ If you want to extract the requested data into other workbooks or share the request with other users, you must save the web request. To do this, click the ▣ tool button, select the location of the file, enter the **File name** then click the **Save** button.

By default, a web request is saved in C:\Documents and Settings\Username\ Application Data\Microsoft\Queries with a .iqy extension. If you do not save the web request in a file it will be saved as a workbook element and will only be usable from that workbook.

▣ Click the **Import** button.

▣ Specify the location for the data: An **Existing worksheet** or a **New worksheet**. In the case of the latter, use the ▣ tool button to activate the first destination cell of the imported data.

*The **Properties** button defines the refresh, formatting and layout options for the imported data (see Modifying refresh settings).*

▣ Click **OK**.

Importing data from a text file

You can use this technique to import data into Excel from a text file (.txt); this method allows the data to be updated.

⊟ Open the workbook for the imported data and select the first import destination cell.

⊟ Select the **Data** tab, go to the **Get External Data** group and click **From Text**.

⊟ In the **Import Text File** dialog box, go to the folder containing the file to import and double-click its name.

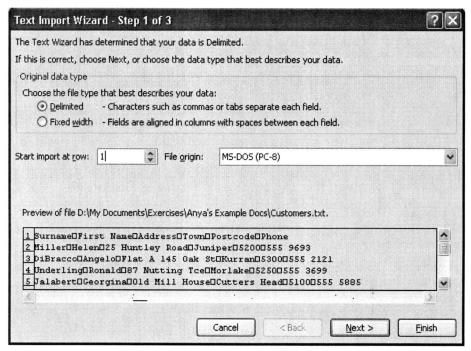

The wizard will interpret the data as being **Delimited** (the data is separated by commas or tabs), or **Fixed width** (separated by commas).

⊟ If necessary, change the **Original data type** in the corresponding frame.

⊟ If you don't want to import the data from the first row in the file, select or enter the required row number in the **Start Import at row** text box.

⊟ Click the **Next** button.

- ⊟ Select the delimiters contained in the data that is **Delimited** or choose the field widths following the instructions in the first frame of the window, if they are **Fixed Width**.

- ⊟ Click the **Next** button.

- ⊟ Select the data format for each column: click the column then choose one of the options in the **Column data format** frame.

  *The **Advanced** button enables you to check or modify numeric data settings on the imported data such as the decimal point and thousands separators.*

- ⊟ Click **Finish**.

- ⊟ Specify the data location: on an **Existing Worksheet** or a **New worksheet**. For a new worksheet, use the button to activate the first destination cell of the imported data.

  *The **Properties** button displays options for refreshing data and layout options (see Updating imported data).*

- ⊟ Click **OK**.

- ⊛ You can also use the **Open** dialog box to import a text file. In this case, however, the data cannot be updated.

Updating imported data

Updating one or more external data series

- ⊟ Click one of the cells in the range of imported data.

- ⊟ On the **Data** tab, in the **Connections** group, open the list on the **Refresh All** button.

- ⊟ Choose one of the following options:

  Refresh all   to refresh all external data series in the workbook.

  Refresh   to refresh the active external data series.

  If several workbooks are open you have to refresh external data in each workbook.

Updating data from an imported text file

⊡ Click one of the cells in the range of imported data from the text file.

⊡ On the **Data** tab, in the **Connections** group, open the list on the **Refresh All** button and click **Refresh**.

⊡ In the **Import Text File** dialog box, select the text file you want to update then click the **Import** button.

Changing data update settings

⊡ Click one of the cells containing imported data.

⊡ On the **Data** tab, in the **Connections** group, open the list on the **Refresh All** button and click **Connection Properties**.

The dialog box that opens is the same as the one that appears when you click the **Properties** *button on the* **Import Data** *dialog box (when you are preparing the import).*

Updating imported data automatically when opening the workbook

⊡ Click the **Usage** tab.

⊡ Select the **Refresh data when opening the file** check box.

⊡ If you want to save the workbook with the query definition but without the external data, select the **Remove external data from data range before saving the workbook** option.

Checking this option limits the size of the worksheet.

⊡ Click **OK**.

Refreshing data at regular intervals

⊡ Click the **Usage** tab.

⊡ Select the **Refresh every** check box, and then enter the number of minutes between each refresh.

⊡ Click **OK**.

Requiring a password to refresh

This procedure does not apply to data retrieved from a text file (.txt) or a Web query (*.iqy).*

⊟ Click the **Definition** tab.

⊟ Clear the **Save password** check box.

Excel prompts for the password the first time that the external data range is refreshed in each session. The next time you start Excel, you will be prompted for the password again if you open the workbook that contains the query and attempt a refresh operation.

⊟ Click **OK**.

Managing existing connections

⊟ Activate the **Data** tab, go to the **Connections** group and click the **Connections** button.

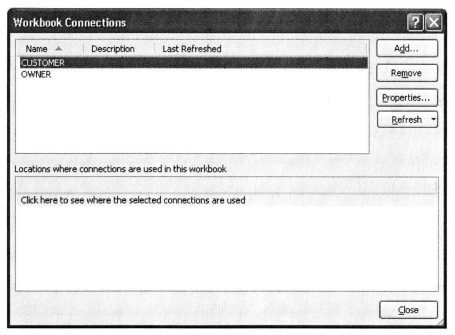

The list of all active connections in open workbooks appears.

⊟ To add a connection, click the **Add** button to display the **Existing Connections** dialog box and select the connection to open.

⊟ To display information about a connection, select a connection then click **Properties** to display the **Connection Properties** dialog box.

⊟ To refresh external data, use the **Refresh** button and then **Refresh** or **Refresh All**.

⊟ To get status information about a refresh operation, select one or more connections, and then click **Refresh Status** on the **Refresh** button menu.

⊟ To stop the current refresh operation, click **Cancel Refresh** on the **Refresh** button menu.

⊟ To remove one or more connections, select the connections and then click **Remove**.

Removing a connection only removes the connection and does not remove any object or data from the workbook.

⊟ To display the locations of connections in the workbook, select one or more connections, and then, under **Locations where connections are used in this workbook**, click the link **Click here to see where the selected connections are used**.

You then see the name of the worksheet, the reference of the cells containing the connected data and the name of the Excel query.

⊟ Click Close in the **Workbook Connections** dialog box.

Inserting an object from another application

This operation is also the way to import data from another application.

Creating a new object

⊟ In Excel, click in the cell where you want the object to appear.

⊟ On the **Insert** tab, in the **Text** group, click the **Object** button.

⊟ In the **Object** dialog box, select the application in which you want to create the object in the **Object type** list.

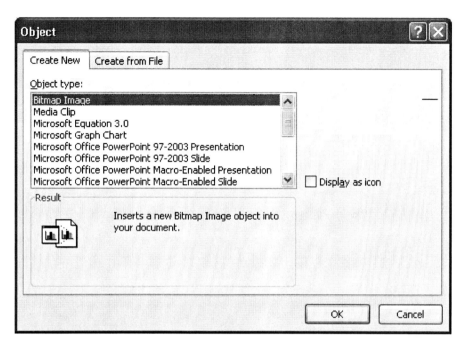

The contents of this list depends on the applications installed on your computer.

- Check the **Display as icon** box to see the object in Excel as an icon representing the application used to create the object.

- Click **OK**.

The selected application opens in a new window or appears in a dotted border in the Excel window (depending on the application).

- Create your object and, depending on the application, use **File** – **Quit** to leave the application and return to Excel or simply click in one of the cells of the active worksheet behind the dotted border.

Inserting an existing object

- In Excel, click the cell where you want the object to appear.

- On the **Insert** tab, in the **Text** group, click the **Object** button.

- In the **Object** dialog box, click the **Create from file** tab.

- Click the **Browse** button to select the file to insert.

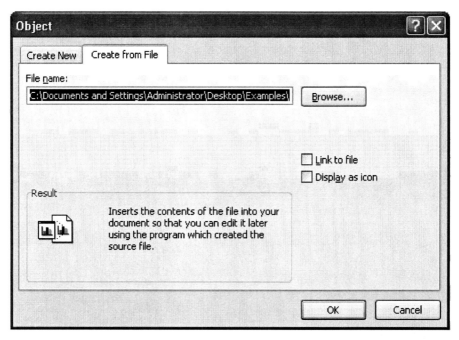

<ul>
<li>Check the **Link to file** box to create a link between the imported object and the workbook.</li>
<li>Check the **Display as icon** box to see the object in Excel as an icon representing the application used to create the icon.</li>
<li>Click **OK**.</li>
</ul>

To modify an object and/or see it in its original application, if it is displayed as an icon, double-click it.

Exporting Excel data to another application

You can copy Excel data to other applications. Note that this is also valid for importing data from other applications into Excel. Three techniques are shown below.

Exporting data by dragging and dropping

You can drag data from one Excel worksheet to another application (e.g. Access or Word).

- Open Excel and the relevant workbook, and activate the worksheet containing the data you want to export.

- Open the application and the file to which you want to export your data.

- Display both application windows on your screen by right-clicking any empty space on the taskbar and clicking the **Tile Windows Horizontally** or **Tile Windows Vertically** option depending on how you would like to see the windows displayed on the screen.

- Select the cells containing the data that you want to export in the Microsoft Excel workbook.

- Point to an edge of the selection.

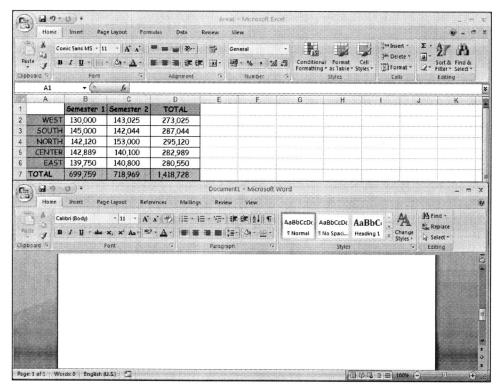

The pointer becomes a four-headed arrow. Be careful not to point to the fill handle.

⏩ Drag the selection to the destination document in the other application, directly to the spot where you want the data to be displayed. To copy the data press Ctrl when dragging.

⏩ Release the mouse button and the Ctrl key.

Exporting data by copying without a link

⏩ Select the cells containing the data you want to copy, or select the graphic object to copy.

⏩ On the **Home** tab, in the **Clipboard** group, click the **Copy** button or use Ctrl C.

- Open the application and the file in which you want to paste the data.

- Click the place where you want to paste the data.

- Select the **Home** tab, go to the **Clipboard** group and click the **Paste** button, or press Ctrl **V**.

Exporting data by copying with a link

When a link is used, any changes made to the data in the original Microsoft Excel workbook are carried over into the file containing the exported data.

- Select the cells containing the data you want to copy.

- On the **Home** tab, in the **Clipboard** group, click the **Copy** button or use Ctrl **C**.

- Open the application and the file into which you want to paste the Excel data.

- Click the place where you want to paste the data.

- If required, activate the **Home** tab, go to the **Clipboard** group and open the list on the **Paste** button.

- Click **Paste Special**.

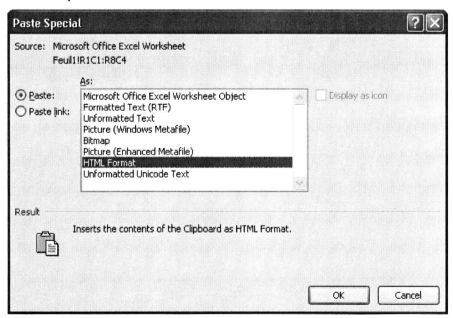

⊡ Select the format in which you want to paste the data using the **As** list, and select **Paste link**.

⊡ Check **Display as icon** if you want the linked data to be displayed in the form of an icon.

⊡ Click **OK**.

You can export a whole file to another application, as long as it manages Excel files. Simply open the workbook in the target application.

Setting up Excel to use Macros

*To create a macro with the macro recorder, you need to use the commands on the **Developer** tab which, by default, is not displayed in the ribbon.*

Displaying the developer tab

⊟ Click the **Microsoft Office** button 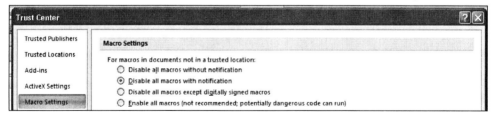 then **Excel Options**.

⊟ Select the **Popular** category and, under **Top options for working with Excel**, select the **Show Developer tab in the Ribbon** check box.

⊟ Click **OK**.

Defining macro security

To record macros, it is advisable to temporarily define the security level to enable all macros. To run macros, you need to perform this operation before even opening the workbook containing the macros you want to run.

⊟ On the **Developer** tab, in the **Code** group, click the **Macros Security** button.

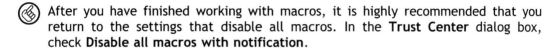

⊟ Under **Macro Settings**, click **Enable all macros** (**not recommended, potentially dangerous code can run**).

⊟ Click **OK**.

After you have finished working with macros, it is highly recommended that you return to the settings that disable all macros. In the **Trust Center** dialog box, check **Disable all macros with notification**.

Recording a macro

A macro automates a command or series of frequently used commands and functions. To automate these repetitive tasks, you can quickly record a macro. Microsoft Office Excel uses the Visual Basic application programming language to record macros.

Start by specifying if you want to record the macro with relative references or not: on the **Developer** tab, in the **Code** group, click **Use Relative References**.

If this button is active, Excel memorises movements in the macro relative to its original position. When you run the macro, it will act on cells relative to the cell from which it is activated. Otherwise, it works with absolute references: regardless of the active cell, it will act on the cells memorised in the macro.

On the **Developer** tab, in the **Code** group, click the **Record Macro** button, or click the button located in the left of the status bar.

In the **Macro name** box, enter the name you want to give to the macro.

Spaces are not allowed in a macro name, and the first character of the macro name must be a letter. Following characters can be letters, numbers, or underscore characters. Avoid using names that are also cell references.

To assign a shortcut (to run the macro), in the Shortcut key box, type any lower-case letter or uppercase letter that *you want to use.*

Open the **Store macro in** list and select the workbook in which you want to store the macro.

New workbook	to store the macro in a new workbook.
This workbook	to store the macro in the active workbook.
Personal Macro Workbook	if you want a macro to be available whenever you use Excel. Excel creates a hidden personal macro workbook, called Personal.xlsb and saves the macro in this workbook. It is loaded automatically whenever Excel starts. In Microsoft Windows 2000 and Windows XP, this workbook is saved in C:\Documents and Settings\Username\Application Data\ Microsoft\Excel\XLStart. In Microsoft Vista, it is saved in C:\Users\Username\Application Data\Microsoft\Excel\ XLStart.

To include a description of the macro, enter the text in the **Description** box.

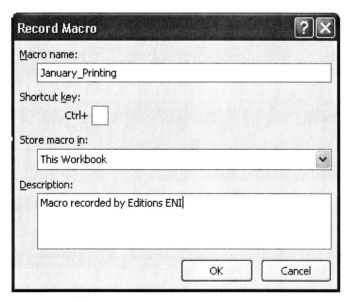

⊟ Click **OK** to start recording.

⊟ Perform the actions you want to record.

⊟ When all the actions have been recorded, click the **Stop Recording** button (**Developer** tab – **Code** group), or click the ▣ button located on the left of the status bar.

Running a macro

⊟ If the macro has been created in a workbook which is not Personal.xlsb, open it.

⊟ On the **Developer** tab, in the **Code** group, click the **Macros** button.

⊟ In the **Macro name** box, click the macro that you want to run.

⊟ Double-click the macro to run it.

🔅 If a shortcut key has been assigned to the macro when it was created, you can simply use the shortcut.

Running a macro on a graphic object

This technique runs a macro by clicking a graphic object.

- Right-click the graphic object on which you want to assign an existing macro.
- Click **Assign Macro**.
- In the dialog box that opens, select the macro in the **Macro name** box.
- Click **OK**.

*In this example, a click on the **Printing** graphic object enables the macro called January_printing to run.*

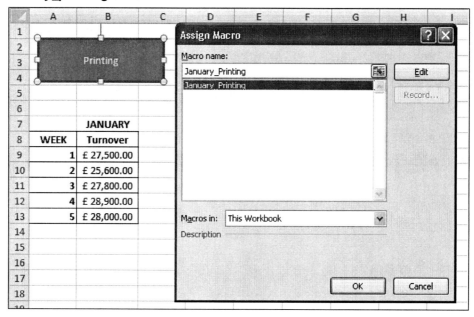

Modifying a macro

- If the macro has not been created in Personal.xlsb, open the workbook; if the macro is stored in Personal.xlsb, display it (**View** tab – **Window** group – **Unhide window** button ▢).
- On the **Developer** tab, in the **Code** group, click the **Macros** button or use Alt F8.

🔲 Open the **Macros in** list to select the workbook containing the macro you want to edit.

🔲 Select the macro then click the **Edit** button.

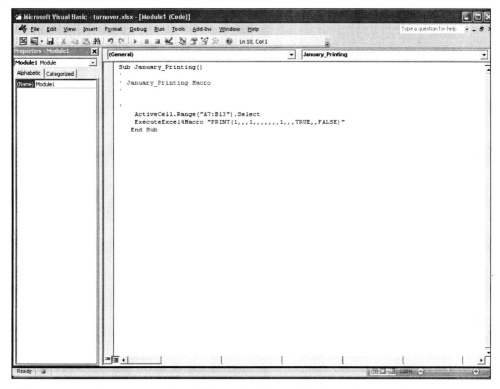

*The macro code appears in a **Microsoft Visual Basic** window. The code to open a macro is always **sub** followed by the macro name, while the code to close it is **End sub**.*

You do not have to know Visual Basic language to make simple changes in a macro.

🔲 To change cell references, do the same as for any entry: go to the place required and enter the references you want, using the appropriate keys.

🔲 To select the instructions, use the drag technique.

🔲 To copy/move instructions, use **Edit** – **Copy** or **Edit** – **Copy** and **Edit** – **Paste**.

⊟ When the changes are complete, close the **Microsoft Visual Basic** window by clicking the close button ☒.

Deleting a macro

⊟ If the macro has not been created in Personal.xlsb, open that workbook; if it has been created in Personal.xlsb, display it (**View** tab – **Window** group – **Unhide window** button ▭).

⊟ On the **Developer** tab, in the **Code** group, click the **Macros** button or press [Alt] [F8].

⊟ If required, open the **Macros in** list to select the workbook containing the macro you want to delete.

⊟ Select the macro, then click **Delete**.

⊟ Click **Yes** to confirm the deletion of the macro.

Saving a workbook containing macros

If you want to be able to reuse your macros later in the workbook, you must save it in a special format that takes account the macros, with the .xlms extension.

⊟ Activate the relevant workbook.

⊟ Click the **Microsoft Office** button ⬚ and move the mouse over **Save as**.

⊟ Click **Excel Macro-Enabled Workbook**.

⊟ In the **Save as** dialog box, optionally change the save-to folder and the file name.

*Note that the **Save as** type box displays **Excel Macro-Enabled Workbook**.*

⊟ Click **Save**.

Web pages

Web pages are HTML format files (HyperText Markup Language), used by web browsers, which lets other users access these pages. Office Excel 2007 has elaborate tools (Excel Services) which let you publish your workbooks on a Microsoft Office SharePoint Server 2007. Even if you don't have access to these services, you can still create web pages for users on your server or network.

Saving a workbook as a web page

This operation is useful when you have Excel but you cannot publish from your computer.

⊟ Open the workbook you want to turn into a web page and, if you don't want to save the entire workbook in a Web Page file, select the relevant cells.

⊟ Click the **Microsoft Office** button 🔲 , then **Save as**.

⊟ If required, change the save-to folder and/or the name of the workbook in the **File name** box.

⊟ Open the **Save as type** list and choose the type of web page you want to create:

Single file web page to save the workbook in a single file as a web page keeping its presentation, including pictures and other files. This format creates files with the extension .mht or .mhtml.

Web page to save the workbook as a web page, with the extension **.htm** or **.html**, and to create an associated folder containing the relevant files, such as highlighting for each sheet, graphic objects, etc. This folder is created in the same folder as the web page.

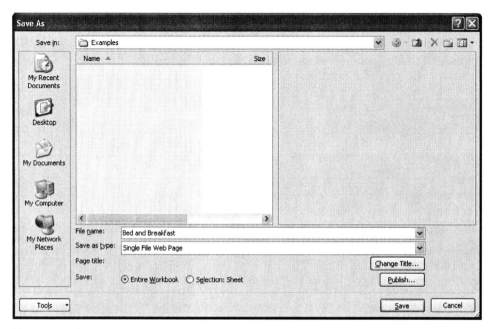

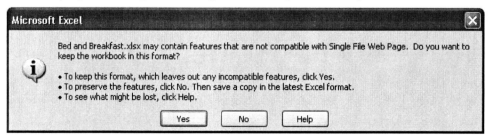

⊡ Click the **Change Title** button if you want to change the text which will appear on the title bar of your browser, then click **OK**.

If you don't edit this title, the text which appears by default is the complete name (with the path) of the Web page file.

⊡ Click **Entire workbook** in the **Save** area to save the workbook in a Web page file, or **Selection** to save just the selection as a Web page file.

⊡ Click **Save**.

Excel displays a message indicating that some features may be lost.

⊡ Click **OK** to continue saving.

The web page is displayed in the Excel window.

If the original workbook is changed, you must resave it as a web page to refresh the changes.

To see a web page in a browser, go to the browser and specify the complete address of the page to display in the **Address** bar, or go to Windows Explorer then to the save-to folder of the page and double-click click its name.

Publishing a workbook

This technique copies a workbook in HTML format so that other users can access it, but also allows the web page to be refreshed if the original workbook is been updated.

Creating the web page

⊟ Open the workbook you want to publish and, if you do not want to publish the entire workbook, select the cells you want to publish.

⊟ Click the **Microsoft Office** button 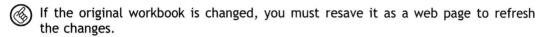 then **Save as**.

⊟ If required, modify the name of the workbook in the **File name** box.

⊟ Open the **Save as type** list and choose the kind of web page you want to create: **Single file web page** or **Web page**.

⊟ Click **Publish**.

⊟ In the **Publish as web page** dialog box, open the **Choose** list to select what you want to publish. If you need to select the cell range to publish use the 🔲 tool button.

⊟ Click the **Change** button to change the text which will appear on the title bar of your browser, then click **OK**.

⊟ In the **File name** box, select the place where you want to publish the web page. If you want to assign a different name to the published copy, specify it at the end of the text entry box.

*You can also use the **Browse** button to select this location, which can be a web server or another computer.*

🔁 Check **AutoRepublish every time this workbook is saved** if you want the workbook to be updated after changes to it are saved.

🔁 Check **Open published web page in browser** to see the page when it is published.

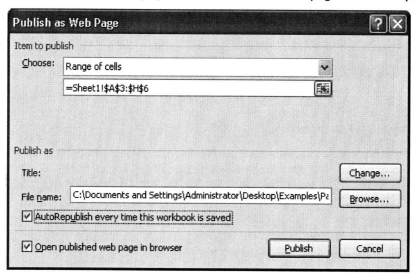

🔁 Click **Publish**.

Updating a published web page

🔁 In Excel, make your changes in the workbook and save them using the 💾 tool button.

*If you have checked **AutoRepublish every time this workbook is saved**, the following dialog box appears:*

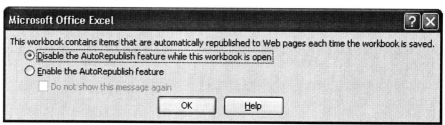

🔁 If you want to deactivate AutoRepublishing for this web page, keep the first option checked. If you want to keep this function, select **Enable the AutoRepublish** feature and, eventually, check **Do not show this message again**.

⊟ Click **OK**.

⊟ In the browser, if the web page is still displayed when workbook changes are saved, refresh the web page to update it.

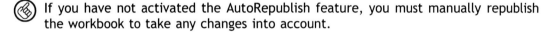 If you have not activated the AutoRepublish feature, you must manually republish the workbook to take any changes into account.

Index

Index

Index

Index

Index

Index

Index

Index

Index

R

REMOVING
Duplicate cells	111
Outline	223

REPLACEMENT
Cell contents	82
Cell formatting	83

RIBBON
Description	14
Display/Hide	15
Using	15

ROTATION
Chart objects	277

ROW
Deleting	104
Displaying/Hiding numbers	33
Freezing the display	37
Height	104 - 105
Inserting	104
Moving and Inserting	107
Printing numbers	227
Printing the same on several pages	229
Removing duplicates	111
Selecting	70

S

SAVE
See WORKBOOK

SCENARIO
Creating	143
Running	145

SCREENTIPS
Displaying/Hiding	26

SEARCH
Using the search feature	136

SELECTION
Cells	69, 71
Cells by name	117
Chart elements	248
From a cell/object containing a hyperlink	333
In a data table	285
Of chart objects	276
Rows/Columns	70
Worksheets	97

SHAPE
See CHART OBJECT, DIAGRAM

SHARE
Activating	307
Managing user modifications	313
Modifying a workbook by several users	309
Protecting the workbook	309
Removing	315
Removing a shared user	314
Tracking user modifications	311
User modification conflicts	311

SIZE
Changing the size	161
Character	159
Formatting	161

SIZE
Chart objects	277

SMARTART
See DIAGRAM

SORTING
By cell colour, font or icon set	203
By several colour/icon criteria	206
By several content and format criteria	207
By several content criteria	204
By several criteria	204
By the content of one column	202
Managing criteria	207

SOUND
Inserting a clip	267

SPELLING
Checking	83
Managing AutoCorrect	85

Index